On the Death and Life of Languages

Published in association with Éditions
Odile Jacob for the purpose of bringing new
and innovative books to English-language
readers. The goals of Éditions Odile
Jacob are to improve our understanding
of society, the discussions that shape it,
and the scientific discoveries that alter its
vision, and thus contribute to and enrich the
current debate of ideas.

Claude Hagège, *On the Death and Life of
Languages* (2009)
Michel Morange, *Life Explained* (2008)

On the Death and Life of Languages

CLAUDE HAGÈGE

Translated by Jody Gladding

Yale University Press
New Haven and London

Éditions Odile Jacob
Paris

Published with assistance from the Louis Stern Memorial Fund.

Translated from *Halte à la mort des langues,* by Claude Hagège, published by Éditions Odile Jacob in 2000. Copyright Odile Jacob, 2000; ISBN 978-2-7381-0897-0.

Designed by Sonia Shannon.
Set in Fournier type by Tseng Information Systems, Inc., Durham, North Carolina.
Printed in the United States of America by Sheridan Books, Ann Arbor, Michigan.

Library of Congress Cataloging-in-Publication Data
Hagège, Claude, 1936–
[Halte à la mort des langues. English]
On the death and life of languages / Claude Hagège ; translated by Jody Gladding.
p.   cm.
Includes bibliographical references and index.
ISBN 978-0-300-13733-0 (hardcover: alk. paper)
1. Language obsolescence. 2. Language revival. I. Title.
P40.5.L33H34 2009
417'.7 — dc22
2009008338

A catalogue record for this book is available from the British Library.

This paper meets the requirements of ANSI/NISO Z39.48–1992 (Permanence of Paper). It contains 30 percent postconsumer waste (PCW) and is certified by the Forest Stewardship Council (FSC).

10 9 8 7 6 5 4 3 2 1

Contents

Preface

Has anyone noticed the alarming phenomenon that an average of about twenty-five languages die each year? Today, some five thousand living languages exist in the world. Thus, by the end of the twenty-first century, only twenty-five hundred would remain. And no doubt that number would be lower still if we consider that the disappearance rate will most likely accelerate.

This catastrophe is taking place, it seems, in an atmosphere of general indifference. Is it vanity, or maybe pure presumption, to want to sound the alarm? I don't think so. That's why I've written this book, with the no doubt naïve hope of making a contribution, however modest, by increasing awareness about something vital: the need to do everything possible to prevent human cultures from sinking into oblivion. Human languages are one of the most elevated manifestations of those cultures, as well as one of the most ordinary and everyday. Languages, quite simply, are the most human thing about humans. So, what are we preserving in defending them? Our very species, as transformed, finally, by its languages, into itself.

Of course, like civilizations, languages are mortal, and the abyss of history is large enough for all. Nevertheless, from our perspective as finite beings, there is something completely different about the death of languages, something exhilarating when we come to realize it: languages are capable of resurrection! For humans, on the contrary, death is what governs life, death directs life, in order to give it a destiny. Of course, languages that come back to life are very rare. But they do exist. There is one case, at least, about which there is no doubt: Hebrew. And other languages that are threatened by death stubbornly remain alive, defying the inevitable, braving all perils.

It is to this dangerous adventure, this wildly reckless game languages play with death, that this book is devoted. The first part, "Languages and Life," will show how closely languages are bound to the vital principles that govern the universe. They are the providers of life, as well as the repositories of past life (chapter 1). The reason for this is that they themselves are, in some way, a natural species (chapter 2). But to understand what provokes the disappearance of languages, and why this is so different from the extinction of other species, one must define an essential attribute: speech. Speech is fleeting, but language never completely dies (chapter 3). And languages' struggle for life is strikingly illustrated by the struggle of those entities within language, its constituents: words, which live, die, are sometimes reborn, and lose their meanings and endlessly take on new ones (chapter 4).

In the second part, titled "Languages and Death," we will see what is meant by the death of a language (chapter 5), what the process entails (chapter 6), what the causes are (chapter 7), what the present tally of dead or threatened languages is and what that means for our species (chapter 8), and, finally, what actions we can take to combat the death of languages (chapter 9).

In the third part, "Languages and Resurrection," I will attempt to point out the sparks left by a dazzling blaze. Those who lit it have brought a language back to life: that language is Hebrew, whose rebirth is a most impressive phenomenon, unique as of now for its significance and its degree of success (chapter 10). Then I will mention a few cases related to this topic (chapter 11).

These notions of life, death, and resurrection may be considered anthropomorphic, or at least metaphoric. In fact, their use helps us to recognize that languages are the most complex of species, because they alone possess traits of a cognitive and social nature. It is precisely because languages are not made of perishable, concrete substances, and because they are creations of the human mind, that their death is not like the death of other components of the living world. Despite the threatening signs now appearing on cultures' horizons, we can hear a few sounds rising from the vast cemetery of languages. In the guise of death, for which the silence of the tomb may be the most compelling symbol in human graveyards, something still murmurs and roams about in the graveyards of language, something that could be called life. That is what must be revived.

Thus, the aim of this book is, very simply, to demonstrate three truths: first, that languages may be what is most alive in our human cultures; second, that they are mortal, and die in impressive numbers, if there is no attempt to maintain them; and finally, that their death is not a definitive obliteration, and that some of them revive, if we know how to encourage them. To defend our languages and their diversity, especially against the domination of a single language, is to do more than just defend our cultures. It is to defend our life.

The present American edition reproduces the French one, which appeared in 2000, but is not totally identical with it. I have updated some data and some references. I have also tried to adapt this book to the present state of scientific research on language endangerment and death.

All my thanks go to my collaborator and friend, Anne Szulmajster-Celnikier, attentive and wise reader, who helped me to set up the index. I am also indebted to Ghil'ad Zuckermann for carefully reading the text and making many good suggestions, and to Colette Grinevald for providing useful references.

Part I. LANGUAGES AND LIFE

1. Languages, Providers of Life

Human Societies and Languages as Vital Sources

When we examine human societies and the relationships they maintain with their languages, a truth that seems a matter of simple good sense presents itself: living languages do not exist of themselves, but by and for groups of individuals who make use of them in everyday communication. That does not mean that languages' only definition is social. As manifestations of the faculty of language, they are complex cognitive structures that reflect the way the mind functions when it produces and interprets utterances; and they bear the marks of the operations by which the universe of perceptions and concepts is expressed. But at the same time, languages accompany human groups. They disappear with them; or, on the contrary, if those groups are large and quick to spread beyond their original environment, the languages can be dispersed, in their wake, over vast territories. Thus, it is from those who speak them that they derive their life principles and their ability to increase their area of usage.

Nevertheless, languages are also one of the essential sources of the vital force that animates human communities. More than any of the other properties defining what is human, languages possess the power to provide individuals with the basis for their integration into a society—that is, on a level different from one's biological framework and mental structure, meaning the very foundations of one's life. This vital power of languages appears in two situations with particular clarity: first, through the enigma of the wild child, and second, in the relationship between languages and the infinite.

THE ENIGMA OF THE WILD CHILD

This is a case of an experience as revealing as it is disquieting. The story of Kaspar Hauser is fairly well known among linguists. Having grown up entirely alone, first in a hayloft and then in the forest, without ever having the slightest human contact until he was about eighteen years old, he appeared in Nuremberg around 1828, where the criminal lawyer Feuerbach took him in and became his guardian. He remained with Feuerbach until 1833, the date of his mysterious murder, whose perpetrators have never been identified and the circumstances of which have never been explained (see Blikstein 1995). As shown in Werner Herzog's 1974 film, despite the devotion of his guardian, who tried to teach him to speak German, Kaspar Hauser never managed to produce any sound resembling human language. Nevertheless he demonstrated a passionate desire to speak, and he made repeated attempts to do so. Without the power to communicate through language, he remained completely outside of everything around him during his brief passage in the human world. He studied faces, objects, and places earnestly and at length; he made gestures and tentative movements that no one had ever seen or used before and that seemed to follow their own peculiar logic. One day he broke down into tears during a reception and then suddenly retreated into a dark corner where he began to knit feverishly. Everything about his behavior seemed to indicate his distress at not being able to use language, and his effort, completely in vain, of trying to compensate for this failing. Deprived of language, he appeared to be surrounded by death, and because his attempts to grasp speech all failed, he was further distanced from life. Truly, languages are life's image and life's principle. Does it bear repeating that, in most cases, the child who is fed normally but never spoken to does not survive very long?

LANGUAGES AS REFLECTIONS OF THE INFINITE

What Kaspar Hauser lacked was not the faculty for language itself. All humans are born with that capacity, and the genetic coding of the wild child is no exception to the rule. But if exceptional circumstances prevent the language faculty from resolving into language, then the potential for living is seriously compromised. Languages are the conduit for life, not only because they provide access to the social plane, but also because they themselves are the manifestation of life.

Language nourishes the one who speaks it, exactly as the air one breathes allows one to live. Language even provides talismans for survival. Thus, it is reported that among the Angmassalik, an Eskimo population in southwest Greenland, some who are old and dying change their last names in an attempt to avoid death's reach. Unable to identify them by their usual names, death will not know where to find them. Thus, for them, hiding behind a pseudonym, as language allows us to do, prolongs life.

But even apart from such subterfuge, and all the clever tricks that humans employ in using words to outwit death, the existence of languages is a very simple and universal means for deceiving nothingness. After all, languages allow for history, in the evocation of the dead through public or private discourse, the notice that reshapes the dust, the "resurrection of the complete past" that Michelet saw as his mission. No animal species possesses the means to evoke its past, assuming that some of them do not lack memory, or at least memories.

It is humans who create the history of animals, in paleontological works in which their language allows them to relate a breathtakingly old past.

Languages change and adapt; they are impoverished and enriched. They have the unexpected traces of life, the sparkle, the pitfalls, the variety. They are life's stubborn instinct for continuity, since, even if they die individually, they do not cease to exist as a whole, realizing through their use the aptitude for language, that defining property by which a single animal species has become different from all others. Nevertheless, there are plenty of other means of communication proliferating and becoming ever more efficient in today's world. In perpetuating themselves, in continuing to defy death even while suffering heavy losses (see part 2), languages present us with a model of immortality. Souls without limits and without contours, languages are reflections of the infinite.

Artificial Languages and Languages Pulsing with Life
AN ANCIENT DREAM: TO DEFY BABEL

As old as the most ancient civilizations, a dream possesses certain minds, a dream of an auxiliary artificial language, a single and universal means of communication. Those who do not acknowledge the domination of an existing language, or the imperialism that ordinarily follows it, consider Esperanto to be a reasonable choice. If this choice became a reality, there would be no theoretical reason to oppose it. That said, does an invented language have the same symbolic power as a natural language? Is it, too, a provider of life? If modern Hebrew has been able to cement the union of all the Jews of the Diaspora, it is largely because, although partly artificial, it was reconstructed from absolutely genuine languages (see chapter 10), each of which had considerable historical and cultural meaning for its speakers. When Zamenhof invented Esperanto, his inspiration was of another order (see chapter 10).

NATURAL LANGUAGES AS REPOSITORIES OF LIFE

Languages Contain Our History

Through speaking and writing, languages not only allow us to trace our history well beyond our own physical obliteration, they also contain our history. Any philologist, or anyone curious about languages, knows that treasures are deposited within them that relate societies' evolution and individuals' adventures. Idiomatic expressions, compound words, have a past that calls up living figures. The history of words reflects the history of ideas (see chapter 4). If societies do not die, it is not only because they have historians, or annalists, or official narrators. It is also because they have languages, and are recounted in these languages.

Languages, Traces of Memory, and Testimonies of Life:
A Language Lover's Remarks

In a collection of reflections and stories from the first third of the twentieth century and recently reissued in French, Dezső Kosztolányi, a great Hungarian writer who, like many other intellectuals from his country, was very devoted to his language, wrote these lines concerning "artificial languages":

> Issuing from the laboratories of reason, they have the durable quality of the celluloid shirt cuff. . . . They never fade. But they are odorless and colorless [. . .] whereas, what gives languages their charm is their human aspect. Entire generations have left the traces of their lives there [. . .]. Words are relics, sanctified

by suffering and disfigured by passion. The rules of the past become the exceptions and superb metaphors are born of simple misinterpretations. Languages are ancient treasures where our familial memories are deposited [. . .]. On the other hand, artificial languages are devoid of memory, rooted neither in time or place. They retain no regional accents. They are unaware of regional variations, and [. . .] have no traditions other than those that follow from the laws of reason. It is impossible to make mistakes in them [. . .]. In these languages never shaped by feeling, how would a drunk bailiff from the seventeenth century, a contemporary young dandy, or a stuffy old gentleman express himself? (1996, 143–144)

In the same work, under the title "On the Infinite Sweetness of the Mother Tongue," the author writes:

Since 1879, when Marton Schleyer gave birth to his Volapuk, artificial languages have flourished. Noble dreamers work night and day to put an end to the Babelesque confusion of languages, which, despite its serious drawbacks, does not lack a certain stimulating charm, much like life itself. It is certainly moving to see finite human reason engage in Titanesque combat to subject to its laws that infinite soul that is language [. . .]. Artificial languages allow us to indicate our place of residence, our profession or the state of our bank account, but prove nearly powerless to characterize [. . .] the lullaby our mother sang or the quick smile the woman we love gives us when leaving us on the street. In short, they can express everything that does not deserve expression [. . .]. Ever since the world began, our fingers have helped us — also — to count, and the inclined head, resting on the hands, means everywhere that one is sleepy [. . .]. Whereas auxiliary languages say nothing more.

Moreover, to do so, deprived of the warmth [. . .] of life, they find themselves forced to multiply the means they put to work [. . .]. Those who enjoy predicting the future [. . .] take pleasure at the moment in repeating that [. . .] national languages are destined to disappear, one day giving way to a single universal language; it is revealing to see such an idea arising precisely in this century that worships the machine and denies the personality [. . .]. Destined for all, a universal language would be no one's [. . .]. Of course, I am resigned to one day disappearing. But I do not accept the idea that the fragment of my spirituality that is my mother tongue should vanish utterly in its turn and that, after my death, the words to which I lent my breath [. . .] should cease to drift over my tomb. They represent the speech of the soul, of a familial continuity that defies death. (1996, 147–148)

In these texts, which don't consider Zamenhof and Esperanto, the assessment concerning artificial languages is partly unjust and results from insufficient information. We do not know if Dezső Kosztolányi actually studied an artificial language closely. It is not true, at least if we consider Esperanto, that an artificial language is a cold mechanism produced by the laws of pure reason. Esperanto was a work of passion, driven by a powerful spirit of idealism. Nor is it true that an artificial language allows us to speak only of everyday things and is incapable of expressing the impulses of the soul. In Esperanto, for example, there exists a lyric poetry. On the other hand, we can understand what faith stirs this inspired Hungarian, why he sees in natural languages an age-old treasure where the life of generations is deposited in successive layers, and why he sings the praises of the mother tongue as the breath that defies death. All that coincides with the testimony of the many for whom languages, because they preserve life's traces, are the providers of life. The sap that so powerfully nourishes languages, and, through them, those who draw from them their identity, issues from roots embedded in a very deep memory; and it is this heritage, maintained and enriched over time, that is a vital, living principle.

2. Languages, Living Species

Vitalism in Linguistics in the Second Half of the Nineteenth Century

LANGUAGES AS SUBJECTS FOR THE NATURAL SCIENCES

One might consider that if languages are providers of life, as we have seen in the first chapter, it is logical to infer that they have something to do with the world of living species. Today we have distanced ourselves somewhat from the vitalist formulations that were common in the thinking and the work of linguists in the nineteenth century. But it is illuminating to reread those works, even with a critical eye, because they show how the properties of languages powerfully tempt us to treat them like natural beings comparable to those that biology studies.

Schleicher, from Botanist to Linguist

The name A. Schleicher (1821–1868) is the one most often associated with the vision of language as a phenomenon falling within the realm of the natural sciences. Like A. G. Haudricourt, the contemporary French scholar (who died in 1996) who was also concerned with the traits in languages that suggest groupings by species, Schleicher was a botanist turned linguist. His thinking was shaped by the works of the great naturalists of the eighteenth and early nineteenth centuries, essentially Linnaeus, the inventor of plant taxonomy, and Cuvier, the proclaimed founder of comparative anatomy. Like other linguists of his generation, Schleicher was later influenced by the works of F. Bopp, whose 1816 essay "On the System of Conjugation in Sanskrit Compared with Those of the Greek, Latin, Persian and Germanic Languages," is considered the founding work of comparative grammar.

F. Bopp and the Principle of Life in Languages

In his famous book *Comparative Grammar of Sanskrit, Zend, Greek, Latin, Lithuanian, Old Slavic, Gothic, and German* (1833) Bopp writes: "Languages must be considered as natural bodies, which are constructed according to laws, and carry within them a principle of life"; and expressions like "the physiology of language" or "linguistic anatomy" constantly recur throughout the work. In fact, this way of seeing goes back to the eighteenth century — to Leibniz, for example, who had studied Semitic languages in terms of human genealogy, especially through the notion of "family."

LINGUISTIC VITALISM AND TRANSFORMISM,
OR DARWINISM AND LANGUAGES
Apparent Harmony

Schleicher's vitalist conception of language, which he inherited from Bopp, predates his reading of C. Darwin's great book, *The Origin of Species* (1859). Darwin's ideas systematize a transformist trend then present in the works of many scholars, among them E. Haeckel, the naturalist attributed with establishing a parallelism between the evolution of beings (ontogeny) and of species (phylogeny) (see Hagège

1990, 18 s.). The one who drew Schleicher's attention to *The Origin of Species* was Haeckel himself. Theirs was a friendship nurtured by mutual influences, the same ones that biology, especially plant biology, and linguistics shared during this time.

When he became aware of Darwin's book, Schleicher was in the process of putting together his principal work (1861), which systematizes and popularizes what had been accomplished in this area, especially by F. Bopp, R. Rask, J. Grimm, and W. von Humboldt. One year after Schleicher published this work C. Lyell, the founder of modern geology, published *On the Geological Evidence of the Antiquity of Man*, a book that had had a certain influence on Darwin (see Jacquesson 1998, 121). A chapter in this book, "A Comparison of the Origin and Development of Languages with Those of Species" (see chapter 4), applies the transformists' theory of natural selection to languages. In 1863, Schleicher wrote a public letter to Haeckel titled "Darwinian Theory and Linguistics," which contains the following passage: "Languages are natural organisms that . . . are born, grow, develop, age, and die; thus they, too, manifest that series of phenomena that is usually included under the name of life. The science . . . of language is therefore a natural science; its method is, generally speaking, the same as that of the other natural sciences. Thus, studying Darwin's book . . . has not seemed to make me depart too much from my positions."

In fact, in a passage in which he wants to make his remarks clearer to readers who are informed less about zoological classifications than they are about more familiar linguistic facts, Darwin himself relies upon the genealogy of languages as established since Bopp. Schleicher recalls that he has always believed in the gradual nature of changes in languages, exactly as Darwin does with regard to living species.

Actually, a Misunderstanding: Natural Selection

By noting in Darwin's work those evolutionist ideas that seemed to him already current among specialists in the natural sciences, Schleicher misses the central point to which *The Origin of Species* contributes something remarkably new, that is, the notion of natural selection (see Jacquesson 1998, 122). Schleicher wants to retain in languages only their property of being living species, like those in nature. He denies that they are also social phenomena. Consequently, he sees the science of languages, which he calls *glottics,* not as a human science, but very much as a natural science. Now if you set about transposing Darwin's discovery to linguistics, you notice that natural selection, provided that it is conceived in economic and social terms, can be interpreted as a driving force in the evolutions that mark the destiny of languages. This will become apparent further on (see chapter 7). It is interesting to note here that, ironically, the treatment of linguistics as a natural science is also to be found in a theory which has almost nothing to do with Darwin's ideas, namely Noam Chomsky's *Theory of Universal Grammar* (see Chomsky 1986).

Languages and the Struggle for Life

The struggle for life as Darwin conceived it in zoology can be transposed to the human sciences, and especially to linguistics. Exactly like animals and plants, languages compete to stay alive, and one achieves this only at the expense of another. The domination of some over others and the state of jeopardy into which dominated languages fall can be explained by the insufficient means available for resisting pressure from the dominating languages. We will see this in more detail in the second part of the book.

Neglecting the Historical Dimension of Languages

Curiously enough, Schleicher dismisses from the study of languages the historical dimension. He carefully distinguishes glottics from philology, writing that, unlike the latter, "linguistic science . . . is not at all an historical discipline, and falls within natural history" (1860, 119). In other words, to him, only the history of human societies is history, and that of natural species is not history, even though it is called that! He separates the history of languages from the history of humans, which deprives the first of many explanations provided by the second. Thus, a theory that sees human languages as living objects to be studied through the natural sciences comes to retain primarily the mechanical aspect of that life. Nevertheless, contradicting himself, Schleicher also insists on one clearly historical aspect of languages. But, as we will see, he does so by imagining one particular orientation.

THE LIFE OF LANGUAGES AS AN EVOLUTION
ALONG ONE PARTICULAR AXIS

The Three Types of Languages for German Linguists in the First Half of the Nineteenth Century: Isolating Languages, Agglutinating Languages, and Inflecting Languages

Schleicher popularized the well-known typological classification that, from the Schlegel brothers (1808 and 1818) to Pott (1849) by way of Bopp (1833–1857) and Humboldt (1836), divided languages into three categories: those in which the words are invariable and independent of each other (isolating languages, for example, Chinese), those in which they are constituted of a root and identifiable affixes (agglutinating languages, for example, Turkish), and those in which they are made up of roots modified through combination with elements more or less amalgamated to them and between each other (inflecting languages, for example, those of the Indo-European family).

The "Evolutionist" Interpretation

Schleicher was not content with simply devoting much attention to this typology in his 1861 book. Systematizing an evolutionist ideology that, as we have just seen, precedes Darwin, Schleicher saw the isolating languages as those of the primitive ages of humanity, the agglutinating ones as the beginnings of progress, and the inflecting languages, which he locates at the peak of evolution, as the only ones permitting the development of refined thinking. Today this vision has long since been abandoned. Just to mention one argument, Chinese is certainly not the language of a primitive people; and furthermore, we possess early evidence (cf. Karlgren 1920) leading us to believe that Chinese was initially inflecting, and that its isolating properties are the result of a change that took place over many thousands of years. It is equally impossible to confirm judgments like this one, regarding another family: "The Indian tribes of North America . . . are unsuited for historical life because of their endlessly complicated languages . . . bristling with overabundant forms; they can only experience decline, and even extinction" (Schleicher 1865). We will see in chapter 7 that the causes for the extinction of many of the American Indian languages — indeed, of any language whatsoever — have little to do with its internal structure.

Thus, Schleicher's thinking does include flaws and ponderous systematizing. But none of that invalidates the vitalist inspiration that feeds it. Provided that inconsistencies and apriority are avoided, it is not at all illegitimate to treat languages like living beings, even if we have a little trouble today condoning the naïveté of a theory that only wants to see them as species within the domain of the natural sciences. It will soon become apparent that Schleicher's successors found a way to reorient his views on languages and life.

The Life of Languages, Parallel to That of Human Societies: Schleicher's Legacy with an Anthropological Component Added

THE TEACHINGS OF H.-J. CHAVÉE

Naturalist language theories continued to flourish after Schleicher's death. His disciples were already publishing in his lifetime. One of the most prominent, H.-J. Chavée, born in Namur, was also a passionate botanist in his youth. He saw to it that Schleicher's work was promoted in Brussels, and then in Paris, where he began to teach what he called *lexicology*, or the science of word formation, by using Indo-European examples to illustrate how words are living beings. He kept company with anthropologists and believed in the parallel evolution of languages and human communities, both animated with the same vital spirit, as he attempted to show in his 1862 book titled, according to the terminology of the time, *Languages and Races*. His inspiration is clearly reflected in the subtitle of the *Revue de linguistique et de philologie comparée*, which he founded in 1867, that is, the "quarterly collection of documents to serve the positive science of languages, ethnology, mythology and history." With this periodical, which opened up Schleicher's theory to the philological preoccupations he dismissed as well as to the human sciences for which he had little concern, Chavée ensured that he would have the support of enthusiastic disciples.

For the members of this group, each word in a language possesses two lives, one phonetic and material, the other semantic and intellectual. The vital burgeoning of languages is inscribed from the beginning of their destiny. Beyond being natural organisms, as Schleicher taught, languages are the reflections of the "races" that spontaneously created them, and the natural history of languages runs parallel to the natural history of these said races. Languages are polygenetic systems; that is, they are born various and not from a single stock.

A. HOVELACQUE AND LANGUAGES AS LIVING ENTITIES TO BE RECONSTRUCTED FROM PREHISTORY

The Anthropological Aim

As Schleicher's reader and Chavée's disciple, with whom he studied general linguistics and a few Slavic and Eastern languages, Hovelacque succeeded his master as director of the *Revue* and founded the School of Anthropology in 1876 with P. Broca (see Desmet and Swiggers 1993). The naturalist trend, for which he is the principal representative in France in the second half of the nineteenth century, draws its inspiration from scientific materialism, which also guided Hovelacque's political activity. He was a member of the Socialist Party and was twice elected deputy for Paris's thirteenth arrondissement, which, much more than his fame as researcher (practically nil today—even, it seems, among linguists), explains why a street near the town hall there bears his name. The linguists he gathered around him, among them J. Vinson, a well-known Tamil specialist, saw languages as living entities whose earliest stages had to be studied, especially their prehistoric development, as well as their relationship with the races. Nevertheless, Hovelacque remains more reserved than Chavée and Broca regarding the parallels between races and languages (see N. Dias and B. Rupp-Eisenreich, in Auroux 2000, 293).

The Problem of the Origin of Languages and the Strictures of the Paris Society of Linguistics

In 1865, only two years before the founding of the *Revue de linguistique et de philologie comparée,* the Paris Society of Linguistics was founded. We know (see Leroy 1985, 219) that Chavée took no part in its activities. Of course, his journal was not explicitly meant to rival the *Bulletin de la société de linguistique de Paris,* created at almost the same time. It did not have its longevity, as the *Bulletin* still exists and the *Revue* ceased publication in 1916. Nor did it have its audience: hardly any historian of linguistics makes mention of Chavée's *Revue,* and most French linguists today do not know of its existence or of the authors who wrote for it. Nonetheless, it seemed to contemporaries that the two periodicals were easy to distinguish even if they were not exactly adversarial. We can see this when the Society of Linguistics, officially organized in 1866, decided in its statutes to exclude any communication concerning the origin of language or the creation of an artificial language. The first exclusion was aimed at amateurs' speculations, then flourishing, on the various origins being flushed out everywhere, especially by those obsessed with Celto-mania (see Decimo 1998). The second exclusion was aimed at language inventors, also numerous at the time.

It has been noted less often that the founders of the Linguistic Society of Paris also wanted to distance themselves from the organicists of Chavée's school and their anthropological investigations. A focus on the vital power that characterizes human languages leads to exploring their origins, and is accompanied by all the scientific risks that such an investigation implies. Likewise, a study confined to the structures underlying the functioning of languages has a tendency to relegate to the unknowable the problem of their genesis, thus accepting the alternate risk of being dry and overly restricted.

The Limits of Naturalism: Social and Historical Factors as Necessary Constituents for the Life of Languages

Hovelacque and his school saw languages as living organisms. They apparently paid no attention to the distinction between species and organism. Nor did they see that it is more accurate to treat languages as species rather than as organisms, because, like natural species, their life and their development are directly dependent upon the environment, which produces significant variations in them (see Mufwene 2001, chapter 7). Living species have two other characteristics that can be assigned to languages, related to each other and observed in biology, recalled above by Darwin: the struggle for life and natural selection. If this conception reawakens the vitalist trend, it nonetheless fails to emphasize enough the social, political, and cultural factors. Even though he assigns them hardly any role in his theoretical construction, Hovelacque cannot avoid recognizing their importance in the concrete cases that he mentions. For example, he cites them expressly with regard to the reasons why Arabic did not take hold in Spain in the Middle Ages, and neither did Turkish in the Balkans later on (see chapter 7).

Paradoxically, the naturalist school likewise did not take historical factors into sufficient consideration. Schleicher's disciples became comparative linguists exclusively, like earlier botanists, examining growth properties separately and in a parallel fashion in each plant, without worrying about reconstructing a common trunk or, for linguists, an original language from which the changes in the various idioms derived from it could be explained. Notably, this criticism of the naturalist school is the one that F. de Saussure formulates in his seminal posthumous work, *Cours de linguistique générale* (*Course in General Linguistics*) (1916, 16–17). The school of neogrammarians, for which Saussure himself was a brilliant representative early in his career (1878), provided the rigor that the naturalists lacked. But it did not refute their principal intuition, that of the rustling life force that travels through languages like a nourishing sap. On the contrary, it provided new, more solid evidence. One great linguist whom Saussure admired and quoted, D. Whitney, shows, admittedly, that the collective will of human groups constructs languages and that, consequently, they cannot be taken for simple natural organisms. But in characterizing what a language is, he also writes that "its birth, its development, its decline and its extinction are like [those] of a living creature" (1867, II, 34–48).

The Diversity of Languages, Symbol of Life

Finally, one essential property of languages must be recalled, one that the naturalist schools do not consider, perhaps because it is so obvious that it tends to be overlooked: their diversity. In the world of the living, the burgeoning of species is one of the images of life, whether it is a matter of insects or grasses. The diversity of languages, a torrential surge of life, is a cause for wonder for those who are not afraid of learning them, and also, one would hope, for linguists themselves.

The Other Side of Life

As mentioned above, despite, or rather in natural symmetry with, that breath of life that moves through and animates human languages, the phenomenon of decline and death is implied by the very notion of life. We could say that, in the domain of the living, death is a part of life. That is also true in the domain of languages. Organicist linguists who most willingly resort to biological terms to speak of the life of languages are also the ones who, according to the same formulation, speak of their death. Hovelacque, for example, says of languages: "They pass away as nations and often individuals pass away: they perish through vital competition, they perish in a desperate struggle for existence. That is a historical fact, that is a fact that takes place before our eyes" (1877, quoted in Desmet and Swiggers 1993, 142).

But do languages perish completely? That is the question that the next chapter will answer.

3. Language and Speech

The Opposition Between Langue and Parole
in Linguistic Studies

BEFORE THE BEGINNING OF THE TWENTIETH CENTURY

The goal of this chapter is not to give a didactic account of the way in which language theories treat the problem of the death of languages. Nor do I intend to yield to the complacencies of the quest of forerunners. I will recall an opposition, well-known to linguistics historians, that Humboldt outlined, making use of Greek terms, when he emphasized that language is an *energeia*, or creative and dynamic capacity, through which humans produce and interpret linguistic utterances, and not simply an *ergon*, or pure result of this capacity. It is often said that this conception, coming through Haman, Herder, and Condillac, owes something to . . . Aristotle himself.

F. DE SAUSSURE

Saussurian Definitions

Whether or not he was influenced by this legacy, F. de Saussure (see chapter 2) makes a largely original and famous distinction between *langue* and *parole*. In fact, both participate in the creative spirit of Humboldtian *energeia*, and there is no real symmetry between the two authors on this essential point. Saussure defines langue as being "at once a social product of the language faculty and an ensemble of necessary conventions, adopted by the social body to permit the exercise of this faculty among individuals" (1962, 25).

Later on he specifies that langue "is a treasure deposited by the practice of speech in subjects belonging to the same community, a grammatical system existing virtually in each brain, or more precisely in the brains of a group of individuals; because language is not complete in any one person, it perfectly exists only in the mass" (ibid., 30).

On the other hand, when it comes to the particular act through which the language system is manifested, Saussure stresses that this act could not be achieved by the whole of speaking subjects. For him, "the execution is never done by the mass; it is always individual, and the individual is always the master of it; we will call it parole" (ibid., 30).

The conceptual opposition thus proposed is fundamental, and Saussure insists upon what it signifies:

> By separating langue from parole, one separates at the same time: 1) what is social from what is individual; 2) what is essential from what is secondary, and more or less accidental.
>
> Langue is not a function of the speaking subject. It is the product that the individual passively registers.
>
> [. . .] Parole is, on the contrary, an individual act of will and intelligence, in which it is useful to distinguish:
>
> 1) the combinations by which the speaking subject uses the code of the language in order to express his personal thinking; 2) the psychophysical mechanism that allows him to externalize those combinations. (ibid., 30–31)

We see that if langue is a principle of life as a dynamic system in which the constructions of words and phrases of many generations have accumulated, it is brought to life, in the literal sense, only by the activity of parole.

Adjusting the Terminology

The term *parole* is perhaps not the most fortunate. Certain linguists have preferred *discours* (see Guillaume 1969, 28, 36, or Buyssens 1970, 40), which is more supple and less ambiguous. Among other meanings, parole evokes the wave of sound produced by the speaker when he opens his mouth, which has nothing to do with Saussure's intention. Moreover, the latter was well served by the chance opposition available in French but less evident in other European languages. We can see this through the difficulty of translating the langue/parole pair into many of them. Of course, Spanish can oppose *lengua* and *habla*, Russian *jazyk* and *rech'*, Hungarian *nyelv* and *beszéd*, but in Italian, *parola*, which very simply means "word" much more commonly than the French parole, is not so clearly opposed to *lingua*. In English, the term *language*, meaning, depending on the context, "language" as much as "tongue," and in some way only having this second meaning when it is plural, is ambiguous, as is speech in its ability to take on the meanings of "discourse," "language," etc. In German, one must resort to compounds that are fashioned especially to express the desired meaning: *Sprachgebilde* ("construction of language") and *Sprechakt* ("act of speech"); in Swedish, *språk* can be used for langue, but *tal* can mean "language" as well as "speech," and almost the same is true for their quasi-homonyms in Danish and Norwegian.

Thus, the terms Saussure uses to establish a fundamental opposition may not be given names that are completely adequate or clearly translatable into familiar languages. It is important to remember the quite remarkable history of the *Cours de linguistique générale*. Full of doubts and aware of the profound complexity of language as an object of scientific knowledge, Saussure refused to write a work in which he had to confine his thinking to an overly rigid form. From 1907 to 1911 he gave a series of brilliant lectures at the University of Geneva, and some of his students and colleagues decided to publish them in 1916, three years after his death. Thus the work that dominates modern linguistics was compiled at least partly on the basis of student notes, which clearly explains some uncertainties. That does not mean that Saussure had not long explored the notion of speech. But he did not have the time to examine all its implications.

Nevertheless, his intuition is rich and opens the way to a better understanding of what must be understood by the life of languages, and thus by their death. But for all that, it makes sense to give some nuances to this opposition, as we will see.

Too Radical an Opposition
The Aporias of a Sharp Split

One comparison that Saussure proposes is borrowed from the musical realm. In the *Cours* we read: "language can be compared to a symphony, whose reality is independent from the manner in which one executes it; the mistakes that musicians who play it may make in no way compromise that reality" (1962, 36).

For pedagogical reasons, at least if the text of the *Cours* faithfully reproduces all his remarks, Saussure often resorts to comparisons. But to compare is not without risks, and here the opposition between langue and parole seems too strong. Caught up in the logic of this opposition, Saussure comes to conclusions that embarrass him, as is clear with regard to the sentence. "Up to what point does it belong to langue?" he asks, then adding: "If it falls into the realm of parole, it could not pass for the linguistic unit" (1962, 148); in another passage, he concludes with this: "The sentence [. . .] belongs to parole, not to langue" (1962, 172).

Saussure probably means that langue contains not sentences but the rules for constructing them. Nevertheless, what good is this split? Could we utter sentences if we did not possess the grammatical system that orders them and the lexical units out of which they are made, that is, all that belongs to langue? Furthermore, we can consider that, in terms of structure, families of sentences exist in langue, just as families of words do. The exercise of parole is the concrete manifestation of structures, for which langue is the locus.

Passing from Langue to Parole

All languages possess tools to be used for actualizing the system, that is, for making it pass into acts of speech. Thus, the demonstratives actualize the nouns and the tenses actualize the verbs. We can give examples of this drawn from one of Saussure's followers, C. Bally, who succeeded him as the Chair of Linguistics at the University of Geneva: the virtual concept of "book," registered in langue, is actualized in parole if one uses the demonstrative *this*, hence, *this book*, which refers to a concrete book, present at the moment one speaks, in the situation or in the antecedent context; in the same way, the concept of "to reign," virtual in itself, is actualized if one says "(he) reigned," a formula referring to a concrete reign located in the past (see Bally 1965, 82–83). Langue is implicated by parole and, in some way, exists before it, since it is langue that provides the tools of actualization. But inversely, it is these tools that keep langue from remaining simply a possibility, defined by the virtuality of the concepts. What is more, we must not overlook an entirely different level from the static one to which we are confining ourselves here. That is, from the perspective of genetics, parole logically preceded langue, since it was surely necessary for our ancestors to utter the first resonant attempts at communication in order for the whole, at the end of a very long period, to organize itself into a system.

Recognizing Reciprocal Conditioning

Despite the sharp split proposed there, Saussure's *Cours* does not overlook the importance of reciprocal conditioning between langue and parole. If it is true that langue is implied by parole, parole, on the other hand, takes priority on two levels, namely that of learning and that of development: "it is in hearing others that we learn our mother tongue; it manages to settle in our brain only after countless experiences. Finally, it is parole that makes langue develop: it is the impressions received by hearing others that alter our linguistic habits. Thus langue and parole are interdependent; the former is both the instrument and the product of the latter" (1962, 37).

These reflections reinforce the idea of a link of reciprocal conditioning between langue and parole, just as it was shown above in recalling that parole makes langue pass from the virtuality of a system to the reality of an act. That does not mean that langue, because it is a virtuality, is an abstraction. Those linguistic signs that are words, as well as their associations, are realities that a community speaking a given language ratifies, and that can be considered to have their locus in the brain even while we await the findings of linguistic neurophysiology that could one day reveal in detail how those connections function.

The Notion of a Dead Language in the Light of the Opposition Between Langue and Parole: Dead Languages, Structures Without Voice, but Not Without Existence

In this chapter, I have a specific reason for recalling and reexamining, as I have just done, the Saussurian intuition of a distinction between langue and parole. That reason is because we can draw from Saussure an essential lesson concerning the subject of this book.

THE DISAPPEARANCE OF PAROLE IS NOT THE DEATH OF LANGUE

Regarding Two Striking Facts

Two facts warrant our attention. First, if someone is deprived of the use of speech following some sort of accident, s/he nevertheless retains language as long as s/he hears the sounds and understands their meaning. Second and more importantly, those languages termed "dead" are no longer spoken, but that does not at all mean that their grammar and even their phonetics cannot be learned, that is, assimilated as organisms, as is done for any living language.

Living and Existing: Two Distinct Situations

An important lesson can be drawn from these two facts. The close relationship between parole and langue matters for languages that are living, but, for all that, it does not follow that a language that is no longer spoken ceases to exist. To be alive and to exist are two different ideas, and two different situations that we cannot confuse. Thus, the distinction between langue as a system and parole as an activity leads us to this essential conclusion: a language termed dead is nothing other than a language that has lost, if we may use the expression, the use of speech. But we have no right to equate its death with that of a dead animal or plant. Here, the metaphors reach their limit. Because a dead language continues to exist.

LANGUAGES, IMMORTAL SPECIES

In chapter 2, we saw that vitalists' formulations in the language sciences constitute a very old temptation. From this is derived the way such notions as life, death, evolution, etc., are applied to languages. But languages possess a completely singular property, as we have just seen: they are virtual systems that, of course, pass into the condition of acts as soon as they are put into speech, but they nevertheless do not need to be put into speech to exist. Not a single living species has this dual nature. For any species, life is a whole, given or withdrawn as such. That is why, for all of them, death is absolutely unremitting. It is, of course, the natural epilogue to life, and, as a preordained annihilation, it is inscribed in the genetic program and thus in the very definition of life. But one does not return from death. A dead person cannot regain the shores of life as one returns from a voyage or awakes from a dream.

On the other hand, it is "enough" for a dead language to be spoken again for it to cease to be dead. The death of a language is only the death of speech. Thus, languages as systems of rules are not mortal, although they have no life by themselves, and live only if communities put them into speech. That does not mean that it is easy to revive a language, that is, to return speech to it. On the contrary, it is an enormously difficult undertaking. But it will become clear in chapter 10 that one group of resolved individuals succeeded in meeting this challenge in the case of one particular language. What is more, that language had been dead since ancient times. What can we conclude from that? Exactly this: the death of languages is not the end of all hope for bringing them back to life.

4. Words and the Struggle for Life

Why Are Words Mortal?

Words die. "Why?" we may ask. We might just as well ask why they should not be mortal. There are many reasons why they do not live forever. I will examine the four principal ones here. The first two involve the death of words themselves, the last two the death of their meanings, replaced by one or many others.

ONE CAUSE OF THE DEATH OF WORDS: ECONOMIC AND SOCIAL CHANGES

Changes in society and economic relations cannot leave the lexicon intact, because words reflect cultures and ideas. To limit myself to one specific case that succinctly illustrates this phenomenon, I will examine the French vocabulary during the period from 1900 to 1960.

Transformations in Technology and Life

What takes place between these two dates (see Dubois 1962)? Electricity and the internal combustion engine, to mention just two phenomena, become essential to production, and they profoundly change modes of life and mass technology through the automobile, airplane, radio, television, etc. Industrial capitalism brings about sprawling networks of urban communities. Small artisans and traditional trades must face competition from vast, complex enterprises. Professions greatly diversify and become specialized, multiplying the number of new objects in daily life. Information and advertising methods, their power increasing continually, soon reiterate the social and technical changes, as well as the political ideologies that allow them to apply ever growing pressures upon the population. The development of cities leads to the extension of a tertiary sector invested in the services. Economic needs tend to involve the whole of the country, not just distinct regional entities. The centralization of political power increases, reflected especially in the ever growing place of social and fiscal institutions. New segments of society are educated. Science rapidly accelerates in its movement toward popularization.

Repercussions on Vocabulary

It is not difficult to imagine the effects of all these transformations upon the lexicon, whether it is a matter of ideology's imprint on everyday vocabulary, advertising jargon reflected in the spoken word (on this point, regarding a more recent period, see Berthelot-Guiet 1997), the unifying effect that centralization has on shared language, or the processes by which technical terms are popularized into everyday words.

A Few Funerals

As I clearly cannot treat all, or even a part, of such a vast domain, I will mention only the consequences such upheavals had for certain French suffixes, which have long been important elements in forming words that the language needs. Let us consider the suffixes *-ard*, *-oir*, *-on*, and *-ure*, which, in the first three cases, are used to form names of instruments, and, in the last case, names indicating the result of a technical operation or event. Between the 1949 and 1961 editions of the *Petit Larousse*, losses are particularly numerous (see Dubois 1962, 60). In the second edition the following words no longer appear, to consider only a small number of the victims of "progress": *accoinçon, acérure, affenoir, avalure, boitard, clysoir, ébourroir, écoinçon, empatture, étoupillon, fingard, lanceron, limure, linçoir, meulard, moletoir, ténure, trésillon,* etc.

Morphological Causes

The morphology of a language is a system with a certain cohesion linking its elements. Thus we cannot forget the strictly linguistic causes for the fossilization of so many terms, no matter how deserving. The derivatives maintain a motivational relationship with their root, which they enlarge through a suffix. Insofar as the derivative ceases to be interpreted as semantically dependent on its root, the value of the suffix dissolves. That is what happened with *écoinçon,* which no longer registered as a derivative of *coin* ("corner"), as well as with *avalure,* an old equestrian term that refers to a change in the horse's hoof, caused by the detachment of the hard part from the skin: *avalure* is a derivative of *avaler,* not in the modern sense of this verb "to swallow," but in the old sense of "detaching itself." Again, we can cite *trésillon* (its root has disappeared), noting that a verbal origin can be found for this word, which used to be a nautical term designating a piece of wood used in tying two ropes together; *trésillon* had itself produced a derived verb, *trésillonner,* as attested in the *Dictionnaire de la langue française* (Littré).

Many terms besides those bearing the suffixes examined here have disappeared for this same morphological reason: the disappearance of their root. To name a few, *affronterie,* which, as indicated in the first edition of the *Dictionnaire de l'académie française* (1694), was derived from the verb *affronter*, for which the meaning was "to deceive"; *affronterie* thus designated an act of deception, and even of fraud; but *affronter* already possessed a second meaning, "to defy," or "to pit oneself against," and had produced a derivative for this meaning, *affrontement*. The supplanting of the "to deceive" meaning led to that of the derivative *affronterie*, all the more so because a lexical field develops, *effronté/effronterie*, that clearly opposes *affronter/affrontement*.

Economic and Social Causes

These facts show that language organizes and reorganizes the lexical fields according to its own laws, and that internal factors cannot be neglected. However, the exclusion of many words is explained by the fact that they correspond to economic and social realities that are outdated, or considered so as soon as relationships of production, types of profession, and techniques change.

ANOTHER CAUSE OF THE DEATH OF WORDS: THE LAW OF TABOO AND ITS DEVASTATION

Over the course of the history of languages and in all parts of the world, words are assailed by many taboos. One human group chooses not to utter a word, whether it is because they want to ward off the evil effects they think they might provoke by doing so (avoidance behavior, or apotropaic behavior, as scholars call it), or because they decide to replace that word with a metaphoric and conciliatory name in order to win over the evil powers by using an antiphrase that presents them as good (propitiatory behavior).

This phenomenon is clearly illustrated by the names of animals with which nomadic hunters from the distant past had some relationship. That is why, in the languages of Slavic populations, to avoid designating the bear by its real name, the custom—apparently shared by all these languages—was to replace that name by a periphrasis meaning "eater of honey" (for example, in Russian, *m'edv'ed'*). There is no external cause that explains this lexical practice: the bear was found everywhere, and it was a very unified species, not involving pronounced or numerous variations which would have justified numerous designations. Nor is there a cause within the languages: the Indo-European name for bear, as it is found in Sanskrit (*rksah*), in Greek (*arktos*, from which comes the English adjective *arctic*), in Latin (*ursus*), involves an -o- stem of a completely common, dissyllabic type, and therefore not too short and not too long to persist (see Meillet 1958, 286); thus this name had no strictly linguistic reason to disappear. In addition, we encounter the same taboo among other northern European populations—Finnish, Estonians, Sami ("Lapps"), "who avoid calling the bear by its name and who describe it as 'the glory of the forest,' 'the old one,' 'the superb honey paw,' 'the hairy one,' 'the wide foot,' 'the eater of white ants,' etc. Moreover, we know that generally speaking, one of the most common vocabulary taboos applies to the name of the animal one hunts during hunting season. Among the Celts, where the name of the bear has not disappeared [. . .] analogous periphrases are found; middle Welsh has *melfochyn* [. . .], literally 'honey pig' [. . .], Irish has [. . .] *maith*, 'good,' Scotch Gaelic *math* 'good'" (Meillet 1958, 285).

The name of another hunted animal, the deer, also warrants a taboo. The Indo-European root which, this time, is retained in Russian (*ol'en'*) was replaced in other languages with an epithet meaning "horned," as in English (*hart*) and in German (*Hirsch*). Comparable vocabulary taboos, of propitiatory inspiration in these cases, apply as well to other animals. Modern French uses the term *belette* ("pretty little [beast]") for an animal that is called *mostoile* in medieval French, from the Latin *mustela*, "which still survives in the name of the fish *mustelle*, and the term in zoological classification *Mustelidae*, as well as in the dialects of the east, the northeast, and many southern French patois" (Rey 1992, 204).

Through the trickery of this flattering term, one avoided naming and sought to win the favor of the weasel, a fearsome carnivore who ravages the barnyard and enters the burrows where it sticks the rabbits.

The Cost for Vocabulary

Vocabulary taboos can have devastating effects. A comparison of Indo-European languages and those of Australia presents striking differences in terms of reconstructing the old lexicon. Indeed, in Indo-European languages, the taboos for which I have just given various examples are few enough, so that it is not difficult to establish associated families in genetically related groups. Regular phonetic correspondences between the words of one language and those of another provide a solid base for demonstrating the shared origin of those languages. On the contrary, in many parts of Australia, after the death of a tribal member the word that forms the root of his name is banned and replaced by a word borrowed from a neighboring language. That is why, among a tribe living where the Murray and Darling rivers meet, the word meaning "water" was replaced nine times in five years, because during that period nine men died whose names included that word (see Dixon 1980, 19–33)! Certain tribes, like the Warlpiri and the Tiwa, keep alternate words in stock, all ready for such situations! Such customs result in a massive, and more or less erratic, transformation of the vocabulary. Typically there is no etymological kinship between the initial word and its substitute.

Similar phenomena exist in Africa, where, among many populations, taboos are applied not only to the names of deceased individuals, but also to those of supernatural beings and certain game animals, and even to words that are etymologically or phonetically related to them. That is also the case among Amerindian languages, like Twana, in the Salish family, formerly spoken in British Columbia, or Comox, in that same family (see Hagège 1981).

Market Euphemisms

It is clear that words are the victims of all sorts of aggression, and that the taboo is not the least of them. It exists everywhere and has been present throughout history, taking different forms, like that of the euphemism, well known today in Western societies. For example, under pressure from the illusion mongers who hope to profit from bowdlerizing the facts, the French words for cancer, blind, deaf, and old, without completely falling out of use, give way to, respectively, a long and difficult illness, poor vision, hard of hearing, and third (or fourth) age. We could give countless examples.

ON TWO CAUSES FOR THE LOSS OF MEANINGS
Circumstances for Transmission: Re-creation by the Child

Transmitting language to children is not a continuous process. If it were, the child would receive the language of the parents intact. But that cannot be the case, since the ontogeny of language learning is also that of the physical being, from childhood to adolescence and then beyond, and since, as a result, the child is not in the same condition for receiving the familial language as an adult would be. Thus children re-create language for their own use, reinterpreting what they hear. They modify not only the forms, which they pronounce as their articulatory capacities allow them, but also the meanings. They designate by analogy, by metonymy, by generalization, calling any animal *dog*, for example, or by transferring from the possessed to the possessor, calling the computer or the violin *daddy*. Semantic displacements become more subtle as the child grows. But they continue to take place. Thus, when a word is used in some special way in the language of adults, the child, who perceives this use, fixates on it. From then on, the first meaning of that word, which the adults attribute to it in most instances, but which the child does not know, is eventually diluted and lost in the following generation. A well-known case is that of the word *saoul*, "for which the old meaning is 'satiated'; this word has come to apply to the intoxicated, who are 'satiated with drink'; the first ones to use the word *saoul* in this way were expressing a kind of ironic indulgence and avoided the brutality of the true name *ivre* (drunk), but the child who heard them simply associated the idea of the drunken man to that of the word *saoul*, and that is how *saoul* became a synonym for the word *ivre*, which it has even replaced in colloquial usage; by the same token, the word *saoul* is the one that now expresses the idea the most crudely" (Meillet 1958, 236).

Dissolving Ties and Diverting Meanings
The Mechanism of Loss

The meaning of a word is not only the one it takes in the context in which it is used. It is also the one it possesses in and of itself, as given by the first part of the dictionary entry. But beyond that, associative relationships construct a field of solidarity between this word and others. We have seen how derivatives that become semantically autonomous are threatened with extinction because they are no longer connected to their roots (see above). In the same way, a word cut off from its group of affinities by historical circumstances is defenselessly exposed to pressures that alter its semantics. That is because it is no longer integrated into a context capable of preserving it.

The Miserable, the Lively, and the Nest

That is why, for Latinophones, the Latin word *captivus*, "prisoner," was not prone to losing this meaning, since it was quite naturally associated with the verb *capere*, "to take." But in the languages descended from Latin, that verb has either disappeared, replaced by the descendants of *prehendere*, like the French *prendre* and the Italian *prendere*, or adopted specific meanings, like the one that appears in the French heir of its frequentative derivative *captare*, that is, *capter*. By effectively isolating *captivus* from the verb it was associated with in Latin, that adjective becomes exposed to external pressures. The contexts of its use finally give it the meaning "bad, contemptible," which is the meaning of its Italian form *cattivo*, or the meaning of "miserable, unfortunate," which is the meaning of its form in old French, *chétif*. This semantic evolution is probably not unrelated to the meaning of "prisoner of sin" that Christian authors in the first centuries gave to *captivus*.

The word then evolved toward the current meaning of *chétif*, but the meaning of "unfortunate" is not completely dead in France, since in one of the proposed etymologies it is the meaning of [*shti*] (Picardy dialect form of *chétif*) that we find in *ch'ti-mi*, "poor me," an interjection that, since the First World War, has become a humorous way to designate the northern French, by imitating them. A clever reconstruction, going in the reverse direction of this spontaneous evolution, will generate *captif* beginning from *captivus* and with its same meaning. A comparable semantic evolution is that of the German adjective *schlecht*, "plain, simple." Its *e* and its use in various contexts eventually distance it from the verb *schlichten*, "to level, to smooth out," from which it is derived. *Schlecht* then takes the new meaning that is its exclusive one today, "bad"; no doubt because a simple man, in a very hierarchical feudal society like that of the Germanic peoples of the Early Middle Ages, was a man without value.

This semantic struggle, over the course of which words eventually lose their ability to safeguard their meanings, is illustrated again by the case of the Latin adjective *vivus*, "living," which, in becoming the French *vif*, loses its ties to the verb *vivere*, "to live." From then on, the acceptation of "living," which was its principal meaning, disappears, except in frozen expressions, transmitted from the past, like *mort ou vif* (dead or alive), *brûlé vif* (burned alive). Secondary meanings dominate, which are those of "lively, animated, swift, abrupt."

A final example is offered by the Latin word *nidus*, "nest," that we trace back to the combination of two Indo-European words: **ni*, "from high to low," and **ʒhdo*, from which comes the Latin verb *sedere*, "to be settled" (the asterisk marks reconstructed forms). In one Indo-European language of the Caucasus, Armenian, the word descended from this compound, *nist*, has retained the old meaning and signifies "residence." The same is true in another language of the same family, Sanskrit (*nídáh*). But in Latin and in the Romance languages, as well as in the Germanic, Celtic, Slavic, and Baltic languages, the word took the particular meaning of "place where a bird has settled." In late vulgar Latin, this word produced the derivation **nidiacem*, from which we get the Italian *nidiace* and the French *niais*, all terms that originally designated, in the language of falconry, the bird taken in the nest. But as speakers are no longer aware of the relationship between *nid* and *niais*, the isolation of *niais* has accelerated its semantic evolution. Thus, this word, belonging to the vocabulary of the hunt like so many others, has taken the meaning of "clumsy, foolish, simpleton."

Wholesale Massacres

DISAPPEARING WORDS, A FEW OF WHICH MANAGE TO LEAVE SOME TRACES

I will consider examples from just one language here, French, in order to examine, through various periods, a coherent whole. Moreover, we might recall that the aim of this chapter is to characterize the way in which languages, by means of words, struggle against decline and adapt themselves by virtue of a kind of vital instinct. Thus what I want to do is not to present lists, but to choose examples that seem to be revealing.

The Lexical Losses of the Preclassical Ages

Lovers of medieval texts will recognize them, of course, but the majority of French speakers today cannot identify such well-coined words as *ardre*, "to burn," *bloutre*, "clod of earth turned over by the plowshare," *chaloir*, "to matter," *convice*, "reproach," *cuider*, "to think," *déduit*, "diversion, pleasure," *dextre*, "right," *s'e(s)baudir*, "to be delighted," *férir*, "to strike," *guerdon*, "reward," *issir*, "to go out, leave," *los*, "praise," *piéça*, "long ago," *pilloter*, "to gather (nectar)," and *soulas*, "consolation." These words have not all disappeared without a trace. We can see that *ardent* is the present participle of *ardre*. We use the adjective *outrecuidant*, the second part of which is the present participle of *cuider*. We still use an erudite compound of *dextre — ambidextre —* and a derivative, *dextérité*. *Férir* survives with its meaning in *sans coup férir*, although that expression is probably understood as a whole that is not analyzed. *Issue* retains something of *issir*, since it is the feminine form of its past participle. *Chaloir* is not entirely dead, since we still say *peu me chaut*, meaning, "it does not matter much to me." But the use of that phrase is accompanied with a smile, which is a standard way of judging one's own expression by injecting some distance in order to indicate that you know it is old-fashioned, or that you are using it for fun. The same can be said for *s'e(s)baudir*, deliberately used as an archaism, as a sign of complicity. As for *pilloter*, which was medieval in origin and which, according to A. Rey (1992, 1521) "had come into colloquial use (1829) and then disappeared," it might also belong to this register of gentle irony, to judge from a recent critical anthology entitled *Pillotage* (Duhamel 1995). To indicate the benefits he has drawn from reading the texts he selected, the author uses as an epigraph a line from Montaigne's *Essais* (I, 26): "The bees gather nectar (*pillotent*) here and there from the flowers, but afterwards they make it into honey, which is all their own."

The Sad Toll of Postclassicism and the Modern Era

The following can be considered among the missing at the end of the classical era, after good service and despite valiant efforts to stay alive: *bobeliner*, "to patch (up)," *controuver*, for which the past participle still manages to survive today in high style, with the meaning of "false, untrue, fabricated," *extoller*, "to exalt," *déclore*, "to open" (which survives in mannered speech — it seems to me that as a modest attempt to keep this word alive, I would not hesitate, for example, to speak of a *"regard déclos sur le mystère"*).

Other words, although almost having fallen out of use since the end of the eighteenth century, still appear in the *Littré* (1877 with the *Supplement*), which nevertheless labels them "old," exactly the sort of thing to hasten their demise: *cavillation*, "false reasoning, shallow subtlety," *chevance*, "goods that one possesses" (and *chevir*, "to have at one's disposal"), *gavache*, "destitute, poorly dressed man," *passefin*, "one who surpasses others in cunning." Certain terms are very Latin in construction, like *patavinité*, "provincialism in culture or style (in reference to the Roman historian Titus Livius, to whom this trait is attributed, and who was born in Padua, or Patavium in Latin)," or *vécordie*, "lack of heart, toughness," where we find the old Latin privative prefix *ve-* of *vésanie*, "insanity."

The beginning of the nineteenth century marked the disappearance of a great number of words that had succeeded in surviving until the end of the Revolution, among them *bailler*, "to give" (of its homonyms *bayer*, "to open the mouth wide [= *bée*)]," or "to stand gaping," and *bâiller*, "to yawn," only the latter survives today, the former no longer attested except in the fixed expression *bayer aux corneilles*). The great number of extinct words is explained by the fact that the realities they evoked had themselves disappeared, as is the case for the nouns with suffixes that I examined earlier (see above).

Obviously we are concerned here only with words that have truly fallen out of everyday use, and not with terms that, even when they are old, still thrive in the technical language of scholarly texts. To consider only one example, in a work on numismatics, we could still find today an expression like *bractéates et autre pièces incuses*, designating coins that are minted concave on one side.

DISAPPEARANCES AND SUBSTITUTIONS OF MEANING

The cemeteries of words are also those of meanings. Nonetheless, a word can endure and its meaning vanish. That is even one of the basic elements of languages, and to the extent that the history of words reflects that of humans and their representations, we can consider such changes completely normal. To respond to external pressures, vocabularies continually restructure themselves by modifying the relationships between words constituting various semantic fields. Again I will consider only a few examples. The words *biberon, candide, dévot, galanterie, meurtrir, offenser, route,* and *séminaire* have lost their earlier meanings, that is, respectively, "one who likes to drink," "sincere," "venerable," "quest for amorous affairs," "to kill," "to attack militarily," "rout," and "planting bed, plant nursery."

Words that lose their meanings acquire one or more new ones. As for those that disappear entirely, to be buried without services in the vast and ever growing cemeteries of words, they are replaced by others. The death of words is only one side of a complex phenomenon, the other side of which is the birth of new words, just as we shall see.

Neology's Rich Harvest

Here I will also limit myself to the single example of French. The authors of the Renaissance, notably the seven poets of the Pléiade, introduced into their works a wealth of new words by drawing especially from regional and foreign languages. A strict attempt at purging followed at the beginning of the seventeenth century, as we are often reminded. Nevertheless, still enduring today are many words that were introduced in the sixteenth century. Some are Provençal in origin, like *auberge,* "inn," *badaud,* "gaper," *bouquet,* "bouquet," *cadenas,* "padlock," *caserne,* "barracks," *daurade,* "sea bream," *escalier,* "stairs," *girolle,* "chanterelle," *luzerne,* "alfalfa," and *triolet,* "triplet." Others, which were threatened even before this epoch and which have become increasingly rare, have nevertheless been able to stay alive even in the modern language. Among them are *affoler,* "to terrify," *émoi,* "agitation," *hacher,* "to chop," *hideux,* "hideous," *rancoeur,* "rancor." Still others were formed at that time through derivation or composition, or through reactivation of old forms: *aboutir,* "to succeed," *bigoterie,* "bigotry," *clairvoyance,* "clear-sightedness," *décomposer,* "to break (up or down)," *déplorable,* "deplorable," *désordre,* "disorder," *marmaille,* "gang (of kids)," *non-dit,* "unspoken," *soussigner,* "undersign." Words are borrowed from Italian: *banque,* "bank," *balcon,* "balcony," *bosquet,* "grove," (*à l'*)*improviste,* "unexpectedly," *soldat,* "soldier," *sonnet,* "sonnet," etc., or from Spanish, like *bizarre,* "strange," *escamoter,* "to make disappear," *fanfaron,* "boastful," *hâbleur,* "bragging," *mascarade,* "masquerade" (see Brunot 1966, III, part I).

We are in the habit of thinking that French leaves the classical age bloodless. The causes given for this are Malherbe's actions, and then, the Académie becoming more liberal, Vaugelas, whose severe words are often quoted: "No one is allowed to make new words, not even the sovereign." But he adds: "if someone can make ones that have currency, it must be a Sovereign, or a Favorite, or a chief Minister [. . .]; that happens by accident, because if these types of individuals invent a word, the Courtiers immediately make note of it, and say it so often that others say it, too, in imitation of them; so much so that finally it is established in the usage, and spread to everyone" (Vaugelas, 1647, I, 40).

Whether by this means, or by that of more spontaneous creations, backed up by the authorities that then ruled over the language, French was enriched in the seventeenth century with more words than one would think. Thus, various nominal suffixes allowed for the construction of derived substantives like *causerie,* "talk," *cirage,* "polish," *discernement,* "discernment," *douanier,* "customs officer," *exactitude,* "exactitude," *félicitation,* "congratulations," *machiniste,* "stagehand," *orangeade,* "orangeade," *plaisanterie,* "joke," *ponctualité,* "punctuality," *républicain,* "republican," etc. The verbs *débar-*

rasser, "to clear," *détromper,* "to disabuse," *griffonner,* "to scribble," *ironiser,* "to ironize," *régaler,* "to feast," and the adjectives *inconcevable,* "inconceivable," *indiscernable,* "indiscernible," etc., can also be considered new. In this same epoch, French continues to borrow heavily from Latin: *diffusion,* "diffusion," *éluder,* "to elude," *insidieux,* "insidious," *sévir,* "to act ruthlessly," *subordination,* "subordination," *surrection,* "uprise," all words attested, actually, for a few centuries already, but that Vaugelas considers new. Borrowing from Greek also takes place: *anachronisme, homonyme, polyglotte* (almost the same in English), etc., as well as from Italian: *bagatelle,* "trinket," *cascade,* "waterfall," *miniature,* "miniature," *riposter,* "to retort," etc., from Spanish: *baroque, disparate, sarabande* (like the English), from German: *halte,* "pause," *sabre,* "saber," etc. (see Brunot, ibid., 215–223).

The eighteenth century created or sanctioned by use a considerable number of new words, especially but not exclusively during the revolutionary period. The *-iser* verbs are only one chapter among many where the creative force of the language is deployed. The adjectives *complémentaire,* "complementary," and *supplémentaire,* "supplementary," for example, or again the noun *éventualité,* "possibility," and the verb *sauvegarder,* "to safeguard," are from this epoch, to cite just words that sound so modern that we would think they were not so old.

The nineteenth century and the contemporary epoch are, as we well know, times of influx for English words. Certain French words that English puts in jeopardy or pushes toward extinction are synonyms of those that English had borrowed from Norman, and then from French, in the eleventh to the thirteenth centuries, following the Norman conquest. Thus, *approche, challenge, contrôle, initier, majeur, opportunité, pratiquement, réaliser, réhabiliter* (close to their English equivalents) are used more and more today in place of *méthode, défi, maîtrise, commencer, important, occasion, quasiment, se rendre compte, remettre en bon état* (see Hagège 1987, 57–58). In other areas, French words, recommended by terminology commissions, have succeeded in asserting themselves in face of Anglo-American words nevertheless favored by the economic and industrial power of the United States and, what is more, backed by the media, in France as in other European countries. For the success achieved by French words like *logiciel, matériel,* and *ordinateur,* which, for more than thirty years, have dominated over software, hardware, and computer, and for other similar successes, I refer the reader to a detailed study of these facts (Hagège 1987).

In this way, words live and die like all other natural beings. It is interesting to reread what was written in 1862 by C. Lyell, a supporter of the transformist theories who took an interest in the life of words, even though he was a geologist (see chapter 2):

> Quite a curious subject of inquiry is the study of the laws by virtue of which certain words or certain expressions are invented and even selected, and take precedence over others. Because, since the human memory has only a limited power, it must also be true that there is a limit to the growth of vocabulary and to the proliferation of terms. Thus it is necessary for old words to disappear [. . .]. The slightest advantages resulting from a new pronunciation or a new spelling, by reason of brevity or euphony, can tip the scale, just as there can be other more powerful reasons for selection that determine triumph or defeat between rivals. Some are: the style, the influence of an aristocracy by birth or by education, the influence of popular writers, orators and preachers. Again, another is that of a centralizing government that organizes schools expressly to propagate the uniformity of diction and to insure the use of the best provincial and local dialects.

This text is dated, of course, by certain aspects of its inspiration, and what is more, the factors involved in the evolution of words and of languages are confused. Nonetheless, the transformist vision is not inadequate for demonstrating the play of forces according to which, when words die, others replace them. We could say that, in a certain way, languages live because words die. The death of words does not threaten the life of languages; on the contrary, it is one of its necessary conditions.

Part II. LANGUAGES AND DEATH

5. What Is a Dead Language?

Dead Language Versus Classical Language

We usually say that a language is dead when it no longer has users (or "locutors," more technically speaking). But there are many ways for a language to be dead. Thus, Latin and Greek ceased to be spoken a very long time ago. Nevertheless, in France, they are both represented among the subjects taught in schools (at least until now, although they are increasingly in danger of being excluded from programs). Academic administrations call them "ancient languages," Greek being justly called "classical" (as opposed to today's Greek, which is called "modern" and which is spoken). Students can choose classical Greek and Latin in the same way as so-called living languages, even though they are dead in the simple sense just described.

That is because the status of Latin and classical Greek gives them a particular place in the culture in France and in the other Romance language countries (Italy, Spain, Portugal, Romania). Indeed, historically, French descends mostly from Latin, and from Greek for a major part of its scholarly vocabulary. The presence of these ancient languages in the official curriculum as it is offered in many states is an indication of at least symbolic, if not actual, continuity.

To further clarify what must be understood precisely by "death of a language," I will give a rough survey of the history of Latin. But besides this revealing example, others exist throughout the world, and I will show that, in each case, we have to do with a language clearly fallen out of use, but nevertheless endowed with prestige and regarded as an inalienable part of the culture. Finally, one other case also deserves to be examined. This is the case of literary Arabic, also taught in the schools in all the countries concerned yet nevertheless absent from everyday communications. Who would maintain that literary Arabic is a dead language? And yet, who would claim that one can hear it used by ordinary speakers in any Arab country? Rich in lessons on what constitutes a dead language, these are the kinds of situations that provide an opportune starting point for this study.

WHEN IS LATIN "DEAD"?
Literary Latin and Vulgar Latin

In the West, quick minds might ask a hard question: when did Latin stop being spoken? To respond, it makes sense to examine at least the last stages of it. In most complex societies that occupy large territories and that are hierarchized into classes, linguistic differences tend to be established. By greatly simplifying things, these differences can often be subsumed into an opposition between literary language and vulgar language, the latter being defined as that spoken by locutors upon whom scholarly and written models exercise a limited influence, and who more easily accommodate external contributions, and so help to hasten evolution.

Such an opposition existed in ancient Rome from a time that we cannot precisely determine but which had no doubt begun long before the Republic. Plautus's plays from the end of the third to the early second century B.C. preserve for us an example of vulgar Latin in which various changes are beginning to appear. As for the much more stable literary Latin, we can get a sense of it from the fragments remaining from the same period by the poet Ennius, who cultivated a careful norm, which compensated for the Osque and Greek origins of this romanized Calabrian. The cultivated elite of this epoch and the ones that followed were aware of the changes brought about by the development of vulgar Latin. As early as the first century A.D., the grammarian Varro established the norms of "good usage," while Caesar chiseled a prose as close as possible to the classical ideal, and while in his *Brutus* Cicero mourned the epoch when the native inhabitants of Rome, not subject to "some barbaric influence within their own families, expressed themselves as was necessary," and deplored the change produced in Latin by "the cosmopolitan throngs speaking a corrupt language" (quoted in Banniard, 1992, 243, other passages of which are used below); a century later, the rhetorician Quintilian insisted upon the choice of speakers worthy of serving as models.

One fact thus becomes clear: for a long time spoken Latin had been in the process of dominating usage when, at the beginning of the fourth century, Constantine began to grant the Christians a significant role in state life. Roman power was then in full decline, faced with continual pressure from the Barbarians. From then on a problem presents itself: literary Latin, obviously promoted by the Church, on the way to becoming the only legitimate heir to Rome, is the instrument of Christian preaching, and, as the prestigious written language, it will not experience considerable changes in relationship to the classical language of Cicero and Caesar; conversely, the masses of the faithful, whom the Church Fathers address in their evangelical mission, speak a vulgar Latin that is continually evolving, like any oral language. It follows that the "death" of Latin will coincide with the moment when vertical communication between learned preachers and the faithful becomes impossible, because of the increasingly insurmountable distance between that written language and vulgar Latin, evolving finally to result in many distinct Roman languages.

The Three Stages in the "Death" of Latin

We can distinguish three stages. From 400 to about 650, that is, from the last century of the Roman Empire to the middle of the Merovingian dynasty (founded in 481), preachers managed to make themselves understood by the masses, even though their attitudes varied. Gregory the Great in Lombard Italy, and Augustine in Africa, who appreciated rustic Latin as the living soil of Christian pedagogy, kept their distance from classicist choices of the translator Jerome and his teacher, the grammarian Donat. In contrast, Isidore of Seville, in Visigothic Spain, or Gregory of Tours in the Gaul of Clovis's successors, lamented what they considered a debasement of Latin, while adapting themselves out of necessity. During a second stage, which we can place between 650 and 750, communication functioned in an increasingly approximate way between the illiterate on the one hand and the learned on the other who were seeking to make themselves understood by the latter, at the price, sometimes, of a vulgarized Latin, as is the case with the monk Marculf.

Finally, in the last stage, after 750 and at the close of the Merovingian epoch, an irreversible linguistic crisis occurs. At the beginning of the ninth century, Charlemagne charged Alcuin, a scholar whose mother tongue was Northumbrian (Old English), with restoring Latin studies. In Carolingian Gaul, where the court and the aristocracy with their Tudesque language were cut off from the population, his efforts had the effect of only deepening the gulf between the latter and Latin. This was a population, of course, that did not participate in the Latin-Tudesque bilingualism of the Frankish intellectual elite. The break was more radical still in Spain, where the educated Latinophones of Cordoba, especially Alvaro and Eulogio, representatives of those Christians who were called, oddly, Mozarabs ("Arabized"), cultivated a language as pure as possible to assert themselves in the face of the Islamic authority, which did not persecute the Church but brought it under its yoke. That intensified the distance from the speech of the masses. Of course, in politically Arab but mainly Romanophone Andalusia, in the middle of the ninth century, the spoken language evolved more slowly than in Gaul. And it was not subject to as strong an influence as Germanic Frank exercised over vulgar Latin to produce, as a result of this convergence, the ancestor of French. Nonetheless, the speech of the Roman masses in Spain was already so far from Latin that communication with Latinophone preachers became impossible. The rupture came later in Italy, but it was complete by the middle of the tenth century.

Thus in the Christian West, the passive competence of the masses with regard to Latin, that is, their ability to roughly understand it while not speaking it (see Hagège 1996a, 246 s.), never stopped declining. But as a corollary, the active competence of preachers declined by the very reason of their effort to adapt to their public. Romania had ceased to be Latin to become Romance, the name that was given to the new languages. They are also called "neo-Latin." And in fact, for quite a long period, probably beginning even before the end of the Roman republic and continuing until the early Middle Ages, foreign users must have thought they were speaking "in Latin," even when communication with Latinophones had already become difficult. Consider, for example, the Romans speaking to mercenary veterans, with their diverse linguistic origins, who guarded the *limes* in the middle of the second century. At the empire's frontier they fought off Barbarian incursions from Dacia, Pannonia, or Mesia (today roughly representing, respectively, Romania, Hungary, and Bulgaria). Much later, Latinophone preachers would address the masses in order to Christianize them. But they would not resort to the common languages the masses used, which explains the difficulties in communication.

It is clear that neo-Latin languages could not have descended from literary Latin. They could have come only from spoken forms of Latin, just as modern Greek is not the descendant of the classical Greek (essentially Attic) that the ancient authors used when Athens was at its height, but very much the descendant of the *koiné* that developed after that epoch, that is, since the fourth century B.C. The promotion of neo-Latin idioms as fully entitled languages is guaranteed since the recognition that writing in Latin has become inadequate for transcribing the words of the masses.

It must be stressed that Latin was a written language not only in the sense of a literary language and a language of prestige, but also to the extent that, for the learned of the early Middle Ages in the West, writing in a language other than Latin was unthinkable. Thus it was necessary to devise a new *scripta* that guaranteed recognition to · Romance languages. Of course we are speaking of languages that are new on still another and essential level, that of their internal form. We must recall the well-known fact that in all the Romance languages since this time, if we confine ourselves to areas other than vocabulary, we can note the following traits: there is no longer any neuter (Romanian is a special case; see Rosetti 1985); declensions are in the process of disappearing, giving way to an increase in the number and the role of prepositions; a new category of articles is developing; the simple future in Latin is replaced by a compound form; the inflections of the middle and passive voices are dying out; the infinitive in complementary clauses is increasingly replaced with a personal mood; and the system of conjunctions is renewed.

Some would maintain that the notion of death does not apply in any clear way to Latin, to the extent that the neo-Latin languages descended from it. That is only partially true, since in fact, as we have just seen, they came from various forms of *vulgar Latin*, and not the Latin transmitted to us through the great classical texts. As for those who maintain that neo-Latin is not distinct from Latin, that position is unacceptable. A recognized genetic origin is not sufficient to conclude that the ancestor and descendant are one and the same thing. Only the nationalist pride of a Spain where Christianity and Latin had been restored to the peninsula after the completion of the *Reconquista*, which had put an end to nearly eight centuries of Arab occupation—which was, incidentally, quite brilliant—could explain the strange impression held by certain Spaniards since 1492. They imagined that they had brought to the American Indians, whose languages were so exotic, Latinity itself, through Castilian, from which comes the notion of "Latin America," a surprising one when you think about it.

In fact, the neo-Latin languages were set free a long time ago in Spain as in France, and their forms, then, were not as far removed as one might think from those they take today. It is only a metaphor to say that Latin lives on in the Romance languages. Moreover, it must be emphasized that vernacular languages have been used in the sciences and in philosophical treatises since the mid-seventeenth century. Though less bold, of course, this was another sign of emancipated thinking in relation to the dogmas of authority, which express themselves in Latin.

That said, we must also recall that in Europe in the classical age, as in the medieval period, scholars and the literati generally continued to communicate in Latin, and that is true even in non-Latin countries: Germany, Poland, Sweden, England, and Ireland. Moreover, Latin did not disappear everywhere from use. It is still the language of the Roman Church, as it formerly was of the Roman Empire. As is typical of the fate of human languages, Latin is not alive nor completely dead.

A language that has fallen out of use can also persist in a state that is not alive, as defined by presence within the daily exchange, but that nevertheless is not truly dead.

Coptic

Thus, Coptic is still used today in the liturgy and religious ceremonies of the Christians in Egypt. In fact, Coptic is nothing other than the "modern" form of a language that goes back to Pharaonic Egypt itself! A direct continuity, stretching over more than five thousand years, links Coptic to the language, written in hieroglyphs, of the ancient empire that was founded in Memphis by Menes in 3400 B.C. This line continues through the Middle Egyptian of the Theban empire (about 2000 B.C.), which still used hieroglyphs, though they were drawn according to a cursive writing style called hieratic, and then through the neo-Egyptian of the new dynasties, those of the Ramses (beginning in about 1580 B.C.), and finally through the Egyptian—called demotic, along with its simplified writing style—of the last dynasties, those of Psammetichus and his followers, before Cambyses' Persians conquered Egypt in 525 B.C. Hellenization followed two centuries later, at the time of Alexander's victories. Thus a "single" language is maintained through this immense stretch of time in successive states very different, of course, from each other. And the vitality of Coptic, the last of these states, will only be compromised by the spread of Arabic in an Egypt that had become primarily Muslim, beginning in the ninth century A.D. Coptic might still have been spoken in the villages in the mid-nineteenth century. In any case, its unfathomably long history cannot help but confer a certain prestige upon this language that lives on in religious use.

Late Archaic Chinese

That is how we can designate the classical language of the Warring States period (fifth to third century B.C.), called *wen yen*, as opposed to the archaic Chinese of the Western and Eastern Chou (eleventh to sixth centuries B.C.). It is the language of the great works that are considered—along with those illustrating archaic Chinese—to be the foundations of Chinese culture: Confucius's and Mencius's Four Books, Mencius's *Writings*, Mo Tzu, Chuang Tzu, and others. Among sinologists, some think that the Late Archaic Chinese in which these famous books were composed reflects a spoken language of the time; others see in this very elliptical language an artificial construction corresponding to no idiom that had ever been spoken; finally, others (see Hagège 1975, 21–22) see it as one of the former states of literary Chinese. Whatever the case, this language never evolved, whereas as early as the end, if not the middle, of the following period, the time of the Former Han dynasty (from 206 B.C. to A.D. 26), the spoken language began to experience increasingly significant changes. *Wen yen* has always been taught in China, where the classic books are read and studied in the academic system. Thus this is not a spoken language, certainly, but one whose "death" does not keep it from being a constant presence in the culture.

Sanskrit and Pali

This is also the status of Sanskrit in northern India, in relation to languages of the Indo-Aryan family, and even in relation to the non-Indo-Aryan languages of southern India, called the Dravidian languages, which have borrowed significant vocabulary from Sanskrit as a result of their speakers practicing the same Brahminical religion as the speakers of the northern languages. The famous grammarian

Pāṇini established the rules of Sanskrit in about the fifth century B.C. Three centuries later, Patañjali, one of his successors, formalized the interpretation of the texts. This gave a sort of rigidity to Vedic Sanskrit, the sacred language of four great collections of versified religious hymns, their commentaries and speculative glosses in prose, and manuals relating to rites. But over the immense span of the millennium that separates the first Vedic attestations from Pāṇini, this language — which may never have been spoken — probably knew oral and evolutionary variants, exactly like the states that succeeded it, among them Buddhist Sanskrit beginning in the fourth century B.C. and, of course, what are called the Prakrit languages, namely the early forms of Middle Indian. They began to develop in the later centuries B.C. to become, in about the tenth century, the many components of modern Indo-Aryan, the source of today's northern Indian languages.

But, for cultural and religious reasons, other Asian languages also drew from the prestigious depths of the Sanskrit vocabulary. That is true, most notably, for Khmer, Javanese, and even Malay, whose later Islamization would nevertheless make it into a borrower of Arabic words. Like Latin and Greek in the European countries of Christian civilization, Sanskrit is taught in India. Some even claim that it is still spoken there, but if that is true, its use is only a scholarly one among the literati. In any case, Sanskrit today is one among twenty official languages recognized in the Constitution of the Republic of India.

Another well-known religious language, Pali, is the one Buddha's successors chose in place of Sanskrit to spread his teachings, taking for its base the vernacular languages of northern India. Pali, the language of the Buddhist canons of Ceylon, retained a liturgical use on that island, as well as in Burma and in many regions of Southeast Asia where it had been the vehicle for Buddhism. But beyond that, and for that very reason, Pali was an important source of borrowings for the religious, philosophical, and administrative vocabulary of Burmese, Thai, and various ethnic languages. Thanks to its status as generous fountain from which so many modern languages drink, we could say that it is not quite dead.

Ge'ez

Attested since less ancient times, Ge'ez, the first form of Ethiopian, also endures today in liturgical and scholarly use. Ge'ez was the language of Aksum, the capital of the Abyssinian realm in the fourth century, when the sovereign introduced Christianity in his states. The Semitic languages of Ethiopia, in particular Tigrinya and especially Amharic, the idiom of Addis Ababa and most of the Abyssinian high plateau, evolved outside of the scholarly influence of Ge'ez, but the latter was and remains for them a source of borrowings. Thus this eastern African language bears the same relationship to modern Ethiopian idioms as do the sacred languages of Asia to the modern idioms of that continent.

IS CLASSICAL ARABIC A LIVING LANGUAGE?

As is the case with Latin, if we use the definition proposed at the beginning of this chapter, we can hastily declare classical Arabic to be dead. Nevertheless, a very common experience demonstrates the opposite. In numerous circumstances marked with some formality, classical Arabic is used today, and not only in situations involving monologue. What can we conclude from that with regard to the definition of a dead language?

We must recognize the complexity of what is called the Arabic language. Its remarkable nature appears as soon as it is named. If "Arabic" is mentioned without an adjective, some will understand this word as referring to classical Arabic, which is also called literary, or written, or Koranic Arabic, although these terms—and what they designate—are far from being equivalent. Others, maybe less numerous, will think that "Arabic" means dialectical Arabic, that is, one of the forms of Arabic spoken in the Maghreb (Moroccan, Algerian, Tunisian, Libyan), or in Saharan Africa (Mauritanian, or Hassaniyya), or in the East (Egyptian, Sudanese, Chad, Saudi Arabian, Jordanian, Palestinian, Lebanese, Syrian, Iraqi, Yemeni, Omani, the dialects of Dathina and Hadramaut), or in one of the sultanates of the Syrian-Arab peninsula, or again, the Arabic used by Christians like the Maltese or the inhabitants of Kormakiti in Crete.

It is likely that the situation of diglossia that prevails in the Arab world, that is, the existence of a literary variant that is reserved for written use and dialectical variants that are spoken in the various Arab countries, is very old (see Hagège 1973, 3). It is also likely that the Arabic of the Koran was not a spoken language from which the dialects descended historically, but rather a prestigious norm in which the Prophet received and transmitted the revelation of Islam. Thus the situation is different from that of Latin, despite the shared opposition between the written and the spoken. Furthermore, unlike Latin, literary Arabic is commonly used today in all Arab literature, since, in principle, the dialects are not written (on the distinction between language and dialect, see the beginning of chapter 8). It is used on radio and television, and in official discourse, scientific communications, and all other formal circumstances.

Nevertheless, what allows us to say that we are not dealing with a spoken language in the ordinary sense of the term is one simple fact: literary Arabic is not, in principle, anyone's mother tongue. The inhabitants of Arab countries speak in daily life and transmit to their children only the dialect of the country in which they live. We know that Arab dialects can be quite different, including those within the same geographical or cultural group, and even more so between two groups: a Yemenite and a Moroccan can experience some communication difficulty when each speaks his own dialect. That is why they may have to resort to literary Arabic in this case. But that assumes that each one knows it well enough to use it in oral exchange, which is far from being always the case, considering the highly variable levels of schooling and education. Furthermore, the use of this language in spoken communication seems artificial and affected to the majority of Arabophones, the dialects alone serving as true instruments of conversation.

From all this, and in light of cases like those of Latin, certain old prestigious languages, and Arabic, it follows that the definition of a dead language as one that is no longer spoken must be qualified. For our present purposes, languages will be considered dead if no locutors speak them anymore, of course, but beyond that, if they have left no living traces in the cultures of the descendants of those who died speaking them.

Dead Languages Without Classical Status

Another case will bring us closer to understanding this idea of the death of a language. Numerous languages that have been dead for many millennia are known to us only through inscriptions, texts, or coins. These are the materials upon which epigraphists, numismatists, philologists, grammarians, and other researchers practice their art. Thus we have to do, here, with scientifically investigated languages. Unlike those I have just presented, these languages have no classical status today, insofar as they are not put to any liturgical or more general cultural use through which they can live on, nor taught in primary or secondary schools, even if they are taught in certain universities and research institutes. But precisely because they have this property of being objects of scholarly investigation and academic study, they can be considered part of the culture in the places where they have left archeological traces. Obviously the number of these traces is very variable. Sometimes there is abundant documentation, and sometimes it is fragmentary.

THE CASES OF ABUNDANT DOCUMENTATION
Sumerian, Akkadian, Ugaritic, Numidian

We possess considerable traces of Sumerian, one of humanity's oldest written languages that is a perpetual enigma because it cannot be connected to a single known linguistic family. We can go back to at least 3300 B.C. thanks to tens of thousands of cuneiform texts: hymns, rituals, contracts, steles, annals, and inscriptions, and legal, medical, and mathematical writings. There is the same fascinating richness for Akkadian, the eastern Semitic language that succeeded Sumerian when Assyrian power began to dominate Sumer, even though Sumerian continued to flourish for some time, and Akkadian prolonged the cuneiform notation of Sumerian. Toward the end of the seventh century, before declining and being relegated to scholarly use and then replaced by Aramaic after the Persian conquest in 539 B.C. (see chapter 10), Akkadian and its evolved forms, Babylonian and neo-Babylonian, would experience a long tenure as languages of the civilizations of powerful empires. That is recounted for us in even more detail since the excavations of Mari, Ebla, and Emar brought to light enormous quantities of new documents, among them a wealth of private correspondences (see Durand 1997).

Two sources of important documentation were also deciphered in the modern period (1929). The first, found at Ras Chamra on the Syrian coast, includes many mythological poems, revealing the ancient existence of Ugaritic (approximately fifteenth century B.C.), another Semitic language, but a western one, close to Cananian. The second is made up of a significant quantity of short inscriptions found scattered from the Sinai to the Canaries that reconstruct Libyan, also a Semitic language and ancestor to the Berber dialects.

Etruscan, Indo-European Languages of Asia Minor (Anatolia) and of Chinese Turkestan

We would like to know much more than we do of the mysterious Etruscan language, which reigned until about 300 B.C. in Etruria, that is, in almost immediate proximity to the very territories where Rome and Latin would supplant it. The knowledge we have is provided by about ten thousand short and monotonous funeral inscriptions, by strips of cloth bearing a series of invocations and ritual instructions, and by glosses, that is, translations of transmitted words in treatises by ancient authors. A contemporary of Augustus, the Greek historian Denys of Halicarnassus already noted the isolation as well as the obscurity of this language that resembles nothing known (see Briquel 1994, 319–321). If it were true, as Herodotus says, that the Etruscans came from Lydia, then perhaps a connection with the Indo-European of Anatolia (see below) would not be implausible, considering certain shared points in the area of syntax, and even though there is nothing Indo-European about the vocabulary.

On the other hand, abundant texts and thousands of tablets unearthed in the early twentieth century have allowed many languages to be saved from oblivion. Two of these are important ancient Indo-European languages, Tocharian and Hittite. The evidence for Tocharian, that is, for its two dialects, are treatises (religious, medical, economic) inspired by Buddhism. They were discovered in Chinese Turkestan and are written in brahmi (the most ancient writing of India, ancestor to nearly all today's Indian writings and used for a long time in all of central Asia). In 1908, two German scholars established that the Tocharian languages belonged to the Indo-European family. The Tocharian languages must have become extinct before 1000, shortly after the conquest of the Anyi and neighboring territories by the Ugaritic Turks in the ninth century (see Isebaert 1994).

At the heart of Asia Minor, Hittite was the language of a powerful empire between the nineteenth and the thirteenth century B.C. Terra-cotta tablets found in the ancient capital of that empire, Hattusa (present-day Bogazköy), have been a source of numerous texts. To these have just been added texts from tablets very recently discovered at Ortaköy, and still not completely studied. The Hittite empire was taken over by other states whose languages, especially Luwian and Lycian, were sometimes close relatives, sometimes evolved forms of Hittite. In particular, epitaphs and legends on coins written in Lycian give interesting clues about this language of a population of the southwestern coast of Asia Minor, mentioned by Homer and Herodotus. It was made easier still to salvage from oblivion by the 1974 discovery of a dedicatory text in three languages, Lycian-Greek-Aramaic. In the same region were found abundant inscriptions in various non-Indo-European languages, not clearly assignable to any family and presenting some Caucasic traits: Hurrian, Elamite, and Hattian, all idioms that had probably become extinct by the beginning of the Christian era.

Gothic

There is another important language we are very familiar with as well, but this time thanks to means other than ritual, administrative, or private inscriptions: Gothic. It must have become extinct much more recently, at the end of the Middle Ages. As the language of the Goths, of whom one branch, the Visigoths, sacked Rome in 410,

Gothic is the only existing evidence of the eastern branch of Germanic, to which also belong the languages of those tribes who, in the fifth and sixth centuries, made Rome, northern Italy, Gaul, Spain, and Africa tremble: the Burgunds, Vandals, and Lombards. Gothic melted in the West with the Roman environment that surrounded it, and this had already taken place when, in 711, the Arab invasion got the better of the Visigothic realm in Spain. But in the East Gothic fared better, thanks especially to the text that preserves it for us even today: the translation of the Bible done in the mid-fourth century by the bishop Ulfila, from the diocese of Moesia, occupied by the Goths. Important fragments of it have survived.

CASES OF FRAGMENTARY DOCUMENTATION

Many languages that knew their days of glory but died out before the beginning of the Christian era are attested only by as few as one or as many as several hundred inscriptions, or by short texts or vocabulary lists that, awaiting new discoveries, do not allow researchers to form a precise idea of these languages, beyond scattered and elementary structural particulars.

Celtic Languages

This family was once widespread in Europe and as far away as Asia Minor, as onomastics attest to: the name of the realm of the Galatians, who settled in that region has the same root as Gaul, Wales (*pays de Galles,* in French), and certain cities like, probably, Gallipoli ("city of the Gauls"), the Turkish port on the European bank of the Dardanelles. The Celts began a continuous decline about the beginning of the third century B.C. Today, what survives of their languages, though clearly in a state of decay, as we will see, is spoken only in remote areas near the ocean, where the advance of the Romans in Gaul and the Saxons in Great Britain forced the Celts to seek refuge: Scotland, Wales, the Atlantic counties of Ireland (Donegal, Galway, Connemara, Kerry), and Brittany (for more detail, see Hagège 1994, 242–245, 250–254).

Other Celtic languages have been dead for nearly two thousand years. The only traces we have of them are, for Gaulish, a hundred inscriptions. There are as many again, all of them on funeral monuments where almost all we find are the names of the individuals, for Lepontic, which was spoken around the lakes of northern Italy. And we find even less for Lusitanian, formerly used in the northwestern part of the Iberian Peninsula. This lack of attestations is all the more unfortunate because Lusitanian, from which the Portuguese dialect of Galicia (another Celtic name!) has retained many vocables, is of particular interest to linguists. Indeed, it occupies a completely distinctive place within its family. It is the only family member to have retained the Indo-European *p, extinct everywhere else, as the words of Old Irish *athir, orc,* and *íasc* show, as opposed to the Latin *pater, porcus, piscis* and the Old High German *fater, farh, fisc* (respectively "father," "pork," "fish"); on the contrary, for "pork," Lusitanian has *porcom.*

Aquitanian

There remain only, on Latin inscriptions from the beginning of our era found in the Upper Pyrénées, two hundred names of individuals and divinities in a language that is supposedly an ancient form of Basque, because of the fact that, in one of the Basque dialects, it is possible to give a meaning to those names. Could this rather be an earlier language having borrowed from Basque? The situation is as enigmatic as that of Basque itself, about which there are many theories regarding its origin (assignment to a Caucasic family, or to the Altaic languages, etc.), although none that are convincing to all the scholarly circles.

Slavic and Baltic Languages

The pressure to Germanicize made German the gravesite of Slavic as well as Baltic languages (see Hagège 1994, 57–65). Of course, many of them are very much alive today, but they owe this to the power of large states, with which Germany waged war unsuccessfully, or to the continual efforts of a national affirmation policy in face of German expansion. On the contrary, the Slavic languages of isolated little ethnic groups have been engulfed.

We have nothing more than short texts and vocabulary lists for a language that died in the eighteenth century, Polabian, which, as its Slavic name indicates, was used along (*po-*) one tributary of the middle course of the Elbe (*Labe*) in the region of Lüchow, as well as with Slovincian, still spoken by two hundred senior citizens in 1903 in two parishes in the heart of Pomerania (another Slavic name meaning "along the [Baltic] sea"). These phenomena show that German pressure allowed only some small islands to remain in a formerly Slavic stronghold that it had totally overrun. Of a Baltic language that died in the seventeenth century, we possess a few more texts: vocabularies, translations of catechisms, and Luther's Enchiridion, a manual for spreading the reformed faith; this language is Old Prussian, spoken in the country that would become German Prussia, and that was called *Prusis* in that Baltic idiom before being crushed in the rush of Teutonic knights.

Indo-European Languages of the Balkans: Pelasgian, Macedonian, Thracian, Phrygian, Illyrian

Almost all we know of Pelasgian is what the *Iliad* suggests about it, its second song giving a catalog of vessels owned by the inhabitants of "fertile Larissa," their capital. The patronymics and toponyms from the Homeric passage allow us to envision a language distinct from Greek, but most certainly Indo-European (see Bader 1994, 19–20).

Another language of the Hellenic domain, Macedonian, is important to the European collective memory as it is to contemporary politics, since Greece, Serbia, and Bulgaria have each claimed ancestral rights over Macedonia since the second half of the nineteenth century, and have based their claims on "linguistic" arguments. Now, not only has Macedonian been dead for a long time (we are not speaking here of the Slavic language of the little republic formed after the 1992 breakup of Yugoslavia), but the available documentation on this language is very poor. No written texts in Macedonian remain. We have only the glosses attributed to Hesychius and, of course, the comments of historians like Herodotus, and later, Titus Livius, without counting a passage by Quintus Curtius, who declares that Alexander the Great (a Macedonian) resorted to an interpreter in order to be understood by the Greeks. We may doubt the merit of this information, knowing that Alexander had people acknowledge his Greek origins in order to be admitted to the Olympic games, and that elsewhere, the same Quintus Curtius has Alexander suggesting that Macedonian is understandable to the Greeks (see Brixhe and Panayotou 1994b). Whatever the case, the little that we know of this language gives way to hypotheses: for some, Macedonian is a mixed language composed of Thracian and Illyrian contributions grafted onto a dialectical Greek base; according to others, it is the language of a non-Greek, historically Hellenized people. In many such cases the fate of languages casts into oblivion the mother tongue of great conquerors of brilliant renown.

The former domain of the language of the Thracians, who lived long ago in the southeastern part of the Balkan peninsula, where they had arrived at the beginning of the second millennium B.C., was noticeably enlarged by their migration, seven or eight centuries later, to the northwest of the Balkans (Propontide, Mysia, Bythinia). In order to form a Thracian-Dacian ensemble, one group of specialists has catalogued their language with those of the distant ancestors of the Romanians, i.e., the Dacians, who fought Trajan's armies. Others have defended a bipartition into Thracian, which was spoken to the south of the northern slope of the Haimos (Balkans) and Dacian-Mesian or Dacian-Getic (the mountains), which was spoken to the north of the Danube (see Brixhe and Panayotou 1994a). This debate, which, as we might guess, sets Bulgarian and Romanian linguists in opposition, is fueled only by very scanty documentation. Beyond toponymy, abundantly exploited by each side, we have only a short Thracian inscription found in Bulgaria. Otherwise, there remains hardly anything of a language that once had its hour of glory.

For their part, the Phrygians occupied present-day Macedonia before migrating into Asia Minor about 850 B.C. and constituting a powerful empire there that, according to the *Iliad* (songs 2, 3, and 14), had the Trojans for western neighbors and allies. They came under the yoke of the Lydians, and then the Persians, and their language was finally engulfed in Hellenism after the arrival of Alexander in 333 B.C. What remains of it are a hundred funeral inscriptions and formulas for consecration and execration.

We can count two hundred epigraphic vestiges in the north of Italy (areas of Trieste and the Piave Valley) for Venetian, and in the south (Apulia, Calabria) for Messapian, languages of the Illyrian group, also Indo-European, that includes Illyrian itself, attested by a short inscription found in Scutari (Albania). The birthplace of these populations was located in the northwestern part of the Balkans, and they played the role of liaison between the Greek, Italic, and Germanic worlds. The precariousness of these languages as objects of knowledge did not prevent southern Slavic patriots, the Serbs, Croats, and Slovenes, from laying claim to this prestigious heritage to launch a national protest movement, called the Illyrian movement, against the Hapsburgs and the Ottomans in 1850. That says something about the symbolic value that languages can take on, even if they are long dead, sporadically attested, and not part of a classical education.

Other Languages of Asia Minor

We have not fully exploited the two hundred some votive and ritual inscriptions written in Urartian, also called Vannic, because it was spoken at the site of Van, which was to become the cultural center of Armenia after the Indo-European invasions.

We are also badly informed about Lydian, which was spoken until the fourth century B.C. in the nearby region of present-day Smyrna. Lydian seems very different from other Anatolian languages. The center of Anatolia and the present-day Turkish coasts to the west (ancient Paphlagonia), to the southwest, to the south, and to the southeast (ancient Pamphylia) are the places where a few attestations of languages were found, respectively Palaic (extinct as early as 1200 B.C.), Carian, Pisidian, and Sidetic, all three extinct about the third century B.C. We are more or less certain about the Indo-European lineage of Palaic, a close relative of Luwian and Lycian (see above). The same lineage is assumed for the other languages, without enough evidence to prove it.

Old Cushitic

The excavations in Upper Nubia unearthed several written texts, sometimes in hieroglyphs, sometimes in demotic. The language of these writings is Hamito-Semitic and seems, if we compare it to the present-day state of Beja, its neighboring language, to be an archaic form of Cushitic. This language is Meroitic, which was the lingua franca of the realm of Meroe (corresponding to what the Greeks called Ethiopia) for more than a millennium until about 350, though not without greatly evolving, as we might well imagine. Meroe tried hard, with more or less success, to maintain its independence from its neighbor to the north, Egypt, whose power, it is true, was in decline.

From the above, it seems that languages do not die completely when epigraphic or archeological monuments and, more importantly, interpretable texts of a certain length allow their structure to be reconstructed, or at least allow their physiognomy to be drawn. Still, this concerns only languages with no direct living descendants, if we put aside the cases of Ancient Greek in relation to Modern Greek, and Arabic for those Arabists who want to see the classical language as the ancient form from which they claim today's dialects have descended. These two cases are closer to others we have not discussed and will not discuss below, because they do not fall precisely into the scope of this book: the cases of languages that are earlier states of languages living today.

For example, we cannot strictly consider medieval French in its successive states to be dead, nor can we for Old English, Old High German, Old Russian, Classical Armenian, Old Turkish, Classical Mongol, Old Tamil, Classical Tibetan, Kavi (Old Javanese), Old Japanese, etc. The modern languages that are the present-day states of all these idioms from the past are the result of a continuous diachronic line. The modification of languages through time is a natural phenomenon, inscribed in their very nature. For example, taken as a whole, the French of the Middle Ages is a stage of French and belongs to its history, whereas Latin is a different language from French, French being one of the outcomes of a transformation that produced the split of Latin into five divergent languages (or eleven, if we add to Spanish, Portuguese, Italian, Romanian, and French the languages of regions not formed into states, that is, Occitan [including here Gascon and Auvergnat languages, to make things simpler], Catalan, Galician, Rhaeto-Romanic, Corsican and Sardinian). Moreover, the link between the languages just mentioned and their past (often prestigious) states, as in the examples of Armenian and Classic Tibetan, vehicles for sacred Christian and Buddhist texts respectively, is further strengthened by this fact: the modern languages that are already descended from them borrow from them further for scholarly words or use them as a source for neological creations.

As a result, the phenomenon of the death of languages that I am going to describe is necessarily very different from those that have just been mentioned in this chapter. It is quite a dramatic phenomenon, because it unfolds before our eyes, even while largely escaping our power.

Now, I will not examine ancient languages preserved by classical teaching as integrated parts of various human cultures. Nor will I examine archaic languages for which traces have been unearthed here and there to be studied by scholars. I will examine languages that, in countless places in the contemporary world, are conspicuously heading to the brink of death en masse, since all of them are simply and brutally languages now threatened by extinction. And as we will see in the next chapter, the stakes are not low. It is the cultures built by human societies that are in danger of being lost forever.

6. The Paths to Extinction

The Three Profiles of Disappearance

TRANSFORMATION

It would seem that there are three ways for a language to disappear. The first is transformation: a language is greatly altered over the course of a process that can take a very long time, so that, at a certain moment, a new language can be said to have appeared. Such is the history of the transformation of Latin into various Romance languages. Another case is the one of modern languages for which certain classical languages represent its former state, such as Russian and Turkish, as described earlier. We have seen that historical continuity is quite direct here; in this case, as in the one illustrated by Latin, we cannot speak strictly of disappearance in the sense of total elimination, even if it is true that Portuguese is a far cry from Latin and that modern French is not at all similar to medieval French. Thus, we will not consider transformation to be a relevant case of death for a language.

SUBSTITUTION

We can say that an exterior language is substituted for another, previously the only one attested in a human group, when the latter ends up being absorbed into the former after having coexisted with the new language for some period of time. This involves a process of increasing fusion, at the end of which neither the structures nor the words of the original language remain in general use, at best surviving in a small minority of usages.

EXTINCTION

The notion of extinction, more metaphoric than that of disappearance, adequately evokes for the imagination what the phenomenon entails. This is a total retreat from the scene, by definition concomitant with that of its last speakers, who pass away without descendants. Thus the extinction of a language occurs with the deaths of the last people of advanced age who still babble in it, or sometimes that of a whole community that spoke it, whatever their ages. Extinction ends in substitution when, as frequently happens, subsequent generations completely abandon the language in question, and adopt another one.

Thus we can say that a language is extinct when it no longer has *native speakers*, that is, users who learn it from birth in a familial or social setting, and upon whom this learning confers what can be called native competence. This latter term is itself defined as a complete knowledge and a capacity for spontaneous use, making the language in question an instrument of communication that belongs to all circumstances in everyday life. According to this perspective, a living language would be defined as one of a community that renews its native speakers by itself. And a dead language, if we choose to retain that term, would be one of a community in which native competence has totally disappeared, to the extent that the native speakers had only imperfectly transmitted their knowledge, and their descendants in turn do not transmit an ability to speak and to understand the idiom of the group.

Two inferences can be drawn from these definitions. In the first place, the individual implication of the notion of death is absent here. The death of a language is certainly not the death of a physical community, since a human society that abandons one language for another does not itself die. But the death of a language is a collective phenomenon. It is the entire social body that ceases to speak this language. Even if it is true that the death of the last native speakers is an individual phenomenon, the extinction of the language that disappears with them must be considered one of a linguistic community.

In the second place, the last native speakers who — inadvertently — initiate the process of extinction can find themselves in two different situations: they may be in the original place, where the language is spoken as the native inheritance, or they may be in a place of immigration, where a displaced community still retains it within an environment that speaks one or many other languages. Thus a language can pass away in situ, but it can also pass away in diaspora. This latter case is illustrated by the examples of Norwegian and Hungarian communities living in the United States for a century or more, in which Norwegian or Hungarian is, depending on the individuals, sometimes extinct, and sometimes threatened by extinction.

Extinction by Stages

In the ensuing discussion I will attempt to characterize the stages of a process for which the final result is the death of a language. I will speak of jeopardization with regard to the initial stages, and of obsolescence with regard to the stages prior to the final outcome. To refer more generally to the process as a whole, I will use other concepts, like that of decay or, drawn metaphorically from geology and law, those of erosion and of escheat.

Total or Partial Lack of Education in the Native Language

The fact that a language stops being transmitted to children as it usually is under natural living conditions is the indication of a significant jeopardization. In many cases, and for reasons that will be examined below, parents are not spontaneously inclined to teach the language of the community to their children, simply through speaking it with them to the exclusion of any other. That does not mean that they entirely give up using it within the framework of education. Nevertheless, sometimes this is very much the case, and thus we can speak of a radical lack of transmission. In other families, the lack of transmission is only partial. Parents are doing two things: first, the elements that they teach are insufficient, and secondly, by not ensuring a transmission beginning from the earliest ages, as is common for any living language, they hand down knowledge that their children do not acquire in a continuous fashion.

For certain aspects of the language, the absence of continuity implies an acquisition that is too belated. It comes at an age between childhood and preadolescence when the eagerness to listen and to learn is diminishing, and when a selective stabilization, if not an ossification, sets in on the part of neurological aptitudes for attention and assimilation (see Hagège 1996a, chapters 1 and 2). In a regrettable coincidence, this is also precisely the age when children become more and more interested in a language or languages present in the near or even distant environment, besides the one used by the community.

The Absence of Children Among the Speakers of a Language as a Portent of Its Death

If a language is spoken only by the adults of a community, and the children know only languages foreign to that community, it is not condemned to die immediately or inevitably. In principle, the youngest adults will still use it among themselves until the end of their lives. And moreover, the possibility always remains for founding schools where children to whom it is not transmitted at home can learn it. Nevertheless, in most known cases, the absence of young speakers can be considered a gloomy prognosis for the survival of the language (see chapter 8, where it is used as a discriminant).

THE BILINGUALISM OF INEQUALITY
AND LANGUAGES AT WAR

The Devastation Caused by Contact in Situations of Inequality

The stage that follows the failure of transmission in the process of a language's jeopardization is a generalized bilingualism among its users. But what is involved here is not just any kind of bilingualism. Contact is permanent in the history of all human communities and is far from being necessarily detrimental. Contact between two languages is not reason enough to predict the death of one of them, nor even, in the many situations where this contact is direct, for one language to constitute a threat to the existence of the other. What we really have here is what has elsewhere been called the bilingualism of inequality, or inegalitarian bilingualism (see Hagège 1996a, chapter 13). This is the situation in which one language exerts formidable pressure upon the other because it is in a much stronger position due to its social status or its widespread national or international use (see chapter 7). The lack of transmission occurs within a framework thus defined. The oldest possessors of the community language, which is no longer in a state to resist competition from another idiom, transmit this community language in an imperfect way to their children, who themselves transmit it more imperfectly still, or no longer transmit it at all, to the subsequent generation.

When the transmission process is disrupted, communication between the last speakers of a language and their grandchildren becomes increasingly inadequate and difficult. As a result, the language is gradually abandoned, to the benefit of the language in a position to claim victory. That is because the two opposing languages engage in a veritable war. The means used by each one are different. We observe an unequally matched struggle between one language at the end of its reign and one language that is expanding its territory. But above all, inegalitarian bilingualism produces a particular type of speaker that we will now consider.

THE UNDER-USERS

Along the inexorable path to extinction, we pass from the bilingualism of inequality thus illustrated to another stage whereby obsolescence is initiated. To characterize this stage, I propose calling *under-users* of a given language those speakers who use it, in varying degrees according to the situation, without possessing what I above have called "native competence." The way in which under-users speak the language of their community is a disquieting sign of the danger to which it is exposed and, in the most advanced cases, a clear announcement of its imminent demise.

Many authors have studied this stage of languages within specific groups. Notably, users who handle the original language with increasing uncertainty have been called *semi-locutors* (Dorian 1977). *Semi-lingualism* has been used (see Hansegård 1968) with regard to a situation that I call *double incompetence* (Hagège 1996a, 261–262). In that situation, recent immigrant families employ the language of their new country incorrectly without having retained complete competence in their own language. We do not have here an obsolescence phenomenon for either of the two languages, even though the circumstances are analogous, but a linguistic deprivation for individuals of a socially and economically disadvantaged group. Thus, in this case we cannot speak of under-users as we can for speakers of languages on the path to extinction. The behavior of such speakers will be examined below and will allow us to see precisely what the notion of under-user entails. Let us simply note here that under-users can be distinguished from subjects who possess a passive competence. For the most part, of course, the latter group does not produce sustained discourse and does not use the language as those who possess a full competence can. But they have not lost their knowledge of the system and, as listeners, at least in principle, can recognize all its traits, which is not the case for under-users.

ALTERING THE DOMINATED LANGUAGE
AND DENYING ITS LEGITIMACY

The type of language that under-users speak in situations of initial obsolescence can be illustrated by many examples. We will consider two of them here.

Quechua in Bolivia in the Face of Spanish

The first example is Quechua, from the city and the valley of Cochabamba in Bolivia (see Calvet 1987). Quechua is the modern state of the language that was spoken in the Inca empire at the time of the arrival of the Spanish conquerors. Cultural and linguistic Hispanization has not made its situation as precarious as that of many other American Indian languages. Quechua is spoken by nearly half of the five and a half million inhabitants of Bolivia. But it is obviously subject to pressure from Spanish. In the urban environment (the city of

Cochabamba and immediate surroundings), tradespeople, as well as the government and the media, acknowledge Quechua's undeniable place, but the form they use is quite different from that used by rural people (in the Cochabamba valley).

On the phonological level, rural Quechua possesses two vowels, *i* and *u*, and no *e* or *o* except as possible pronunciations of some words: *i* can sometimes be pronounced *e*, which it resembles, and likewise for *u* in relation to *o*. That means that when Quechua is less influenced by Spanish, there exists no pair of words in which the members, basically identical, contrast with each other only because of the presence of *i* in one and *e* in the other, or *u* in one and *o* in the other. On the contrary, in urban Quechua, which borrows heavily from Spanish, the vowels *e* and *o* are phonemes (the set of sounds' traits serving to distinguish words) by right. Indeed, these sounds work their way into urban Quechua at the same time as the Spanish words that contain them. Thus the phonological systems of urban Quechua and of rural Quechua in the Cochabamba region are different enough to speak of two distinct languages.

The evidence does not stop there. We have just seen that the contamination of urban Quechua's phonological system by Spanish is a corollary of the influx of borrowings, which is a lexical phenomenon. But grammar is affected as well. On the grammatical level, the more conservative rural Quechua possesses very different characteristics from those of Spanish. Thus, the verb is in the final position in most sentences, which are usually short. In Spanish, the verb is in the final position as infrequently as it is in French, where it is not common practice to say *ils ont leur maïs au marché vendu* (they have their corn at market sold). Consequently, the omnipresent influence of Spanish on Cochabamba city Quechua alters the word order so that the great majority of sentences do not have the verb in the final position.

In a warlike environment between languages where there is great inequality, the legitimate language is the one of the economic "elite." Now, in Cochabamba, these elite are precisely the users of an increasingly Hispanicized Quechua, on its way to disappearing as Quechua when the phonological, grammatical, and lexical absorption by Spanish is complete. That is why these semilocutors are hardly looked down upon socially, even though their original language is scorned. The process of extinction for Quechua is one of a language whose former legitimacy finds itself challenged. In turn, this process is legitimized by the very status of the semilocutors. Thus we see that the legitimization of the threatening language and the overthrow of the menaced language are part and parcel of the same process of affirmation.

But, of course, another large category of under-users exists. Belonging to the disadvantaged classes of Bolivian society that speak rural, or true, Quechua, these speakers also use a "bad" Spanish, called "Andean Spanish," which is stigmatized. Consequently, the effort to advance socially leads them to imitate the increasingly Hispanicized Quechua of the urban under-users. If the number of under-users, partly urban, partly rural, continues to grow, Quechua may well face obsolescence, and then extinction, in this region.

The Situation in Creolophone Circles in the Caribbean

The other example involves one of the languages of the West Indian islands of Trinidad and Tobago, located off the eastern coast of Venezuela. English is the official language of this dominion of the British Commonwealth. The language spoken by a majority of the population is an English-based creole, as in Jamaica and other Caribbean islands. But half the inhabitants have another language as well. These are actually the descendants of workers who, after slavery was abolished in 1838, surfaced in the sugar plantations before 1917. They came from the east-central region of northern India, a region where the language which is spoken is related to Hindi, the dominant language of this country, as its dialects are used by almost seven hundred million Indians. This language is Bhojpuri. Thus, the Indians of Trinidad have the local variant of Bhojpuri, or Trinidad Bhojpuri, for their vernacular language.

Nevertheless, if certain criteria are used to test the degree to which Bhojpuri has been maintained on Trinidad, a clear difference can be noted between speakers older than seventy-five born in India, those between fifty-five and seventy-five born on Trinidad, and those under fifty-five also born on Trinidad. Research done on these speakers (see Mohan and Zador 1986) established that the knowledge of Bhojpuri decreases noticeably from the first to the second group, and then from the second to the third, if one uses as criteria the correct and frequent use of certain elements belonging to this language as it is spoken in India and absent from English as well as from the local creole. Following are these elements: honorific personal pronouns, compound verbs, nouns and verbs reduplicated distributively, and echo-forms (forms with two elements, the second of which repeats with changes an initial element x, having for a semantic result "x and other things of this type").

If we also consider how the speed of elocution clearly decreases from the first to the second and then again to the third group, and how the rate of borrowings from English increases dramatically in the same direction, we must conclude that, unlike the oldest speakers, who transmit their competence only imperfectly, the youngest speakers have become under-users of the ancestral Indian language. It is characteristic in this regard that the youngest speakers no longer recognize the ruined language they use in this very faltering way as Bhojpuri. They believe it is "bad Hindi," according to their own self-mocking expression. Bhojpuri's extinction on Trinidad is no longer far off.

INVASION BY BORROWING

The Hard Kernel and the Lexis Faced with Borrowing

Borrowing, essentially lexical borrowing, that is, the borrowing of vocabulary words, is one of the living conditions for languages (see Hagège 1987, 75–79). No language exists, not even one spoken by communities living in almost complete isolation (islands very far from any other land, high valleys separated from neighboring populations by cliffs difficult to circumnavigate, etc.), that does not borrow from one or many other languages.

We can consider the most structured parts of a language to be its hard kernel, that is, the component most resistant to the wear of time and the influence of a foreign language. These parts are the phonology and the grammar. In contrast, the lexis (inventory of available words at a given moment in the history of the language) is a less structured domain, and much more open to borrowings. Of course, we are speaking only of a general tendency, but despite the many counterexamples we can adopt it as the framework for studying such phenomena.

It is important to note that borrowing is not, in itself, a *cause* of the extinction of languages. It is a disquieting *sign* of extinction when it is invasive and leaves no area intact, as we will see.

Code Switching

Borrowing vocabulary is a phenomenon belonging primarily to discourse; vernacular phrases are cluttered with words taken from other languages. This phenomenon is called code switching within a single utterance. Code switching is far from always being a sign of decay. It is extremely widespread. Without linguistic training, any attentive listener can hear two protagonists in a conversation pass from one language to another even within a single sentence, provided that the scene takes place in a multilingual environment.

Who has not noticed how often the Arabophones we hear in the Latin Quarter in Paris, for example, use French words and even whole expressions by inserting them in the middle of discourse that seems to be essentially Arabic? Many Mexicans who have settled in California, Texas, or other areas of the western United States (territories that belonged to Mexico until the United States won them militarily in the nineteenth century) constantly alternate codes in a similar manner, passing from English to Spanish and vice versa. Cultured Malayans do the same thing, inserting numerous English words into Malayan discourse.

In all these cases, it is not a matter of a bilingualism of inequality. Because even if the speakers consider one of the languages (French for those Arabophones, English in relationship to Spanish or to Malay in the other two cases cited) to embody a rich country valued for its higher education or certain socioeconomic patterns, they do not reject the native language, or strip it of its legitimacy. And when the situation is not unequal, or when various factors compensate for a high rate of importation of foreign words, borrowing is not a sign that the language is threatened.

The Bilingualism of Inequality and Borrowing by Under-Users
Borrowed Discursive Markers, the First Wave
in a Lexical Invasion

If, on the contrary, the situation is one of inegalitarian bilingualism, then the influx of borrowings, especially when there is code switching, is facilitated by the multiplication of little words, as practical as they are formidable. These are the discursive markers, that is, the terms or expressions that punctuate discourse, or attract the attention of the interlocutor, or solicit his approval, or acknowledge something to him. For example, these are the kinds of expressive French elements inserted within a dialogue between students, Arabophones or Africans, in a French university, and reflecting their solidarity: elements like *tu vois?* ("you see?"), or *c'est ça!*, or *voilà!*, or *et alors*, etc. We can say that they are "the first wave in a lexical invasion" by the loan language (see Tosco 1992). To the extent that, when the situation is one of unequal bilingualism, discursive markers from the dominant language begin to proliferate in the discourse of the dominated language, along with code switching, the way is prepared for lexical borrowings to swallow up the original lexis. The ultimate stage in this process is substitution. And this process can very easily unfold without the users having any idea at the time that it is happening.

Borrowings and the Major Offensive

Various examples can be given to demonstrate how the dangerous power of borrowing often leads a language to the next stage, once it passes the threshold of tolerance. In Kusaiean, the Micronesian language of the easternmost island of the Caroline archipelago ("freely associated" with the United States), the proliferation of borrowings from Anglo-American has so westernized the vocabulary that speakers hardly know anymore how to use the twenty-eight or so terms that designate the different phases of the moon in the language's unaltered state. This impoverishment of the lexis runs parallel to the Americanization of customs. For example, the custom of accompanying greetings of welcome with touching the genitals shocked and astonished Protestant missionaries, whose apoplectic responses in the face of this innocent spectacle are explained by the fact they were used to not only extremely prudish relationships in America, but also maintaining a certain distance, as studied by the founder of proxemics, E. T. Hall (1966). Countless words have disappeared from Kusaiean due to the changing social conditions of discourse, the decline in public debate, and the invasion of the media that acts as a substitute for it. We can consider this state of the lexis, impoverished by being stripped of its own resources and assailed by borrowings, as a phase in the jeopardization of the language.

Similarly, we can find examples of advanced decay among the members of the Tibeto-Burman linguistic family in Nepal and Thailand. Kusunda has disappeared in the flood of borrowings from Nepali, and Hayu is almost inevitably going to follow suit, while Ugong, besieged by borrowings from Thai, could very soon die out. Likewise, Thai exerts formidable pressure on other language families in Thailand. Tin and Mlabri, languages in the Khmuic family, for example, are spoken by isolated tribes in the mountainous eastern regions of the country. They are both subject to very strong Thai influence. This contact has contributed to the impoverishment of the vocabulary, originally rich in designations for natural phenomena. Mlabri is in an even more precarious situation, since the tribe is exposed to changes that result from its migrations across the Indochina peninsula. The Mlabri people use Thai overwhelmingly for everything unrelated to domestic life, and we can predict the imminent disappearance of the Mlabri language, unless we consider that it is increasingly becoming a mixed language, and therefore, to that extent, it could survive (see chapter 9).

The Tidal Wave of Borrowings: From Lexis to Grammar

In the example languages above, Quechua in Cochabamba and Bhojpuri in Trinidad, it is through borrowed words, and models of phrases in which these words figure, that foreign traits are introduced, Spanish in one case, English in the other. This phenomenon is an important indication of decay. We can observe a correlation between the rate of borrowing and the degree of destabilization in the phonology and the grammar. A language exposed to this kind of pressure replaces its own systems with other systems. Their expansion announces the death of that language. The accelerated decline of Australian Aboriginal languages is explained in the same way. Warlpiri, for instance, borrows a great number of words from English, not only for ideas that were originally foreign to the ethnic group (*turaki*, from "truck," *pajikirli*, from "bicycle," *lanji*, from "lunch," etc.), but even for objects with native origins. Thus, in place of *karli* and *wawirri*, the Warlpiri now use *boomerang* and *kangaroo*, respectively. The invasion of these words is not without irony, since we know that English had itself borrowed them from another Australian language, Guugu-Yimidhirr, according to James Cook's journal of 1770. And in the wake of the invasion of vocabulary, we soon observe the invasion of the hard kernel itself, a prelude to the obsolescence of a language.

In particular, we can note that detachment from a language whose own lexical base is in decline correlates to a deactivation of the processes for forming new words. Having acquired superior competence in the dominant language, under-users introduce a considerable number of words borrowed from that language into their discourse in the dominated language. Consequently, these words are integrated into the lexical inventory, and pass from chance discourse into the workings of the system. At the same time, native words, which imported words make redundant, begin to disappear.

The morphological calque is also characteristic of the borrowing phenomena. Welland French in Ontario (see chapter 8) provides a very simple example where the calque of the English *the one* and *the ones* gives us *le celui, le celle, la celle, les ceux, les celles* (see Mougeon and Beniak 1989, 300), usages in which, in relation to French not exposed to this morphological influence, we can note the addition of the article and the mix of genders.

THE PROCESS OF EROSION AND THE INDICATIONS OF ITS PROGRESS

A General Profile of the Process

The Range of Situations

The process of erosion is variable and largely depends on circumstances specific to each community. Thus, according to a recent study, about eighteen years ago the last speakers of Cayuga were in the process of losing the names of many animals. Cayuga was an Iroquois language spoken by a tribe living in the Great Lakes region, before being moved to reservations in Oklahoma. Nevertheless, they had preserved many of the complexities of the morphological system in much the same condition as the Cayugas of Ontario had (whose language is better maintained) (see Mithun 1989). This suggests that the jeopardization of the language had not led to a true state of obsolescence, and illustrates the complexity and the diversity of situations of extinction for languages, linked to multiple factors that sometimes contradict each other. Dahalo, a Cushitic language of the coastal province of Kenya, is subject to strong pressure from urban centers like Lamu, where Swahili dominates, a language used by many bilingual Dahalo, whereas in the past they were only monolingual. Dahalo has retained its wealth of consonants, some of which (like / ɬw/, a consonant that phoneticians call *a lateral fricative with labiovelar appendix*) are quite rare. But it has lost the opposition of genders, despite its deep roots in Cushitic, as well as another deeply rooted trait, namely the diversified marks of the plural, characterized by reduplications and numerous alternations.

Alterations in the Hard Kernel

Nonetheless, if we look beyond the considerable variations in particular cases and try to establish a general profile of the erosion process and the way different components of a language are affected by it, we will recall that, in the majority of cases, the tough parts are resistant longer than the vocabulary. When they are affected in their turn, what disappears first is the phonemic and grammatical system. There is, among other things, a loss of essential oppositions constituting the most specific aspects of the phonology, and, in morphology, there is a great reduction in the variations between forms. And, within the system of grammatical categories, syntactical constructions, word order, mechanisms of subordination—those traits most characteristic of the endangered language—are affected as well. In those languages that possess them, the distinction of case endings, tense, aspects, and moods of verbs is lost. In languages where there is a significant output of new words, the most common rules for forming them cease to be productive, and the rarest ones disappear, as do the variety of forms in certain languages.

Thus, the Estonian of some twenty-six thousand immigrants to Sweden at the end of the Second World War, and especially that of their children, lost the distinction between the nominative, genitive, and partitive as marks of the object, leaving it to the word order to mark those functions, according to the Swedish model. Kore, the language of a Masai tribe composed of a few hundred people living on the Lamu island off the northern coast of Kenya, has lost many traits due to contact with Swahili and Somali, the lingua francas of the region: the distinction of genders, most of the morphemes marking the tense and the aspect of verbs, as well as the productive use of personal suffixes. We may note as well the loss of the exuberant verbal morphology of Kemant, a Cushitic language of Ethiopia. That is a trait we find among under-users, as striking as the conservation of this morphology among the old people of Gonder, the prestigious former capital of Ethiopia, where this language strives to survive. That said, we note only a general tendency here, and examples exist that run counter to that of Kemant. Even in decline, certain languages still retain a good portion of their grammar for a long time.

Loss of Recessive Traits

But it remains true that there is a tendency toward losing recessive traits, that is, statistically rare ones if compared with all other human languages, and directly linked to a very specific organization of the world. Thus, in New Guinea, one can observe (see Laycock 1973) that, over twenty-five or thirty years, the Papuan languages Duna, Murik, and Arapesh had lost the complex systems of nominal classification that characterized them and that consisted of a series of a dozen marks differentiating as many classes of nouns according to the object of the world to which they refer.

In almost the same period of time, Kiwai, another Papuan language, had lost the differentiation it made between singular, dual, triple, and plural; moreover, there remained only one present, one past, and one future, whereas it had formerly possessed two pasts and three futures. Closer to Paris, the Bigouden and Trégorrois speakers of Breton have lost an original trait that consisted of adding the plural suffix twice to nouns with the diminutive mark -*ig*, which gives us, for example on *paotr*, "lad," *paotre-ed-ig-où*, "little lads," where the noun receives the mark of the plural of the animate, -*ed*, and the suffix -*ig* receives the other plural mark, -*où* (see Dressler 1981, 8).

Farther from Paris, in Ayiwo language of the Santa Cruz archipelago, at the eastern end of the Solomon islands, the sixteen nominal classes, the same kind as those of languages cited above, have also disappeared, or almost disappeared, between two surveys, the second following twenty years after the first. This disappearance is complete among the youngest users, the oldest exhibiting only the vestiges of the former system. Kamilaroi, an Australian language now dying out in north-central New South Wales, has lost nearly all the fine distinctions its verbal system made between the different times of the day that, from sunrise to sunset, served to frame events.

One of the recessive traits quickest to disappear is the often original numeration systems that languages possess, according to which one counts objects by referring to parts of the body: not only a hand for "five," both hands for "ten," a man (= two hands and two feet) for "twenty," but also an important series of corporal indicators conventionally taking on numerical values assigned to each, as in Wambon, a Papuan language of Indonesia (see Hagège 1998, 51).

Analogical Leveling, Diluted Formulations

Most frequently, the type of knowledge that under-users retain of the language in decline can be defined by two characteristics: first, the elimination of irregularities by analogical leveling, and second, the loss of dense structures and their replacement by diluted formulations, in many cases where, no longer possessing the rule to produce the adequate word or expression, underusers express themselves through periphrasis. Calques are also used when a native word is lacking, like Finno-American under-users replacing the Finnish word *takka*, which they no longer know, with *tuli-paikka*, a calque of the English "fireplace," in order to say "hearth" (here we have an example of Finnish disappearing not in situ [in Finland] but in diaspora [in the United States]). An example of analogical leveling is provided by an Irish speaker using a form *nócha*, through analogy with *fiche*, "twenty," in place of *deich is cheithre fichid* ("ten and four twenties") to say "ninety." This speaker is abandoning the former vigesimal counting system, which we find surviving also in *quatre-vingt-dix*, the French word for "ninety" in France, whereas French-speaking Belgians say *nonante*.

The Case of Expolitio and the Reduction
of Registers of Style

Sometimes, a sign of the advanced decay of a language among bilingual speakers who are switching over to a foreign language is *expolitio*. I use this term from classical rhetoric here specifically to designate the use in immediate succession, in the same sentence, of a word from the dominating language and then its equivalent in the native language, as when a speaker from the county of Donegal says, in Irish contaminated by English, *bhí sé black dubh* (it was black-black), "it was all black" (see Watson 1989, 50). We can interpret such uses as illustrating a deficiency in expressiveness, since the use of two adjacent words with the same meaning, a native one and a borrowed one, to render an intensive sense assumes that the means originally used to express intensity have been forgotten. Thus, another mark in the decline of the language appears among under-users. This mark, a corollary of the preceding ones, is the reduction in the registers of style.

The Survival of Strata

When languages disappear due to pressure from other idioms, after a period of mixing, the survival of strata, that is, of traits ascribable to the dead language, must be considered a sign by default, since otherwise the language is submerged. Thus, Vumba and Chifundi, languages spoken in southeast Kenya, are now considered dialects of Swahili, which absorbed them, whereas they belong to another subgroup, from which they retain some erratic but clearly identifiable vestiges, particularly in their phonological system.

Fluctuations

In the final stages of a dying language, we can observe continual fluctuation from one phoneme to another, one form to another. All the rules seem optional, as everywhere free variation reigns, and under-users orient themselves in expression according to what little bits of competence remain to them, as if we had to do not with languages, but with objects adrift, governed now only by some chaotic progress. To consider but one example, specialists who have studied what remains of French in Newfoundland (see chapter 8) note that in the mid-1980s, there was no longer a single rule for deciding if a verb with a plural pronoun for a subject agrees in plural or in singular. Whereas five or six monolingual octogenarians still opposed *ils allont à la côte à tous les matins*, "they go to the coast every morning" (agreement of the verb), to *ya des gars qui va pas à la côte*, "there are guys who does [*sic*] not go to the coast" (lack of agreement in relative clause), other speakers had them agree or not with no observable regularity (see King 1989, 142).

Linguists who love the futile game of formalistic confrontations can get caught up in these fluctuations. They come to believe that they have discovered the very rare properties of flexibility and individual variation in a language, worthy of theoretical interest, or they set about stubbornly researching the underlying factors of invariance that cover the appearance of oscillations, when in reality and without their knowing it, the language is in its death throes. Thus, the semi-competence of under-users is capable of creating illusions, even for professionals.

The diversification that we find universally in healthy human languages correlates to the variables of sex, age, profession, and ethnicity that sociolinguists have thoroughly examined. Nothing comparable can be found in the penultimate phase of erosion.

The Mute Old People

The final stage is that of aged informants who are questioned by the linguist wanting to record a final testimony and who, although they used their language fluently in the first stages of their lives, have literally forgotten it. Among the illustrations of this common phenomenon we can cite the example of Armenians of advanced age in Marseilles or other French cities who are no longer capable of coherent discourse in Armenian and babble almost incomprehensible syllables. Their behavior cannot be attributed simply to emotion (account of Mme. A. Malian-Samuélian).

Inadvertently, certain linguists have found themselves facing an older person introduced to them as mute, because he no longer remembers his language and just stammers incoherent bits of speech. This charge of muteness against those one does not understand has long been a sign of the distancing that takes place when one is faced with the impossibility of dialogue. Many Slavic peoples called the Germanic peoples "mutes" (and modern Slavic languages still designate the Germans in this way; "German" in Czech is *nemecky*, and "mute," *nemy*), because they heard only meaningless rumbles in the Germanic discourse. But here we have an entirely different kind of muteness. A scene from W. Herzog's film *Das Land, wo die Ameisen träumen* ("The Country Where the Ants Dream") shows a pathetically mute old Australian (this bit of information comes from Mme. H. Albagnac). Here, the linguistic wound takes on the aspect of a dramatic circularity. No doubt the user still possesses some memories, but his language is nearly destroyed because he no longer has anyone with whom to speak it. It is this very awareness of his inadequacies that gives his expression a semicataleptic form; and conversely, it is exactly this suspension between speech and silence that signifies death for a language in its final death throes.

A Comparison with the Case of Pidgin

Some of the traits of escheated languages seem to increase the transparency by reducing the irregularities and the number of forms. Transparency is also a characteristic of pidgin (see chapter 11), so the comparison of pidgin to dying languages has been suggested. Admittedly, the two situations do have some properties in common: the tendency toward invariability, analyticity, and the use of universally recurring traits in the languages, rather than recessive traits. Another trait shared by dying languages and forms of pidgin is that, in both cases, the youngest speakers are not subject to the normative intervention of adults, acting as regulators in the language's acquisition, and prescribing the rejection of analogical formulations that violate common usage, as well as all other deviant forms. Indeed, both types of situations are characterized by the importance of variation and the absence of a fixed norm, in one case (pidgin) because it is no longer established, in the other (languages in obsolescence) because it has been eroded.

Nevertheless, other traits distinguish forms of pidgin and dying languages from each other. The random nature of the destruction affecting a dying language is especially obvious in the way that underusers often retain elements that have no function or clear meaning, and that are residue, surviving amid the decay of the language. This phenomenon has not been noted in forms of pidgin, where every element responds to a specific function.

Other characteristics mark significant differences between pidgin and dying languages. The process of *expolitio*, which was illustrated above with regard to Irish, is also found in certain written styles of pidgin, like the one in New Guinea (called Tok Pisin) which, in recent editions of the Port-Moresby newspapers, allowed the insertion of English words in the middle of a sentence, immediately followed by a translation (see Hagège 1993a, 30). But, unlike in the case of a dying language, here it is not a matter of contamination: this pidgin is very much alive, and the users who read this paper often do not know English, which explains the pedagogical need to translate the borrowed words used here and there.

The Pace of Erosion and Speakers' Awareness

The changes undergone by an endangered language are much more rapid than the everyday ones characterizing the life of healthy languages. Under-users are not always aware of the pace at which their language is falling apart, even when it is dizzying. Often they are convinced that they are still speaking a normal language, even though it is dying. Most often the forms that give the illusion of continuity are already those of another system in the process of being established, the prelude to total extinction.

THE ILLUSION OF LIFE

Studies in various places where languages have begun the process of decay can reveal phenomena that seem to refute the prognosis of extinction, but that, upon closer examination, confirm it. Three phenomena of this type are presented below.

Addresses of Solidarity

Several cases have been reported in which the vernacular language can still be heard in the discourse of certain subjects in communities that are in the process of switching en masse to another language. These subjects thus hope to establish a link of complicity with partners capable of understanding them. One study (Mertz 1989) mentions the case of Anglophone speakers on the island of Cape Breton, which is part of Nova Scotia, the Atlantic province of Canada (where many Francophones formerly lived but who now make up only 5 percent of the population, as French becomes extinct in the Anglophone Canadian environment). At the beginning of the twentieth century, Scottish Gaelic was still spoken by a great many Scottish descendants living on this island. Since the 1940s it has been subject to a process of elimination, to the benefit of English. This process has transformed the members of this traditionally bilingual community into monolinguals.

Nevertheless, the language has not completely disappeared from use. One can hear Gaelic used, in the form of interjections or short phrases, by speakers not belonging to the current generation. They utter addresses directed at the interlocutor, or reflections of a general nature, or again, words expressing an emotion, or vigorous approval, or a comic reaction, or finally, greetings, obscenities, or snatches from old legends. Some of these addresses are aimed at the speaker himself. This use in a monologue can, of course, mean that an intimate relationship is still retained with the language. Nonetheless, it cannot support a serious argument in favor of true preservation, since the speakers who have been heard in these situations otherwise use English almost exclusively.

The same may be said for the use of a threatened language as a secret language between old people, and sometime young people, forming a complicity of initiates that excludes foreigners. This integrative function of using a ghost language to mark membership in a group can also be observed among monolingual speakers of Spanish, as in Lima with Quechua, or in Mexico with Nahuatl (Aztec), even though these two languages are very much alive in most of the bilingual communities and, of course, among those inhabitants of rural regions who are monolingual in one or the other of them.

The Creativity of Under-Users
The Proliferation of Inventions

It has been observed that in certain cases of predicted extinction, the under-users demonstrate a striking creativity. Since at least the beginning of the twentieth century, some have maintained that Hungarian in eastern Austria is on the verge of disappearing. In the little suburb of Oberwart, for example, less than twelve kilometers from the Hungarian border, two thousand inhabitants, representing a third of the population, ought to have long ceased being bilingual, speaking only Burgenland German, abandoning their ancestral Hungarian. Now Hungarian continues to survive, as adverse as the entirely Germanophone environment is for this survival. But the way in which it remains alive is quite extraordinary.

According to a study done between 1974 and 1983 (Gal 1989), many Oberwart inhabitants, and not only the oldest ones, construct nouns and verbs with elements not part of standard Hungarian. No longer remembering common words, they may forge new ones that, even though they do not exist, are close in structure to words that have fallen out of use. Or, lacking knowledge of the adequate word for certain meanings, they may give new meanings to words that they still possess in their lexical inventory. They make up verbs composed with the help of elements that standard Hungarian combines in certain cases, but not in others. They no longer know how to activate certain mechanisms. For example, according to the study mentioned above, one under-user said *tanult nekem* (to study [third-person singular past tense] to me) "he taught me (things)," instead of *tánit*, the causative verb meaning "to make learn," the only correct form here because the meaning is "to teach." Thus, the vocabulary of these under-users abounds in neologisms that a Hungarian from Hungary can easily understand, even while identifying them immediately as belonging to speakers with an inadequate knowledge of the language.

There are many other cases of under-users' creativity. One notable example involves the last speakers of Arvanitika, a southern Albanian dialect that was introduced in northwestern Greece by Albanian colonists at the end of the Byzantine Empire. The emergence of a Greek nation, and then a state, after the 1821 revolution against Ottoman domination reduced the Albanian enclave to a fragile cultural minority. This process was intensified further by the overall expansion of Greek in education and administrative systems. Today Arvanitika under-users speak a very Hellenized Albanian, especially on the lexical and even grammatical levels (see Tsitsipis 1989). The attention they give to finding the most adequate formulation using continually declining resources is an indication of how little time is left to their language before its apparently inevitable death.

Native Speakers and Under-Users

This example, as well as others of the same type throughout the world, make under-users appear very capable of invention. Their linguistic attitude is explained by the value they attach to the vernacular language and by their conscious desire to promote it, knowing that formidable competition is ready to besiege and eliminate it. Moreover, even if the under-users' feats often defy established usage, they do not compare to those of foreigners who might have learned the language badly or are still learning it. Nor can they be considered similar to those of children in the initial stages of acquiring their mother tongue, as some linguists claim. The means by which French-speaking children of at least five years of age, for example, compensate for their gaps by analogical extensions like *il a mouru* "he is dead" (where *a mouru* is made up, instead of the correct *est mort*) are less rich than those of under-users, at least in periods of obsolescence when death is not yet imminent.

Thus, even if they do not possess native competence as defined above, under-users do have a certain competence: their relative ease at forging and combining elements to generate formulations that general usage does not accept denotes a level of competence between that of native speakers and that of foreigners. We do know that one characteristic of foreigners who do not master a language, but have enough shrewdness to know how to thoroughly exploit their incomplete knowledge, is increased periphrasis. They convey through glossing what the single word they do not possess would say more quickly. However, even if cases like the Oberwart Hungarians lead us to qualify any simplistic notions of a language's life or death, and to refine the notions of native speaker and native competence, we have to admit that the behavior of these creative under-users reveals the serious impoverishment of their linguistic knowledge. They are forced into inventive detours. Their faulty, if comprehensible, formulations lead to a growing ignorance of their language, dying from the pressure of another language and outside of its country of origin.

Purist Rigor and Laxist Fluctuations

Communities in which a language is in obsolescence often signal this in two unconscious ways: first, a concern for fixed styles, and second, a purist rigor that, paradoxically, does not prevent the language from falling into a state of fluctuation which knows no norm.

Conserving Ritualized Usages

In the final stages of an erosion process, the loss of everyday use of a language in private and public life is often accompanied, if not revealed, by the exclusive presence of ritual uses of that language. Their elevated style contrasts sharply with that of everyday speech. Thus, according to Campbell and Muntzel (1989), the last speaker of Chiapanecan, an Oto-Manguean language of the state of Chiapas in Mexico, remembered, almost exclusively, a religious text meant for formal recitation. Beyond that, he knew only a few words. The inhabitants of the island of Trinidad (other than the Indians mentioned above) who are losing the Yoruba of their African ancestry (from the lower valley of the Niger) no longer know more than a few traditional songs. The last speakers of Kemant have not only lost its very diverse verbal forms, as we have just seen, but also signal its imminent disappearance by the way they can spiel prayers in an archaic version of the language, creating the illusion of their competence.

The texts still committed to memory can be very long. The only existing "speakers" of a southeastern dialect of Tzeltal (a Mayan language), formerly spoken fluently in the state of Chiapas, were able to recite some prayers, one of which was made up of symmetrical couplets, was rich in metaphors — important to their culture — and was shared with users of Tojolabal, another Mayan language, although a healthy one. In any case, this single attestation of formal phraseology in a ritualized style, to the exclusion of any natural use, signals the reduction of the language to museum fossil.

The Purism of the Less Competent

Most societies, either through the voice of official power or through that of specialists with established authority, determine a norm for their language. They can devise it with varying degrees of flexibility. Notably, the most finicky defenders of the normative model are sometimes those who have the most uncertain command over it, in communities where that language is in the state of decay. Thus, in

Mexico, where Nahuatl is holding out very well in certain parts and less well in others, the last quasi-speakers of dying Nahuatl dialects establish a stringent norm (see Hill 1987). For example, they reproach others for using a Spanish structure for the expression of possession, as well as for stressing the last syllable of borrowed words, even when this stress is found to be the norm in Spanish. Ordering fidelity to Nahuatl accentuation, which stresses the next-to-last syllable, they require the wrong pronunciations *ciúdad* ("city"), for example, and *lúgar* ("place").

Those who prescribe this norm are the very ones for whom the language is in the process of being destroyed. They have long since lost some of Nahuatl's most typical grammatical traits, such as verbs with incorporated nouns (such as "I meat-eat" to mean that one is an eater of meat), or the construction of subordinate clauses. Here, the defensive purism of Nahuatl zealots is an indication of the erosion of their knowledge. Of course, purism might very well be recommended by those with a good knowledge, and even an excellent knowledge, of the language. But then the situations are different. In the case we are dealing with, this attitude is typical of obsolescence, as if, in a preterminal phase, the quasi-speakers want to give themselves the illusion of full competence by artificially maintaining a stringent norm that runs counter to the healthy image of life.

Hypercorrections

Among the characteristics of under-users' eroded language, one must be entered into the file of signs that seem to indicate renewed life while in fact pointing to approaching death. I am speaking of hypercorrections, or faulty use through too general an application of a limited rule, or through extending an obsolete usage into modern language. Let us consider two languages that may still be known by a few older people but are probably extinct today: Xinca (southeastern Guatemala) and Pipil (Salvador, belonging to the Aztec family). Studies done between 1975 and 1985 found that speakers used in all contexts a few consonants of complex articulation whose appearance, in the norm, was strictly limited to certain contexts. Hypercorrections are hardly unknown in healthy languages. In contemporary French it is a hypercorrection to say *j'y pense*, "I am thinking of him/her" (where *y* refers to a human), thus restoring the classical usage, or *je n'ai pu m'empêcher de le vous* (instead of modern *vous le*) *déclarer*, "I could not refrain from saying it to you." But in the normal course of evolution, hypercorrections do not occur with the frequency we find in cases like the one cited here.

The dominant trait in these phenomena is, in fact, instability. There is no observable limit to hypercorrections, nor any rule that organizes the distribution of them. Neither is there concerted, or even precise, delimitation of the domains where purist prescriptions ought to be applied. Much to the contrary, quasi-speakers severely lack a coherent view of what could constitute a defense of the norm. As we have seen for certain Nahuatl dialects, purist impulses, when they exist, are deployed only to stem the tide and not to implement a general defense plan.

7. The Battalion of Causes

The Three Groups of Main Causes

PHYSICAL CAUSES

The Violent Death of a Language

Through the Extinction of All Speakers: Natural Catastrophes,
Genocides, Epidemics, Migrations

This is the simplest case, if one may dare to say so. Here, the speakers disappear, every last one of them, without assuring any transmission of the language, even to foreigners. It could be a matter of a natural catastrophe, like the 1815 volcanic eruption that caused the death of all the Tambora people, inhabitants of the Sumbawa island in the Indonesian archipelago of the Lesser Sunda Islands that separates Java from Timor. All we have of Tambora is the short vocabulary list an English traveler made at the beginning of the nineteenth century. Although they have not yet been destroyed, the small tribes of the Goliath mountains in Irian Jaya, and their languages, diverse and little known like nearly all those of Borneo, are currently under threat from landslides and earthquakes, which are particularly frequent in this region (see Dixon 1991).

The phenomenon of the death of languages can coincide with an ethnocide, that is, the elimination of a culture and a language, without involving a massacre of its bearers. But it can also be the result of a genocide. Thus, in 1226, Genghis Khan's Mongols annihilated the Xixia (or the Tangut), a Tibeto-Burman people of western China (modern-day region of Kansu) who had developed a flourishing culture and had invented an original ideographic writing system. Their language was destroyed with them. In 1621, the Dutch depopulated the archipelago of the Banda Islands, in the center of the Moluccas, by massacring its inhabitants. Likewise, we have no remaining trace of the language or languages that were spoken in Tasmania, because the Aborigine inhabitants of the island were annihilated.

A massacre (*gran matanza* in the popular memory) took place in El Salvador in 1932, claiming the lives of more than twenty-five thousand Indians. With them, two languages totally died out, Cacaopera and Lenca. The Andokeans, an Amazonian population of southeastern Colombia and northwestern Brazil, were decimated by a series of atrocities perpetrated by companies exploiting wild rubber over the course of the twentieth century (see Landaburu 1979). Again in Colombia, Indian massacres took place in the twentieth century. The border wars of 1982 and 1995 between Peru and Ecuador brought many Indian tribes from both countries to the brink of extinction, and, in the last decade, so has the violence on the high Andean plateaus of Peru, instigated by the organization called the Shining Path. Hitler's programmed destruction of European Jews from 1933 to 1945 got the better of Yiddish and Judezmo (see chapters 10 and 11). A comparable extermination program also deprived Gypsy dialects of a large share of their speakers.

Beyond massacres, epidemics as well as wars can leave no survivors. But there is rarely a single and simple cause. Mexico in the second half of the sixteenth century offers a dramatic example of what the convergence of several factors can produce. Possessing, as we can imagine, considerable power to exterminate populations totally lacking immunity and not armed with antibodies, bacteria and pathogenic agents of all kinds wrought havoc as soon as this group had contact with Europeans. But other factors added to this potent threat: radical changes in relationships with agriculture, the displacement of peasants to almost barren lands, driven from their fertile fields by the Spanish who seized them.

Dispossessed of their traditions, their goods, and their civilization, haunted by the feeling of being abandoned by their gods, many Indians gradually lost their taste for life. From this followed sexual abstinence, abortions, and suicides, which explain the disappearance of a great number of tribal languages. To all these factors were added the massacres, thus making the death of humans an essential and dreadful cause of the death of languages. And what is true for Mexican Indian ethnic groups applies as well to Australian Aborigines, ravaged by syphilis, smallpox, and influenza, and decimated by the violence of the Whites (defending hunting territories when those they had expelled reentered).

Finally, a language can disappear as a result of its speakers leaving their homelands. Often, communities where traditional occupations are in decline seek ways to make a living elsewhere. This can be a slow process. It can also be rapid, as in the case of inhabitants of small islands settling on the mainland and subject to the influence of the expansive powers of the language spoken there.

Through the Disappearance of the Last Speakers
and Lack of Transmission

The death of a language can also be linked to the pure and simple physical disappearance not of an entire ethnic group, but of the language's last speakers, the old people who still know the group's idiom but who leave no descendants who have acquired that tongue. Various works cite the names of the last monolingual users of numerous languages, notably Amerindian languages. After the death of these speakers who used the languages among themselves and yet did not pass them on to others, the languages have clearly not been able to survive.

Abandonment as Survival Strategy

We are not dealing here with a physical extinction, although the situations of oppression or danger in which populations find themselves can be attributed to physical causes, at least indirectly. To escape grave dangers, unbearable persecutions, or death, a community can abruptly abandon its language as a survival strategy, to the extent that concealing one's language is an act of self-defense, considering the tragic fate of those who openly use it. That is why, in El Salvador during the 1932 massacres mentioned above, the speakers of Pipil abruptly renounced their language, witnessing many among them suffer the same fate as the Cacaoperas and the Lencas. Pipil became moribund in the years that followed, and today it is probably extinct.

Deportation

This situation is likewise not a matter of physical extinction. Nevertheless, deportation is a physical constraint, along with the consequences that result from it. In Australia, the United States, and Canada, many communities have been uprooted from their ancestral lands and deported against their will. The effect of such violence on languages is easy to understand: everywhere deported tribes find themselves mixed in with other deported tribes, knowing neither them nor their languages. The languages of the oppressors or various emergency jargons born of such situations then become the only means of communicating. Initially reduced to family use only, tribal languages gradually lose their reason for existing, given the new life these populations face and the close relationships that begin to tie them to one another. In most cases, these languages finally disappear. For the past two hundred years, this scenario has dominated the history of many Australian languages, as well as the languages of communities in the United States deported to the Oklahoma territory.

ECONOMIC AND SOCIAL CAUSES
Pressure from a More Powerful Economy

We may wonder why Dutch was not maintained in the regions of New York, Delaware, and New Jersey, which were controlled by "New Netherlands" colonists from 1623 to 1664; why French disappeared in the state of Maine, where French-speaking immigrants from Acadia were numerous; and why, finally, African languages did not survive in Black American communities (see Mufwene 2001). We may not have to look very far for an answer. The economic machinery and, consequently, the colonial and postcolonial administrative structures had one, and only one, means of expression: English. Of course, this preeminence was not immediate. Colonists quickly dominated agriculture, but the industrial revolution, which had started in the first decades of the eighteenth century in England, came later in the United States, where political structures had to be constructed and damage from the Civil War had to be repaired. But in the last third of the nineteenth century, English, and not the other languages, had become and would increasingly become, the linguistic vehicle for, and even a sign of, economic progress.

This in itself no doubt explains the decline in Amerindian languages. The economic structures established by the English-speaking population, now the majority, rendered knowledge of English increasingly necessary for Indians, now the dominated minority in their own territories, who wanted to enter into and find ways to integrate themselves professionally to the new system. Henceforth maintaining a bilingual aptitude became less and less justifiable, if one follows these communities' standard reasoning, clearly open to criticism. This entails the majority of parents posing the question of language learning in terms of cost and return. According to a movement of increasing magnitude, the transmission of Indian languages tended to be judged as too costly with regard to the dividends — measured in terms of skills and integration — that it could yield to the children.

The Creation of an Upper Social Class

Within a community, a group of individuals often forms that takes its inspiration from foreign models in order to gain control. If this group manages to assert itself, and if it grows, then the time may come when the external language it has adopted, which represents economic power, exerts pressure on the vernacular language. Insofar as the intrusive language extends its audience thanks to the appearance of native speakers, its pressure becomes more powerful still.

Generally speaking, that is the process responsible for the decline of Welsh in Wales, despite its healthy appearance if we compare it to the precarious situations of the other major Celtic languages, Breton and Irish among them. Indeed, a politically dominant upper class formed in Wales as early as the Tudor period. This class was more and more drawn to London and its economic and cultural domination. In the second half of the eighteenth century, the decline of Welsh, which this situation had begun to produce, accelerated again with the immigration of Anglophone speakers to the coal mines in southeast Wales.

Of course, obvious counterexamples exist. Linguistic phenomena, which bring the human element into play, are not predictable or without exception, and even less so when external forces, like economic and social factors, intervene. Thus, the case is reported (see Poulsen 1981) of the Frisian dialect spoken on the islands of Föhr and Amrum (in the North Sea, off the eastern coast of Schleswig-Holstein). After the decline of traditional herring fishing, a school was founded in the sixteenth century to teach sailing to the men of these islands, who consequently found employment with seafaring Dutch companies. To speak the Frisian dialect was an advantage, and it was in immigrants' interest to learn it if they wanted to become part of this tightly knit circle of sailors. This was one of the main factors in preserving a dialect previously in danger of disappearing. But such counterexamples are rare, and, moreover, we have here an economic microsystem and a limited professional environment, unimaginable for a vast community confronted with a dominant language.

Dominant Language and Dominated Language: An Ecological Interpretation of Socioeconomic Models

It is possible to interpret the phenomena in question in ecological terms. If we broaden the notion of *ecolinguistic* proposed previously (see Hagège 1990, 196), we could say that, in order for languages to survive, they must adapt to the new necessities of the ecolinguistic environment. Pressures exerted by a previously unknown ecolinguistic environment can become too strong so that communities confronted with a radically new way of life have neither the means nor the time to resist by adapting their languages. Consequently, these languages are replaced by others representing a more powerful economic and social status. In other words, the renunciation of a native language, and the adoption of the language that is seen as more effective on the linguistic values market, seem to be the means of economic promotion and social advancement.

Here a dominant and a dominated language confront each other. The dominant language is in the position of assailant. The territory for it to conquer, and for the other language to defend, is truly an exploitable resource. This territory is nothing other than the linguistic community itself that was built around the original language, now taking on the status of dominated language. We can speak of a functional *erosion* of the dominated language, in the sense that its productivity as a means of communication continues to diminish in inverse proportion to the expansion of its rival language, which is associated with a revolution in economic standards.

Natural Selection

The phenomenon by which the language of a more economically powerful population tends to threaten that of a weaker population could also be interpreted in the Darwinian terms of natural selection. But then the confrontation between economic systems must be considered as the locus of forces produced by nature and environmental conditions. Such a treatment is conceivable. Certainly the conscious will that produces economic domination differentiates human societies from other animal societies in a profound way. We cannot forget that language, a natural species by many of its characteristics (see chapter 2), is also the product of an innate cognitive aptitude on the one hand, a social institution on the other. But we can admit that relationships of domination are themselves natural phenomena, the metaphoric representation of social givens. In the struggle for life, many factors make certain languages dominant. That is true in no matter what territory and at every scale, as another example, this time drawn from Africa, will make clear.

The languages of hunter-gatherer societies are particularly threatened. This phenomenon can be observed especially in eastern Africa. Hunter-gatherers are small, often impoverished groups who traditionally had a bad reputation in comparison to farmers and livestock breeders, because their nomadic ways — seeking game and plants, and living unhygienically — were considered close to those of animals. Even though these groups have taken initiatives to modify their living conditions, their social status is still quite low. Thus they are subject to very strong pressure from the pastoral model, which allows them to reduce their poverty as well as enhance their status.

It follows that hunter-gatherer societies are driven, for economic and social reasons, to abandon their languages in favor of those spoken by the group into which they want to be integrated. There are many examples of this situation. We will consider only two of them here. The Kwegu of southwestern Ethiopia, partly settled in the poor villages along the Omo river, cultivate corn underwater on a small scale, but live especially by hunting hippopotamus and keeping bees. They sell mead, as its intoxicating powers are appreciated on the high Ethiopian plateaus, but keep the meat for their own consumption because their neighbors, the Mursi and the Bodi, consider the flesh of many animals taboo.

The Kwegu maintain cliental relationships with these neighbors, who look out for their interests, and whose herds they tend in hopes of becoming livestock owners; they often marry the daughters of their patrons. The resulting couples will be much less motivated to transmit Kwegu since the mothers do not speak it and consider it difficult even though it has many similarities with Mursi and Bodi, which belong, as Kwegu does, to the Nilo-Saharan language family. Most importantly, the inegalitarian bilingualism that generally develops does not benefit Kwegu, a language without socioeconomic value. Another example, also African, involves the Dahalo, hunter-gatherers numbering in the few hundreds, who live in the coastal province of Kenya, opposite the island of Lamu, and whose language, as discussed in chapter 6, is greatly eroded under pressure from Swahili, spoken by the majority of the population in the cities.

The hunter-gatherers who tend to become livestock breeders and farmers sometimes retain the identity of belonging to a certain ethnic group. But in abandoning their means of existence and changing their social status through intertribal marriages and cliental and protection relationships, they also abandon the cultural activities and traditions linked to the use of their language. These two losses combine to lead them to sacrifice the language itself. From then on, the preservation of a truly distinct identity, even if it is strongly desired, becomes largely illusory. The same is true in other societies, like fishing societies. To consider only one example, the Elmolo, former fishermen of the southern shores of Lake Turkana in Kenya, have partially lost their language (Cushitic family), by moving to the language of the Samburu, a Nilotic people to whom they have assimilated themselves economically and culturally.

The Decline of Rural Life

Just as hunter-gatherers and fishermen, in their desire to attain higher status, assimilate themselves to farmers and livestock breeders, so too are rural people often drawn to urban life, where they hope to find a better economic situation. Here again, in the long or short run, the linguistic consequence is extinction. This might become, at least in the cities, the fate of Nubian, a language in the Nilo-Saharan family, still spoken, theoretically, by two hundred thousand individuals in Egypt and the Sudan. In Egypt, great numbers of the youngest Nubians go to Cairo or Alexandria, drawn by the better job prospects that the cities seem to offer. The presence of electricity, and thus of radio and television, does much to promote Arabic among them, and thus the men become vehicles for it. This is because they are more present at home, due to the proximity of their work places to the villages, and they tend to speak Arabic to their children. Only the Nubian spoken in rural areas still escapes the decline that threatens the language in urban zones.

This process, with a few variations, seems to apply everywhere. The decline of regional languages, dialects, and patois in France was linked to the population drain of the countryside, to professional mobility, and to the attraction of the (relative) comfort of urban life. The widely held opinion is that the French peasants who renounced their local languages, except when being harassed by teachers charged with spreading the national language, acted freely. They were attracted by progress, or what is designated as such. But did the rapid evolution of lifestyles put them in a position to choose?

Abandoning Traditional Occupations

When a population renounces its way of life for economic and social reasons, one of the consequences is that old occupations are phased out and soon abandoned. Now, the language in which these occupations express themselves is the traditional one, the whole of cultural symbols by which an ethnic group recognizes itself. Thus the ethnic language is threatened with extinction at the same time as the culture for which it was the vehicle. Of the examples of this process, let us consider the Aborigine languages of Australia. In most groups, hunting and fishing have disappeared or are now practiced only on a small scale. The same is true for nocturnal celebrations called *corroborees* (through reinterpretation according to the closest English word, "corroborate" [although there is no semantic kinship], of the word *korobra*, meaning "to dance," probably in Wunambal, still spoken in the northern part of western Australia). Over the course of these festivities celebrating a tribe's victory or some other fortunate event, people dance and hold forth, obviously in the vernacular language. At first, Aborigines used their own languages in these circumstances, as they did in their private and family lives, while they used English in professional activities and in their relations with Whites. But to the extent that assimilation entails a decline in traditions, they devoted less and less time to such celebrations. Consequently, they used their own languages less and less, and English more and more. This is how changes in cultural landmarks can lead to the death of languages.

Cases of a direct correlation between the decline of traditional activities and the erosion of grammatical systems can even be observed. Thus we can understand why, at the time of the last study done in the 1970s, the last speakers of above-mentioned Kamilaroi had almost completely lost the elaborate system by which verbs allowed the specific times of day for an activity to be distinguished morphologically. The cultural importance of this system stemmed from the fact that it was based on the cycles of behavior adopted between sunrise and sunset by the animals that the Kamilaroi had formerly hunted. In fact, the last old people had long since given up hunting, and the youngest members of the tribe had abandoned this traditional relationship with the environment.

POLITICAL CAUSES

Languages Sacrificed on the Altar of the State

States and Multilingualism

The establishment of centralized political powers and concern for extending control over all regions that are supposed to fall under their authority are not always compatible with maintaining small ethnic groups scattered over vast territories. The development of states aware of their political clout often leads to enterprises that are particularly disastrous for these groups: the destruction of habitat, deforestation, displacement of populations, forced assimilation. Such is the history of the Spanish colonization in Central and South America, for example, and the English and then American colonization in North America. The colonial policies of other countries—Portugal, the Netherlands, France—did not differ much from this pattern.

The linguistic consequences are easy to perceive. The ideology of states built around the domination of a nation is hardly favorable to the burgeoning of languages and any implied attempts to further them. The constant reduction of the role of regional languages is the most visible effect of the linguistic policy in France, under the monarchy as under the republic. The decree of Villers-Cotterêts in 1539 only punctuates a series of royal acts that, even before the reign of Louis XI, had no purpose other than to extend the language of the state, curtailing the role of Latin, certainly, but also those of regional languages. During the French Revolution, the abbot Henri Grégoire's remark is significant, as he invokes the necessity for a single language, without which understanding on the scale of the whole nation is impossible, and consequently guaranteeing the circulation of merchandise and ideas is likewise impossible.

This policy is one of the causes (but not the only one) for the decline of regional languages, as well as dialects and patois, in present-day France (see Hagège 1987 and 1996b). France is hardly an isolated case. In most societies established as states, a fundamental characteristic of their conception involves bases of national unity, often built upon linguistic unity. It may be that the conception of national cohesion as linked to linguistic unity was widespread in Europe and in America more than elsewhere, to judge from the more flexible attitudes toward multilingualism found in India, Thailand, and Malaysia, and even, to some extent, in China (see Fodor and Hagège 1983–1994).

The State and Linguicide

Political powers do not confine themselves to measures that limit the use of minority languages. Often they do nothing to prevent a predicted and certain death. But sometimes they go even further. They hunt down languages, even if they do not exterminate their speakers. State linguicide, that is, the concerted elimination of one or many languages through explicit political measures, is illustrated most notably by the war that the United States waged during the first decades of the twentieth century on the languages spoken on the various islands of Micronesia, like Chamorro (or Guameño) on Guam, as well as other languages on Saipan, Rota, Tinian, Pagan, Anatahan, and Alamagan. American power, even more than Spanish power before it, did its best to annihilate Chamorro through very strict administrative measures, and achieved a spectacular reduction in the number of its speakers. Nevertheless it seems that the language is not dead.

Another well-known example also pertains to the same region. In the early twentieth century, after Spain was evicted between 1898 and 1901, American political authorities in the Philippines set out to virtually eradicate Spanish by sending English-speaking auxiliaries all the way to the mountain villages. Nearly five hundred years of colonial power had served as a forceful introduction to Spanish for the elite, although that power had been undermined, of course, since the beginning of the seventeenth century by a long series of rebellions.

Sometimes linguicide has been perpetrated by a dominant group belonging to the population of native speakers itself. For example, the education act adopted by the Scottish parliament in 1616 stipulates that in each parish, the schools should bring English into general use and eradicate Scottish Gaelic, declared the source of all barbarity, and consequently, "to be abolished and removed" from all teaching.

The Instruments of Deferred Execution

Of course, states are not obliged to take administrative measures against the languages they have condemned, explicitly designed to exterminate them. For executing languages, they also have instruments at their disposal which may be slower but just as effective. These instruments are well known, and will be mentioned only briefly here: the army, the media, and school. Only the army and the media will be considered here. I will examine the effect of school later.

The Army

We know that the mixing of conscripts in France during the Third Republic, just like one century earlier when the revolutionaries rose en masse to face the perils on the frontiers, was one of the means for the general diffusion of French, which amounted to allocating regional languages, dialects, and patois to the reduced status of private idioms. Russian played a similar role in the twentieth century in relation to the many languages of the rank-and-file soldiers in the czarist and especially the Soviet armies, since they were originally from the Caucasus, Islamic republics of central Asia, areas of eastern Siberia where scattered ethnic groups live — Turks, Mongols, Tungus — or elsewhere. In all parts of this country, the most powerful language, Russian, meant to be the language of union, assimilated all the others.

The Media

Bombarding the masses with radio and television programs in any of a few internationally spoken languages (English, Spanish, French, Portuguese) can play only a pernicious role for unrepresented tribal and regional languages spoken by a portion of listeners and viewers. There is no need to stress this transparent cause of extinction among poorly defended languages. It is enough to recall that, among the isolated tribes in remote areas, the number of those without access to television and radio and who can thereby escape this daily assault grows increasingly smaller. We must also stress that the most exposed are those equipped with least knowledge, and among whom the transmission of jeopardized languages is declining, even though these are the key to their survival. The new generations provide the ideal market for the (lucrative!) religions preached by the predominantly Anglophone media—notably pop music, fashion, and sports.

The Imperialism of English
The Hierarchy of Languages

Today, the imperialism of English is key among the factors contributing to the death of languages. Of course, economic and social causes must be considered first. But English, being the language of the most industrialized societies, is the principal beneficiary of the collision between communities of unequal economic strength. By the very fact of its supremacy, it acquires even more political clout, which, in turn, increases the pressure it can apply. American English reaps all the rewards of the almost hierarchical opposition we find increasingly pronounced in the world today between a local language reserved for private relationships and an international language intended to be the vehicle for commercial transactions on a vast scale, and thus also the vehicle for political and cultural ideologies.

The Promotion of Monolingualism and Monolingual Thinking

One consequence of this situation is the supremacy of those who speak only one language, and the favor that their attachment to this single language wins them. This promotion of monolingualism and monolingual thinking takes place to the benefit of English. Instead of being appreciated for what it is, that is, a rich resource, the competence of multilingual speakers finds itself devalued as a handicap. Monolingualism in English is seen as a guarantee, if not a necessary condition, of modernism and progress, whereas multilingualism is associated with underdevelopment and economic, social, and political backwardness, or is considered a stage, negative and brief, on the inevitable path to English alone. Speakers find themselves implicitly condemned to the narrow cell of a single choice: either retain their mother tongue, a minority and politically impotent language even if the majority speak it, or learn English and thus give up their mother tongue. Various studies (see especially Lambert 1967) demonstrate that this choice is very much the trap in which many communities find themselves, such as the immigrant communities in Canadian provinces other than Quebec, for example. Thus, the devaluation of bilingualism goes so far as to make people forget that learning a new language does not require renouncing their original one.

Of course, in this fundamentally unequal situation, native English speakers have nothing to lose. On the contrary, for them the acquisition of another language is conceived of as possible without costing their native language anything. Language learning is considered an addition, as is natural, and not a substitution. In contrast, for others it is very much a matter of substitution, because every effort is made to persuade them that bilingualism is a costly luxury, and only the dominant language is worth learning, since it alone can provide gratifying and lucrative results. Again, such overt pressure is not always necessary. Among most dominated peoples, inegalitarian bilingualism itself devalues and finally condemns the native language, confronted with an economic and social model that appears so much more prestigious.

The Anglophone School in North America, a Death Machine for Indian Languages

We have just seen that states are capable of adopting education policies aimed purely and simply at eradicating one or many languages. Explicit measures of prohibition and promotion are only one aspect of the role schools play in the death of languages. More importantly, the school is the place and the instrument of long-term aggression.

At the end of the nineteenth century, the policy of federal governments, in Canada as in the United States, was to integrate the Indian communities through Anglophone schools. It was explicitly stated (see Zepeda and Hill 1991) that the only means of "civilizing" Indian children was to remove them from the "barbaric" influence of their native environments and transfer them into boarding schools far from their villages. This uprooting operation was sometimes carried out by force. Families were too poor to afford to bring their children home, even for summer vacations. In all schools, whether they were federal, parochial, or even secondary schools on a local town level, the use of Amerindian languages was absolutely forbidden, and all infractions were punished in a manner as severe as it was humiliating, even when the children were still very young. In certain regions, this system still existed in the early 1970s.

Elsewhere the policies became unnecessary because the corporal and moral harassment of Indian children who still dared to use their mother tongue had been so effective. Still very much remembering those days, the old people of the Tlingit and Haida ethnic groups, whose languages, formerly spoken in southeast Alaska, are now dying out, still shudder when they happen to speak among themselves in the language of their community. Clever productions, replete with grimacing actors and frightening characters, were performed in the American schools in order to eradicate all attachment to Indian culture. Indian languages were portrayed as diabolical creations, and any impulse to use them was expelled through fear. Was it possible to still retain some attachment, hearing their teachers assert that God, who must be obeyed absolutely, did not like Indian languages?

To consider only one example, we could mention the schools in Alaska directed by Jesuit, Moravian (a Hussite inspired order, begun in Moravia), and Orthodox missionaries. Until the early twentieth century (see Krauss 1992), these schools taught Indian children in their own vernacular idioms, using materials in Aleut, central Yupik, languages in the Eskimo-Aleut family, as well as many languages in the Athapascan family. But in about 1912 the last Aleut religious school was closed. A strict policy was instituted, under which any recourse to Indian languages in education was expressly banned. This measure of absolute ostracism remained in effect for sixty years.

This policy had devastating effects. It led Indian families to believe that their vernacular languages had no future, and that teaching these languages could only harm their children. In 1979, only one Athapascan language remained in southeast Alaska, Kutchin, then spoken along the lower MacKenzie and the mid Yukon rivers. Only one Aleut community still had children speakers. As for the Eskimo languages, Yupik and Inupiaq, they were on the way to disintegration. Recent studies confirm that their deterioration is leading them to the brink of death.

The Same Scenario and the Same Results in Australia

The discussion above involves American Indian languages as victims of Anglophone schools, but it also applies, and in nearly the same terms, to languages from an entirely different part of the world, those of the Australian Aborigines, also brought to the brink of death by the pressures of English in all areas, and in particular, at school. Beginning in 1814, and for almost a century, 30 percent of native children, that is, many tens of thousands, were sent to school after having been forcibly removed from their families. They were placed with white families, in orphanages, or just simply in prisonlike boarding schools, where they were, of course, categorically forbidden to use languages other than English. It was only in the late 1960s, when it was already too late, that the Australian government revised its policy of complete eradication of Aboriginal languages.

Political Pressure Exerted on "Little" Languages by Languages Other than English

The education policy of France and, to a lesser extent, of Portugal, in their colonial empires (the case of Spain in Latin America is another story), was assimilation. If it did not have a negative effect upon the masses, it did among the elite, who were sometimes won over by the temptation of monolingualism, to the European language's advantage.

But beyond that, other languages besides English, given the status of official language in certain states, can exert formidable pressure on ethnic languages. Africa offers clear illustrations of this situation. Contrary to what is sometimes believed, the threat to regional and tribal languages in Africa today no longer comes from European languages, even though that is very much the case in northern Asia (Russian), Central and South America (Spanish), North America (English), and Australia (English). If European languages were able to exert pressure in the colonial period in Africa, their present use is limited to select society, a situation which makes them compatible with preserving the ethnic identities of the little languages. The true threat comes from African languages that are widespread and meant to unify, their promotion coinciding with that of the state structures. Such is the case of Swahili in Tanzania. The prominence of Swahili as the official language promoted to cement national unity makes it a source of borrowings, to the extent that even languages belonging to its same genealogical group within the Bantu family draw many neologisms from Swahili, although they could easily construct them, since they possess identical derivational properties.

A paradox lies hidden here. In the years after former British and French colonies in Africa gained independence, the first governments' policies of adopting English or French as official languages was presented as the means of preserving national unity by not promoting the linguistic heterogeneity that characterizes Africa and thus furthering separatist temptations. As a matter of fact, in the African environment, the choice of an exogenous language favors regional languages. This is because those of the elite and the propertied class are the only ones who know European languages very well, whereas the masses remain attached to their vernacular idioms. In contrast, the promotion of an African language, viewed by the ruling power as an act of national affirmation, puts the minority idioms at risk: they are not in a position to compete with it, all the more since it is reinforced by education measures and the media. If speakers switch en masse to the promoted language, minority idioms find themselves threatened.

That is the situation today for many languages in Tanzania and, to a certain extent, in Kenya. Swahili is the beneficiary in both these cases. We can foresee a comparable development furthering two other languages used by a great many speakers: Fula, widespread in nearly all central African countries, from Senegal to Chad and the Central African Republic, and Hausa, which has, like Fula, served as the vehicle for Islam in vast areas. Fula's pressure on other languages is particularly felt in northern Cameroon (under its local variant, or

Fulfulde of Diamare). Hausa's pressure is similarly felt in northern Nigeria. Will the future of these two languages in their respective countries be as brilliant as what seems promised to Swahili? In Tanzania, the success of Swahili indicates an uncertain fate for English itself. Moreover we can note that, following a comparable path, Lingala is in the process of seizing French strongholds in Kinshasa and a northern part of the Congo Republic, which is not necessarily good news for the little languages of this country.

The Multiple Substitutions

The most common consequence of the various aggressions suffered by a language deprived of effective means of defending itself is that it is supplanted, and finally replaced, by another language. But sometimes not just one but several languages besiege it. In this case, the assailed language is challenged at various levels at once, and it is often forced to withdraw. An example of this situation can be found in West Africa. Basari, spoken mostly in the border region between Senegal and Guinea, is exposed to three conjoined pressures in Senegal, at the local, regional, and national levels. Locally, its neighbor is Fula. Commercially, Fula and Basari speakers are in constant contact, and Basari women often marry Fulbe (Fula) men, with the children of these unions becoming Fulbe in status and language. At the regional level, Basari is at a disadvantage in relation to Malinke, which has official status in southeastern Senegal and which, therefore, is actively promoted as the written language of education, used in the media and taught in the schools. At the national level, a Senegalese who wants to pursue nontraditional occupations is well advised to know Wolof and French. The former is used in all the country's urban areas and is known by the majority of Senegalese: it is, in fact, the true national language of the country; the latter is omnipresent in higher education and in all the avenues of power.

Nevertheless, outside of Senegal, in Guinea, where Fula and Malinke dominate as well, Basari benefited from a certain amount of promotion under the Sékou Touré regime, which favored indigenous languages. After Sékou Touré's death in 1984, the military regime that succeeded him reversed this completely, holding the indigenous policy responsible for the country's woes in the areas of education and the economy. Thus, Basari finds itself exposed to the formidable competition of languages much better equipped to assert themselves, both within Senegal and without. This is reason enough to predict Basari's extinction.

The Invaders Invaded

In general, languages disappear due to the political pressure of a superior power, which is often invaders who create state structures in the midst of the vanquished. But this process admits to a few obvious exceptions that are worth examining. We know that the Franks did not impose their language on the Gallo-Romans, whom they had conquered, and that, from the Merovingians of Clovis to the Carolingians, Gaul was the theater for the development of a new language, the future French, which is essentially neo-Latin, even if its phonetics and its vocabulary have Germanic traits as a result of this contact.

The warriors of the Danish chief Rohlf, those Vikings who, between the end of the ninth and the beginning of the tenth century, continually frightened Gaul's populations with their devastation, received from the king of the Franks, Charles the Simple, the province that still bears their name, "men of the North" (Normands). But in settling there they adopted the customs of the country and even its language (the Norman variant of French as it was developing), without managing either to introduce their language or to safeguard it, despite efforts like those of Rohlf's son, William Longsword, who sent his son to Bayeux, where there was a Scandinavian school, to learn the dialect of Old Norse spoken by his ancestors (see Hagège 1996b). Thus the Vikings established themselves in what is today Normandy, just as they adopted a Romance language from another conquered country, Sicily. Elsewhere, their relatives, the Varangians, did the same thing when, at the end of the ninth century, having organized the first Slavic state, embryonic Kievan Russia, they became culturally and linguistically Slavic. There are other comparable cases. The Tutsis, a Nilotic people supported by the power their pastoral economy conferred upon them, overran their hosts, the Hutus. Nevertheless they adopted the Hutus' Bantu languages, Kirundi and Kinyarwanda, as they settled (see Mufwene 2001).

Nevertheless, shouldn't the political and military power of these invaders have led to the extinction of the languages in those lands they invaded? Two reasons, equally essential, explain why this was not the case. The first is that the populations of the Franks, the Normans, and the Varangians were much smaller than those they besieged. But that rationale alone is not enough, because how then to explain the lethalness of the Castilian intrusion to so great a number of American Indian languages? The Spanish, as fierce and as well armed as they were, constituted only a small troop of warriors occasionally augmented by local populations with which they formed alliances. But the Spanish, escorted by their missionaries, were not simply gaunt and greedy visitors with violent ways. They were bearers of a lofty civil and religious ideology, and they were convinced of their superiority over all others.

We can deduce from this that the invaders' idiom must reflect a very self-aware civilization in order to dominate the language of the vanquished people and make it disappear. Otherwise, the normal fate of nomadic minorities that attack sedentary communities and dismantle them by force is to settle into, be absorbed by, and even adopt those communities' languages. This was also the case much farther away, in the Far East, with China's invaders, the Yuan (Mongols). And later, exactly as it had done with the Mongols, the old Chinese culture's power of absorption totally engulfed and altered the Ch'ing dynasty (Manchus), which lasted until the death of the empress Tzu Hsi in 1911. Nothing distinguished either the Mongols or the Manchus from the purely Chinese dynasties of the Han, the Tang, the Sung, and the Ming. Even though Manchu was still the language of diplomacy and official records in 1644, the date when the last Ming emperor was driven from Peking, the fascination these newcomers felt for Chinese civilization and their respect for Mandarin Chinese eventually led them to replace their ancestral language. Today, Manchu is virtually dead among the four million Chinese of Manchu origin who live in China and who have long borne Chinese names.

If the language of the Arabs has not suffered the same fate, this is because, like the Spanish, they were the soldiers of a confident and conquering religious ideology that led them, almost in a single sweep, to carry Islam to the Atlantic coast of Morocco in the west, and as far as the Caucasus and the Sind in the east. Under the first three caliphs and then under the Umayyad dynasty, they succeeded in dominating Spain, North Africa, Syria, Mesopotamia, Persia, Egypt, and central Asia. At the end of the tenth century, the Turks spread Islam even further still, and by the beginning of the fourteenth century it had penetrated as far as Malaysia.

Why, then, didn't Arabic, the bearer of one of the world's most brilliant civilizations in the Middle Ages, dominate and drive to extinction the languages of the conquered countries? The reason is simple: most of those countries possessed old cultures. Islamization was a matter of mutual enrichment, and the languages that expressed those cultures lost none of their brilliance in the process. To consider only one of many examples of this cultural symbiosis, the great grammarians, whose penetrating analyses of Arabic between the eighth and eleventh centuries constitute one of the most remarkable chapters in the history of linguistic thought, were, in fact, Arab Persians. In Christian countries like Spain, attachment to the Christian religion and strong convictions regarding its superiority usually had the effect of repelling Islamization, and thus Arabic, which was the vehicle for it. Later, Turkish encountered a similar situation in the conquered Balkans with regard to Greek, Bulgarian, and Serbian, which borrowed words from it but were not replaced by it.

The Loss of Prestige and the Death of Languages

The loss of prestige does not seem to play a direct causal role. Languages without particular renown easily endure, as long as no decisive economic, social, and political factors are involved. The loss of prestige is, in fact, one of the most common consequences of these factors. When prestige is unequally distributed between competing populations, it appears as a sort of currency of exchange on the stock market of linguistic values. When, on the contrary, it is equally distributed and when a rivalry is established between the groups, each of which claims it, prestige is capable of reducing the devastating effects massive pressure can have on the life of languages.

PRESTIGE, EXCHANGE CURRENCY ON
THE LANGUAGE MARKET
Prestige and Languages
The Transfer of Attributes

The belief that a language's prestige is an inherent attribute is illusory. Languages are complexes of evolving structures that play an essential role in the cognitive development of individuals and that are, moreover, used by them in communication. There is nothing in itself—in the phonology, morphology, syntax, or lexis of a language—that is the bearer of prestige. Prestige, that is, a reputation of value and eminence, given the implications of these notions, can be attached only to humans. Thus, when a language is said to be prestigious, this word actually applies to those who speak it or to the books they use. By a process of transfer, which is common in relationship to the world and to the values one gives it, the respect or admiration that a group or its achievements inspires is extended to its attributes. And language is one of the principal attributes of any human community.

The Extinction of Gaulish

Prestige clearly depends upon circumstances and places. Gaulish disappeared at the beginning of the Christian era because the upper classes of the society became Romanized. These people distanced themselves from their language as they did from their culture, as we can see with the history of Druidism, a flourishing religion at the time of Caesar, which was later reduced to the debased image of a witchcraft practice relegated to the wilds of the lonely countryside (see Vendryes 1934). In about the third century, Latin engulfed the last linguistic islands of Gaulish that still survived in the forest-clad mountain groups at the country's center.

The Decline of Irish and Scottish

By the beginning of the seventeenth century, the Celtic languages of the Scottish and the Irish had long suffered a clear decline in the British Isles and, thus, a fall in prestige. They were associated with the popular culture and folklore. They were not the means of expression for people, institutions, literary works, and academic education with any national importance. This decline intensified further in the eighteenth century due to the Industrial Revolution, as English was its language. Later, in the mid-nineteenth century, the great famine in Ireland prompted a dramatic exodus. But Scottish and Irish immigrants in America who, with the English, were the first cultivators of the lands they had seized, often to the detriment of the American Indians, used English in the New World. And, by the end of the nineteenth century, for the survivors of slaughtered American Indian communities, the prestige of the colonists had become the prestige of English. Likewise in all the rest of America, Castilian (the old designation for Spanish in these places, and still very much alive), the language of the conquerors, missionaries, the richest and the most powerful, became the language of prestige as early as the sixteenth century, despite (or because of) violence, massacres, and the confiscating of lands. Portuguese played this role in Brazil.

Prestige and the Language Stock Market

Thus, originally, the prestige of languages is nothing other than that of their speakers, which itself is based on economic, social, and political factors. But by its transfer onto languages, it becomes a sort of currency, according to the standards by which each one is assessed. The most prestigious languages are the highest in demand, as are the most lucrative values on the stock exchange. The least prestigious languages seem less profitable, and create less demand. That is how their own speakers come to disown them, and to deem their transmission to the following generations unprofitable. Thus, prestige, the exchange currency on the market of linguistic values, comes to decide, apparently, the fate of languages.

How to Measure the Loss of Prestige

The prestige of a language is not an objective fact, nor is it easily measured. It belongs to mental representation. Thus, it can be evaluated only according to the standard that symbolic thinking constructs as a gauge. And that construction is the work of speakers among whom the relationship between languages, such as they internalize it, is experienced either positively or negatively. In the second case, the language becomes the victim of a loss of prestige.

The Association with Rural Life and the Past

Many languages are associated with rural life or with the past, as opposed to languages that are associated with industrial work in the cities and with the future. For example, such perceptions placed German and Hungarian at odds with each other in the Austrian village of Oberwart (see chapter 6). The Hungarian minority associated German with political power, modern education, and the mobility that facilitates access to professions more lucrative and less grueling than farming. On all these points, Hungarian is considered retrograde, which strips it of all prestige and even makes it appear useless.

The Mimetic Impulse with Regard to Returning Emigrants

In communities leading a traditional life but in which certain members have left for the city or abroad and then returned, the impulse to imitate the novelties that they bring back with them is very strong among the youngest generations. Here, prestige defines itself as a function of innovating models and detachment from old models. Speech styles occupy a choice place in this schema of thinking and behavior. Each individual wants to express himself like those who return with money and experiences or new stories. On the high plateaus of New Guinea, for example, the pidgin English that is spoken in the coastal cities, and particularly in the capital, Port-Moresby, is being adopted by a growing number of Papuans who have left their hill villages. When they return home, pidgin becomes the vehicle through which new schemas of thinking are introduced, thus dislocating the old schemas, and the local languages that bear them. A parallel process affected Breton when the soldiers who left from Trégorrois, Finistère, Vannetais, etc., returned from the First World War, where they had learned the French names for innovations that prompted their interest.

The Failing of National Consciousness

When a community fails to recognize its national identity, it can strip its language of all symbolic value. If it considers a neighboring community superior, it may come to identify with it, to the point of denying its own autonomous existence in extreme cases. That is what was observed in the Caucasus among the Svans, who, attracted by their more numerous and more powerful Georgian neighbors, threatened their own identity by passing themselves off for Georgians and calling their language Georgian, which, even though it is related genetically, is nevertheless quite different from Georgian. The youngest Svans refuse to learn the language of their fathers.

The Absence of a Literary Tradition

Even when they are not well-read, and as if to give themselves still better reasons to disown it, the speakers of a dominated language often stress that their tongue has not been chosen by great writers to create literary works. As a result, they argue, it lacks prestige, because it has not given rise to good books that everyone knows and can quote.

The Marks of Shame

The Illusion of Inadequacy

A language in good health is willingly valued by its speakers, who find it beautiful, rich, and precise, simply because, knowing it better than any other (unless they are perfectly bilingual), they can truly express themselves to their liking only in that language. On the other hand, if another language becomes appealing to speakers, they stop valuing their original language and even begin to feel ashamed of it, which, in return, leads them to like it even less. They are tormented by a kind of anxiety at the idea of still using a language that no longer has anything to recommend it, and that language becomes the locus of all sorts of negative associations, which they find very hard to relinquish. They convince themselves in particular that it is unsuitable for expressing modernity and incapable of articulating abstract ideas, obviously unaware that any language has that power, as soon as one takes the trouble to create neologisms.

Abandoning a Debased Language

These are the feelings that researchers in the field have observed, for example, in the Tlingit community in southeast Alaska. Parents, who learned to shun their language in childhood (see above), go so far as to think that to still speak Tlingit is to risk appearing like a half-wit or a peasant, and they fear that teaching this language to children will hinder not only their learning English at an early age, but also their mental development. They further fear that such teaching will benefit traditional beliefs, which they want to disown as if they were some mark of humiliation. Similarly, the Rama (Nicaragua) declare that Rama is "ugly," that "it is not a language," and that they are ashamed to speak it (see Craig 1992). Another example involves the youngest and the most urbanized Nubians who assert that Nubian is not a language, "since it is not written," unlike Arabic, and that only backward old people use Nubian, even though in reality this language is still spoken by rural populations of all ages.

A Stark Consequence of the Loss of Prestige: Voluntary Renunciation
The Public Decision of the Yaaku

We know of a few spectacular cases where, instead of leading gradually to the extinction of the devalued language, the loss of prestige has prompted a collective decision at a certain moment to abandon that language. The best known of these cases is that of the Yaaku. This north-central Kenyan population spoke a language belonging to the eastern branch of the Cushitic family. The Yaaku hunted, gathered, and fished, and lived quite poorly, as is common among the nomads who basically maintain this subsistence lifestyle. To improve their conditions, many of the men found work with their neighbors, the Masai, whose herds they watched. The Masai culture and language exerted a growing influence upon the Yaaku. They abandoned the strict endogamy of the past. Marriages became more and more common between the two ethnic groups, and the Yaaku's lifestyle began to change, as a result of acquiring livestock, to a pastoral economy. It was the same process as among other hunter-gatherers. If Yaaku wives adopted the language of their Masai husbands, Masai wives did not adopt the language of their Yaaku husbands. This resulted in reduced numbers of children speaking Yaaku.

The consequence of these profound and rapid changes was a public meeting of the prominent Yaaku in the 1930s. Over the course of this meeting, the greater prestige of Masai language and customs was stressed. Yaaku's vocabulary, which gave an important place to hunting, was declared ill-suited to a society of livestock raisers. Thus it was decided that a language so inauspicious to their future could not be transmitted to Yaaku children, and that, consequently, Yaaku would henceforth be abandoned in favor of Masai as the ethnic group's means of expression in all domains.

Other Cases of Renunciation

There is evidence of comparable cases on a more reduced scale. Many Saami (Lappish) communities living along the fjords refuse to transmit Saami to their children, and raise them speaking Norwegian instead. Still another example is that of certain languages in the Khoisan family of South Africa, like Khoekhoe, whose speakers decided early in the eighteenth century to switch to Dutch, the language of the colonists whose slaves they were, and which, because of this situation, necessarily had the most prestige. I do not know of another case of an entire African ethnic group switching voluntarily to a European language.

Reversals in Fortune: Aztec and Inca Languages, or from Prestige to Debasement

The mechanics of prestige and of its eclipse are implacable. Just as the Tarpeian Rock was located at one end of the Roman Capitol, thus symbolizing the vicinity between glory and decline, when the objective causes of decline are set into motion, and the loss of prestige ensues, the memory of ancient glory is powerless to restore past brilliance. The Aztecs had greatly extended their empire since the formation of the 1429 triple alliance between Tenochtitlán (Mexico today), their capital, founded a century earlier, and the states of Texcoco and Tlacopan. Within this alliance, they had quickly acquired a dominant position. At the beginning of the sixteenth century, thanks to their conquests, they controlled vast territories, extending from north of the future Veracruz on the Atlantic to as far as the present-day state of Guerrero, on the Pacific, and as far as the Isthmus of Tehuantepec to the south. In all these territories, their language, Nahuatl, had acquired prestige, linked to their political and military domination. Even the names they gave to the peoples they subdued clearly reveal their condescending attitudes and the power Nahuatl's dominant position granted it: Popoloca "unintelligible," Chontal "foreign," Totonac "rustic, rude" (see Heath 1972, 3).

Now, it was precisely at this moment in its history, exactly when the Aztec empire reached the height of its power and influence, that destiny brought the Spanish to loom on the horizon. With them, almost from the beginning, came the ravages of extreme violence. After some minor setbacks, Cortés and his troops annihilated the Aztec empire in an astonishingly brief period of time, even if we take into account the greater efficiency of their weapons (firearms), their horses (then unknown in America), and their divisive skills. The linguistic consequences of this outrageous fraud, and of the cultural aggression perpetrated by the conquistadores, were, as we know, catastrophic. A considerable number of languages died violently, along with the majority of their speakers, from the first half of the sixteenth century.

As for Nahuatl, after a certain period of time it lost its status. From the language of the conquerors, it became the language of the conquered. Until then, it had enjoyed great prestige. Even the Mayas, outside of the zone of Aztec influence, knew it, if we are to believe the legend that identifies Malintzin, Cortés's translator and companion, as an Aztec princess who, during her captivity in the Yucatan, communicated easily in her own language with the inhabitants, who spoke Maya Yucatec, before she learned their tongue. But Spanish became dominant. Today, Nahuatl still suffers from having thus become a dominated language, further proof that, on the market of linguistic values, a language's worth is directly linked to the place its speakers occupy on the ladder of prestige.

The Incas, too, had extended their empire from the late fifteenth century. From the Cuzco valley, it spread over a vast area: north to the site of Quito, and south beyond the regions that now coincide with a large part of Bolivia and with northern portions of Chile and Argentina. In the same way, Quechua, having become the official language of the empire, had begun to spread, posing as a rival to the languages of the Andean world, but without yet managing to supplant them. The civil war between the two sons of the last Inca emperor, who died in 1527, certainly aided Pizarro's conquest. As in Mexico, this conquest was violent and rapid. Spanish replaced Quechua as the language of prestige. Nevertheless, Quechua played, and continues to play, a role. The idioms of small, more dominated ethnic groups are its victims. Far from preventing such losses, Spanish provided the necessary means, as we will see below.

The Promotion of Common Languages
Lingua Franca

Languages that have lost prestige through domination by another community and its idiom are not always exposed just to this competition alone. Their positions are also reduced by the spread of other idioms that various circumstances have promoted to the status of common language. But these idioms are not all equally dangerous. Actually, it can be a simple makeshift jargon that allows for nothing more than a basic relationship between two individuals, each of whom speaks a language impenetrable to the other. A historical form of such jargons served as the means of communication from the time of the Crusades between Muslims and Europeans, who, since the confrontations between Clovis's Merovingian descendants and armed Arabs (stopped at Poitiers in 732), were called Franks, from which we get the name given this language, lingua franca.

In much of the Mediterranean, on the coasts of Italy, France, Spain, and the Maghreb, lingua franca was used throughout the Middle Ages and the classical period, until the beginning of the nineteenth century, in commercial, political, diplomatic, or hostile relationships that the sovereigns of Algiers and Tunis had with the French, as well as by other merchants and travelers, soldiers and sailors. The dynamic of these very unstable relationships, no doubt along with the colorful and picturesque nature of a jargon that mixed words of heterogeneous origins (especially Italian, but also Provençal, Catalan, Castilian, French, Greek, Turkish, and Arab), made lingua franca a subject of literary fantasies, as becomes apparent in the plays of Goldoni and Calderón, as well as in Molière, in the famous Turkish scene from *Le Bourgeois gentilhomme*.

Spontaneous Commercial Promotion

Lingua franca did not possess particular prestige. On the contrary, it was often the object of derision. But it had the properties of a common language that can foster contact between linguistically heterogeneous communities. As long as a common language is not a jargon, but one of the idioms present in a multilingual zone where it allows for communication and commercial relationships, its promotion over some other language and its habitual use among inhabitants there can confer upon it a kind of primacy. But it is true that situations can vary, and that many factors come into play that naturally alter this process and may not allow a language of prestige to emerge.

On the northwest coast of the United States and in parts of the interior of Washington and Oregon, the Chinook, originally inhabiting the Columbia River valley, were the most important indigenous ethnic group demographically until the beginning of the nineteenth century, and one of the most dynamic in terms of commerce. One of the dialects of their language, Lower Chinook, spread, under the name of "Chinook jargon," among many American Indian peoples. It facilitated the circulation of goods among them as far south as northern California and as far north as southern Alaska.

We find comparable situations in many other parts of the world and on variable scales. For example, on the island of Timor, situated between the Indonesian archipelago and Australia, a recently developed form of Tetum, in the Austronesian language family, is used as the means of communication in commercial relationships and more generally in social relationships between speakers of different languages. It has even become a kind of national language in this country (see chapter 11).

Deliberate Political Promotion

The promotion of a lingua franca cannot simply be the result of practical habit adopted by local populations, but must involve a massive influx of foreigners. That is how Araucanian became the lingua franca, and even the mother tongue, of the Tehuelches and other populations in southern Chile, when its speakers, the Mapuches (see chapter 8), having crossed the Andes cordillera, came to settle in the Tehuelches' territories. As a result, the Tehuelches' language disappeared (see Clairis 1991, 4–5).

In other cases, the promotion of a lingua franca results from an official choice by a political authority. The effect of prestige can thus come into play. That is the case for Sango, recognized as the national language in the Central African Republic (see chapter 11). Such promotion cannot help but confer upon the language a privileged status, with competing languages consequently losing prestige.

Quechua in the Inca empire before the arrival of the Spanish was a comparable situation to that of Sango in Central Africa. As we have seen, the spread of Quechua, probably in the form used at the end of the fifteenth century in the Cuzco region, accompanied the conquests. Contemporary evidence of this phenomenon is precisely the dialectical diversity of Quechua today, present in seven countries. This diversity is the consequence of many centuries of independent development throughout a vast territory, from Colombia to Argentina. But another factor, which will be considered below, must have ensured an even greater influence for Quechua, and other languages throughout the world, to the detriment of the disadvantaged idioms.

Decisions of the Conquerors and the Missionary Church

The Franciscan missionaries who arrived in Mexico in 1523, two years after Cortés's men conquered the Aztec site of this city, soon became aware that the linguistic landscape was widely varied. No doubt it must have seemed parceled out to them. Seeing this multitude of indigenous languages as an obstacle to evangelization, as well as to the Church's domination, the missionaries set about promoting certain ones as common languages. They chose the most likely candidates, which were the ones with the greatest numbers of speakers or the widest distribution. In the process they compiled remarkable works on certain South American languages. In sixty years of Franciscan presence, more than eighty books, grammars, vocabularies, and catechisms appeared, among them the famous descriptions of Nahuatl by A. de Olmos (1547) and A. de Molina (1555).

According to the customs of the period, these works imposed the

Latin model as the framework for study; the prestige of Latin among the Spanish Catholic elite was such that the Franciscans even taught the art of composing Latin poems to certain gifted subjects among their Indian flocks (see de Pury-Toumi 1994, 492)! Nahuatl grammars modeled on the Latin would be inconceivable today. Nevertheless, these works give us a precise idea of what Nahuatl was like in the late sixteenth century, just as the works on Quechua and Tupi do, compiled by other missionaries in that same period in Peru and Brazil, or, in the early and mid-seventeenth century, the works compiled on Aymara in Bolivia ("High Peru" in that epoch) and on Guarani in Paraguay, respectively.

Nevertheless, in Mexico, relations were not always simple between Franciscan missionaries on the one side, and conquerors and then governors as well as the hierarchy of secular clergy on the other. In the sixteenth century, the Spanish victors had noted the spread of Tarascan in the realm of Michoacán and of Otomí in part of the central Mexican plateau. They had also noticed that the Mayan languages were expanding even more, from the Yucatán to the southern part of present-day Guatemala, despite the breakup into city-states held together only by local alliances, which had facilitated the Spanish conquest as quickly as 1511. The Spanish saw that these three language groups were almost the only ones that were still spreading beyond their original speakers since the Aztecs had begun to implant Nahuatl in many regions through their conquests a century earlier. Cortés and his successors quickly understood that this linguistic hegemony could serve their plans for domination by fostering unity and easy communication.

Nevertheless, they also began to spread Castilian at the same time, so that it could one day replace Nahuatl. But even though they were supported by the political powers in Spain, they ran up against the will of the Franciscan missionaries, who considered their mission to be converting the Indians to Christianity and not to Castilian. This prompted a decree from Charles V in 1550, recommending the widespread use of Spanish for converting and educating not only the Indian aristocracy, as that process had already begun, but all the Indians. Nonetheless, in Mexico the struggle continued for a long time between those who wanted to impose Spanish to support colonial domination, and those who wanted to promote a few great Indian languages. This antagonism ended only with the arrival of the Jesuits, who, of course, greatly admired Aztec, but who, unlike the Franciscans before them, evangelized in Castilian. Now the population was no longer simply conquered, as at the time of the Franciscans, but colonized. Thus, contrary to the Franciscans' desire (see de Pury-Toumi 1994), Nahuatl did not become the "general language" as did Tupi in part of Brazil (see below). Nevertheless, in Europe the Jesuits defended the cause of indigenous American languages.

The linguistic policy of Spanish missionaries was more successful in Peru. Quechua offers a typical example. Paradoxically, the many Andean languages not already supplanted by Quechua when Spanish invaders seized the empire fell victim to it as the Catholic priests chose it for a language of evangelization. They promoted it by imposing its use on all their converts. By being promoted as a common language, and thus becoming a prestigious language, Quechua quashed Puruhá, Kañari, Kakan, Kul'i, Uru-Pukina, and many other languages. This movement lasted into the twentieth century: thus the Zaparos of Ecuador's western lowlands have generally switched to Quechua. The evangelists even managed to spread Quechua into regions untouched by the Inca conquest, like the present-day Argentinean province of Santiago del Estero, or the regions of upper Caquetá and upper Putumayo in southwestern present-day Colombia.

There was also another Andean language that the missionaries promoted as an instrument of conversion: Aymara, spoken by more than one and a half million people in Peru and Bolivia. This figure is probably higher now than it was at the beginning of the sixteenth century, because since that time numerous Indian communities abandoned their languages to adopt Aymara.

Also in South America, but this time in the region southern Brazil and Paraguay occupy today, missionaries made extensive use of two related, and already major, languages — Tupi and Guarani — because they were spoken by a large number of Indians. The Jesuits, who governed and converted in Paraguay until they were expelled in 1768, did much to spread Guarani (see chapter 9). It is to the Jesuit A. R. de Montoya that we owe the most famous description of Guarani, still useful today despite the outdated nature of its Latinizing analyses. And during the colonial period in Brazil, coastal Tupi, under the name of "língua-geral" ("general language"), was the idiom of communication in the countries of the lower Amazon and in the southeast. As in the examples cited previously, this chosen status as common language was a factor in the extinction of various tribal languages that could not withstand the pressure of idioms already favored by their natural diffusion and the demographic clout of their users.

All this must not lead us to forget that the true beneficiaries of colonial politics in Latin America were, in the end, the European languages: Spanish and Portuguese. Some people marvel especially at the astonishing history of Spanish, spread over such vast territories and in so many countries, which are all culturally unified by it today. But there was a price for this success: the death of a great number of Indian languages.

Russian, Lingua Franca in the Soviet Union

Unlike the czarist regime, which had no true linguistic policy, the Soviet Union considered the languages of the many ethnic groups scattered throughout its immense territory to be major pieces in the definition of national entities, and thereby granted them an important place. Until the early 1930s, and the proliferation of dictionaries and manuals, they experienced a period of distinct good fortune. Nonetheless, it is revealing that in the official terminology of that time, Russian was called the "common language," or the "international language," or even the "second mother tongue." In an empire where more than 130 languages were spoken, this status almost seemed to respond to a natural necessity. An important education reform in 1958, which gave parents the choice of the school language, had as its intention and its effect a strong promotion of Russian, the language of prestige, not only because it was the language of socialism, but also because it was the language of industrial occupations and scientific and economic progress (see Hagège 1994, 220–238 and 255–264).

Apart from Russia, most of the republics enacted linguistic laws beginning in 1988, that is, when the Soviet Union had not yet broken up but had begun to suffer more and more serious splits. These laws recognized Russian's lingua franca status, explicitly designating it the "language of relations between nations," but they also defended the other languages, many of which had been weakened by the significant rate of borrowing from Russian in all areas of vocabulary reflecting modern life. If we add to such a state of affairs that, in many of the autonomous republics, autonomous regions, or national districts, the Russian-speaking population was significant and often the majority, and that, furthermore, a strong dialectical fragmentation characterized many languages in the USSR, we can understand why the status of a language of prestige serving as the instrument of daily relations between so many peoples had played a role in the demise of Uralic, Turkish, Mongolian, Tungusic, and Siberian dialects. These were dialects that, except in very rare cases, had hardly any means of resistance.

The Implications and Consequences of Choosing English

The loss of prestige for many idioms confronted with a lingua franca that represents effective communication on a vast scale is, in the contemporary world, still more life-threatening when the language in question is Anglo-American. The situation, then, is no longer that of a simple linguistic exchange in a language with some prestige, chosen as a response to a consensus and thus gaining more prestige, because that process takes place only on a local level. Of course, Russia itself exerted great pressure in the Soviet Union, as we have just seen, but as vast as the country was, the phenomenon remained regional.

In contrast, the adoption of English as the lingua franca does not facilitate a multilingual environment. Rather, it involves integration into a linguistic space where, as native speakers, belong the citizens of one of the most powerful countries in the world, a country that dominates in economic, political, scientific, and cultural realms. It is unlikely that such considerations played a decisive role for speakers of the many American Indian or Australian languages that were becoming or were already extinct. These speakers "simply" adopted the language of the dominant society, present in their workplaces and in their environments. They were simply lowering the barriers that the expansion of tribal languages seemed to erect. But the choice of Anglo-American could not be innocent given the circumstances in the world since the mid-nineteenth century. A common language that is also, everywhere, the language of power and money is not a neutral means of communicating.

RIVALRY OVER PRESTIGE AND ITS EFFECTS ON THE FATE OF LANGUAGES

Speakers besieged by another language, apparently well equipped to ensure its domination, do not always surrender to the intrusion. In at least two cases, they have continued to promote the prestige of their original language and its cultural values in such a way that this language emerges from the confrontation unharmed. The first is a case of massive borrowings countered by a heightened national consciousness. The second involves a bilingual elite.

When Massive Borrowings Do Not Lead to Absorption

When bilingualism is egalitarian, massive borrowing of vocabulary can occur, without foreshadowing the disappearance of the borrowing language through absorption into the lending language. Three cases merit consideration here. The first takes place in England, the second in the Islamic East, and the last in East and Southeast Asia.

Anglo-Norman and the Tenacity of English

The form that Norman took in England, after that country was conquered by William the Duke of Normandy in 1066, is known by linguists as Anglo-Norman. It was mixed with Picard, spoken by some of the conquerors, and took on an important Angevin component in the twelfth century with the arrival of numerous merchants, replaced later by contributions from the Ile-de-France. The French influence increased further because the users of this neo-Latin dialect from western France claimed as a model the literary French then developing and becoming unified around the French court, where some speakers had old connections. However, these users were, in fact, a minority. Only the court, the feudal aristocracy, the rich merchants, the bishops, the priests, and others in privileged positions spoke this Norman variant of incipient French.

As for most of the population, they spoke only English (see Hagège 1996b, 32–36). Nevertheless, they absorbed the massive borrowings that were made, according to the period, from various forms of French, and that give English, at least to the ears of a French speaker, its very distinct appearance as a Latinized Germanic language. Yet English had begun to be Latinized by the Roman occupation in the first century B.C., then by Christianization in the sixth century, shortly after the Jutes, Angles, and Saxons drove the native Celts back to the west. These three groups were the first to use the Germanic language from which English arose. Thus, the considerable contribution of Anglo-Norman words is the natural result of a Latinizing hybridization begun much earlier. As evidence, I will mention here just the conservation of the old meanings of borrowed Anglo-Norman words that have lost those meanings today in French, the alteration in the meaning of other words, and the preservation in English of medieval words that modern French has lost, like *to remember, mischief,* or *random,* etc. (see Hagège 1994, 36).

This independent manner of assimilating a conqueror's language accounts for, and demonstrates the extent of, English's resistance. The annexation of Normandy by Philippe Auguste in 1204 had isolated England from the continent, and contributed to the appearance of a national English consciousness that exerted nationalist pressure, especially through the criticism of the open policy toward foreigners under the reign of the son of John Lackland, Henry III. In the late thirteenth century, a bourgeoisie formed that increasingly asserted itself in the fourteenth century. Now, this English-speaking bourgeoisie had nothing but disdain for the variant of French used by the ruling circles. For them, that foreign language of the invaders' descendants was the symbol of subservience, and prompted growing impatience among their ranks. This bourgeoisie wanted to impose the use of English, to make it known that English was no longer the idiom of the unschooled masses.

And so, in 1362, the Chancellor delivered his address to London's Parliament in English for the first time. By the end of the fourteenth century, French had lost its privileged role in education. Writers, Chaucer among them, no longer wrote in anything but English. The accession of Henry IV in 1399 would mark the first reign of a monarch whose native tongue was English. Thus the Norman aristocracy in England met with a fate parallel to that of their tenth-century ancestors in France. Their ancestors had been Gallicized; they became Anglicized. Far from definitively Gallicizing England, the descendants of the Norman barons finally, after three centuries, became Anglophones. There were three reasons for this: they had lost their connections to Normandy; they had married women of the local aristocracy because there were not enough Norman women and because such marriages granted some legitimacy to power initially obtained by force; and, most important, they had come up against a population very attached to their language.

Thus French domination in England did not harm English in the least, much less set it on the path to extinction. The structures of feudal society prevented the Norman variant of French from imposing itself beyond the privileged minorities. A native English-speaking merchant class rose from the masses and was able to assert itself, and to assimilate borrowings, despite their enormous number, giving modern English its first appearance. Having no reason to denigrate their language, despite the initial prestige of Anglo-Norman, the English of the Middle Ages withstood the shock of French with great fortitude.

Persian and Turkish Put to the Test by Arabic

We know of the conquest and Islamization of Persia under the reign of the second caliph, Omar, between 634 and 644, and later, the gradual Islamization of the Turks by the Islamic Iranians with whom they traded. As for the Islamization of the Mamelukes, Turkish mercenaries in the service of the Abbasids, it resulted in one of them, Alp Tagin, founding the first Turkish Islamic empire, the Rhaznevides', in 962. In a process extending over many centuries, Persian and Turkish borrowed thousands of words from Arabic. In the case of Persian, an almost thousand-year-long intimate symbiosis with Arabic—the language of the Islamic religion, in its Shiite version, adopted by a vast majority of Iranians, but also the language of science and international relations with the rest of the Islamic world—resulted in penetration of the hard kernel itself. An Indo-European language, Persian, like other languages in that genetic group, possessed the usual processes for word formation through affixation and composition. But by borrowing across entire families of Arabic words, the Semitic process of multiple derivations upon the base of a three-consonant root was added. The syntax and phonology of Persian were themselves subjected to the influence of Arabic.

But it is clearly the vocabulary that was the most profoundly affected. Persian still drew from the lexical stocks of, first, Avestan, its ancestor codified under the Sasanians in the fourth century, long extinct as a spoken language, and second, Pahlavi, middle Persian, in use at the time of the Arab conquest. But it also borrowed enormously from Arabic in all domains over the course of centuries. Nevertheless, Arabic's high position did not have the power to cost Persian its prestige. The 1906 revolution in favor of a constitutional government was followed by a nationalist movement exalting the glories of ancient Persia but advocating modernization at the same time. Beginning in the 1920s, modernization prompted a debate over the comparative merits of Arabic words and pure Persian words for the neological enterprise needed to adapt to the novelties of the Western world. Those promoting and defending Persian claimed especially that it was a language of urban culture, whereas Arabic had adapted to desert life before finding itself in fruitful contact with the brilliant

Iranian culture, and moreover, that Arabic processes for word formation were less clear than those of Persian (see Jazayery 1983).

The awakening of a Turkish national consciousness at the time of the early twentieth century military defeats further explains the astonishing measures of the Kemalist regime. For many centuries, the ruling classes of the Ottoman Empire, a theocratic Islamic state, had been subject to intense Arab-Persian acculturation, which invaded the written language to the point of making it an elite scholarly idiom inaccessible to the masses, and in which it was said that only the linking words with purely grammatical functions were Turkish. From that point on, when Atatürk announced the replacement of the Arabic alphabet with the Latin one in 1928, it was a revolution, in the guise of purely technical modifications. What the Arabic letters wrote was that language of the former Ottoman powers, whereas the Latin letters recorded the language as it existed among the masses (contrary to their function in Christian Europe, before the sanctioning of spoken languages).

The Kemalist revolution was populist- and nationalist-inspired. It was not satisfied with simply changing the writing. Henceforth, it was from the deep lexical wells of Turkish and other Turkic languages that one drew new word sources, as well as from the popular language, which had admittedly assimilated many Arabic and Persian words over much time in this Islamic land, but far fewer than official Ottoman. In the schools, where it had no standing, Turkish took the place of Arabic and Persian. Finally, all unnecessary Arab-Persian elements were purged from the language. If we consider the degree of permeation and how far it dated back, this was an immense undertaking. It is said to be still going on today.

Thus, despite the extent and the duration of Islamization, neither Persian nor Turkish has disappeared through merging with Arabic. To what can we attribute this endurance, even though Persia and especially the Ottoman Empire have long embodied Islamic power itself? To a tenacious awareness of their cultures, even among the Turks, who are nevertheless descendants of nomads.

Still other languages—and also for reasons linked to the Islamization of their speakers—have experienced an influx of Arabic words without being destroyed by it. But it is true that borrowings have not been as numerous as in Turkish and in Persian. We know that Malay includes an Arabic stratum, of Hadramawt origin especially, and that Hindustani (to evoke this term that designates neither Sanskritized Hindi nor Persianized Urdu, but the roots of the language that they share) contains a certain quantity of Arabic-Persian terms that it has assimilated, and that continue to be commonly used in the spoken language, despite a significant contemporary contribution of English words.

The Affirmation of Japanese, Korean, and Vietnamese Faced with the Pressure from Chinese, the Cultural Matrix of East Asia

A considerable part of the vocabulary of Japanese, Korean, and Vietnamese is made up of Chinese borrowings. Their significance is so great that the lexical components they form are called, respectively, Sino-Japanese, Sino-Korean, and Sino-Vietnamese. They amassed in the wake of the borrowing of ideograms from Chinese writing, only dispensed with in Annam in 1651, the date of the first dictionary in the Latin alphabet notation system, compiled by the Jesuit priest A. de Rhodes. In North Korea they were officially banned in 1949, and in South Korea, after a series of contradictory measures, a 1974 decree limited the number of "basic characters" taught in the secondary schools to 1800. As for Japanese, it continues to be written essentially in Chinese characters as it has been for more than fifteen centuries, combined, it is true, with native syllabaries.

The question of the writing is fundamental. Just as eliminating the Arabic alphabet in Turkey, and thus eliminating written Arabic words, led logically to Turkish word replacements, so too did abandoning Chinese characters in Annam take aim at Chinese itself. Annamite had been particularly exposed to its influence, since Annam, conquered by China in the second century B.C., became independent only in the tenth century. Nevertheless, even after that date, the Confucian moral code continued to permeate the country, serving the interests of the Annamite kings through its conception of society as a hierarchical system in which each individual is assigned a place. Chinese remained the language of the great official examinations for recruiting bureaucrats, abolished only in 1919. During World War II, the French were replaced by the Japanese. According to colonial logic, the French had tried to put French in a position to replace Chinese. But nothing truly reduced the importance of the latter, despite the promotion of Vietnamese as the official language for education in 1945. Chinese borrowings continued to abound, especially in the official and journalistic language in South Vietnam, and in the Marxist political phraseology of North Vietnam. Nonetheless, a heightened national consciousness always allowed the Vietnamese to retain confidence in their language, and it never lost its prestige.

Beginning with King Sejong's 1446 invention of a Korean alphabet, still in use today, Sino-Korean words ceased to be written in ideograms. But their number was so great (60 percent of the vocabulary), and they were so firmly established (contact between the ancient country of Choson and Chinese culture dated back to the first millennium B.C.), that no attempt was made to replace them. Some are borrowings from Sino-Japanese, and, like the Sino-Korean words, they form part of the structure of a mass of compound words that could not be abolished by Kim Il Sung, the longtime leader of North Korea, responsible for many attempts at Koreanizing the lexicon, and condemner of South Korean, too Japanized and American-ized in his view. Whatever the case, neither earlier Chinese borrow-ings nor today's English borrowings have uprooted Korean, and the cultural nationalism of its enlightened speakers has had the effect of maintaining its prestige in the face of "intruder" languages.

The same may be said for Japanese, since in our own times we see a tidal wave of American words succeeding the enormous influx of Chinese words. But even if it is undoubtedly even more permeated with English than Korean is, Japanese has retained the Chinese char-acters, despite a few unsuccessful attempts to Latinize the writing. Characters render not only those words that proliferate in scholarly terminology and that correspond to the Greek or Latin roots of tech-nical French words, but also, quite simply, the vast majority of the words in the standard vocabulary. Just as in Persian, Turkish, Viet-namese, and Korean, mixed words continue to be created in Japanese with the help of a borrowed term accompanied by a "to do" verb from the native fund. These processes are very old. The borrowed words do not in any way prevent users from having a clear awareness of their own culture. Their language has gleaned from other presti-gious languages for centuries, but, for all that, it has never lost its prestige. Japanese is in excellent health.

When Bilingualism Involves Only the Elite: Greek in Cicero's Rome

On Two Famous Sentences by Caesar

The ready-made culture of former Latin students includes two fa-mous sentences attributed to Caesar at two decisive moments in his life. When, returning from conquering the Gauls in 49 B.C., he crossed the Rubicon, thereby violating the Senate's order and the custom, he supposedly said, "*alea jacta est!*" "the die has been cast!"; and on the Ides of March in 44 B.C., the day of his assassination, he was supposedly heard saying to Brutus, who delivered the last thrusts of the knife, "*tu quoque, mi fili!*" "you, too, my son!" In reality, Caesar uttered neither of these two "historic remarks," for the simple reason that if he said them, he did so in Greek, and not in Latin. With regard to Caesar's last words, Suetonius writes expressly (*Vies des douɀe Césars* [Jules César], 79): "It is recounted that, seeing Brutus prepared to strike him, he supposedly cried out in Greek, "And you too, my son!" Dion Cassius corroborates this testimony (A.D. 229, XLIV, 19, 5). Thus Caesar said, "*kai su teknon,*" that is, word for word, "also you, child!" The *tu quoque, mi fili,* often repeated and appearing in no ancient text, is a translation by Renaissance grammarians, adopted by Lhomond in his *De Viris Illustribus* (see Dubuisson 1980).

And this translation is still not exact, because *kai su* — "you also" — was actually a formula for cursing. What Caesar wanted to express was not his pained observation at seeing his mistress Servilia's son, whom he considered his own son, rush at him to finish him off with his stiletto, but, in reality, a curse; in dying, he said to Brutus, "May the same thing happen to you!" As for the words pronounced crossing the Rubicon, it is established (see Dubuisson, ibid.) that they were also in Greek: *anerriphthô kúbos,* that is, literally "may [the] die [= fate] have been cast!" The Latin translation accepted as authoritative, and its French equivalent, *le sort en est jeté,* are used when one makes an audacious decision, and are even less accurate, because *anerriphthô* in ancient Greek is a passive perfect imperative. Thus it is a retroactive order indicating the result of an action, and it makes sense to adopt Erasmus's correction for the Latin translation of this well-known Greek proverb, *jacta alea esto,* let alone that *alea jacta est* means, in fact, "the die *was* cast," which is strange, since the Latin perfect refers to the past, and not, as with the Greek perfect, to the always-present results of an act that one has just accomplished.

Greek, the Primary Language of the Roman Patricians

Why did Caesar speak Greek in two situations where he was overcome by emotion—first, when he made a very bold choice, and then when he felt himself succumbing to death? Precisely because Greek was the language learned since childhood, and thus the one to come to the fore when trouble was at its worst and self-control at its lowest.

All the texts are perfectly clear on the status of Greek in the education of children belonging to privileged Roman families. One of the most famous is Book One of the *Institutio Oratoria*, where, more than a century after the death of Cicero, Quintilian could still write:

> I prefer that the child begins with Greek, because Latin is more used and we will be permeated with it in any case [. . .]. I would not wish, however [. . .], that the child speak or learn only Greek for too long a time, which is most often the case. This habit leads to a great number of pronunciation faults [. . .] as well as incorrectness in the language.

How did this situation come about? We know Horace's remark: *Graecia capta ferum victorem cepit:* "Greece subdued its coarse conqueror." In fact, the discovery of the enlightened Greek civilization, from 146 B.C., when Rome conquered Greece and made it a province under Roman authority, produced among the Roman elite a feeling of inferiority, still very strong in Cicero's time. In no time, learning Greek seemed to them an education in refinement and the only true culture, whereas not knowing it was evidence of being a rustic or, for someone representing the upper classes, an anomaly. Varro, the grammarian, even defended the wild theory of Latin's Greek origin, without, of course, a single argument that could convince us today, nor undoubtedly even persuade himself, since his aim was primarily to enhance Latin's prestige (see Dubuisson 1981). The Hellenization of the Roman aristocracy possessed more hidden aspects. Knowledge of Greek among the ruling classes became a political tool to the extent that the practice of Athenian rhetoric, by improving oratory, provided them with an effective weapon for winning and retaining power. At the end of the second century B.C., measures were even taken to prevent schools of Latin rhetoricians from forming.

The Ambiguities of Bilingualism in Rome (at the End of the Republic and the Beginning of the Empire)

At the end of the first century, the poet Juvenal, in one of his *Satires*, attacked the way that certain Roman women (of the leisured classes) used Greek, even in intimate sweet talk. This penetration — if we dare to call it that — of Greek into the private lives of the rich cannot be separated from the idea of Latin's inferiority to Greek, very widespread among many of the literati. Writing his *De natura rerum* in the first century B.C., Lucretius complains of the *patrii sermonis egestas* ("the poverty of our paternal language") for expressing the doctrine of Epicurus. Like many other bilingual intellectuals, Cicero adopted a nationalist and anti-Greek attitude in public, refusing to confirm Lucretius's remark, boldly claiming that Latin was richer than Greek, crediting Latin, before Seneca and Quintilian, with power and seriousness in its eloquence as opposed to the delicacy and subtlety of Greek. But in correspondence, he resorts completely naturally to Greek each time he cannot find the adequate phrase in Latin.

The bilingualism of the elite, and the strong presence of Greek, which affected even official life in Rome, could not help leading to very sharp reactions. A famous text by Valerius Maximus, a contemporary of Tiberius, longs for the time when the Romans defended their language more fiercely:

The magistrates of the past were careful to preserve [. . .] their own dignity and that of the Roman people [. . .]. One can cite [. . .] their constant concern over never conceding to answer the Greeks in anything but Latin. What is more, one used to eliminate the loquaciousness that worked to the Greeks' advantage in forcing them to make use of an interpreter, and not only in Rome, but even in Greece and in Asia, in order, of course, to spread the honor of the Latin language to all peoples and to render it more respectable. For all that, these men of the past did not lack culture; but they thought that the Greek mantle ought to be subordinate to the toga: according to them, it was an indignity to offer to the attractions and the charm of literature the weight and authority of power.

Praise for Marius follows, warmly approved of for not having "overwhelmed the curia with speeches in Greek," and about whom we know that, even though he knew Greek very well, he considered it ridiculous (unlike his adversary Sylla, from a higher social class) to learn the literature of a population the Romans had reduced to slavery, since this refinement had not secured freedom for those who professed it. Furthermore, Valerius Maximus refers implicitly to the Romans who defended Latin against Greek, notably Cato, who, coming to Athens in 191 B.C. as military tribune, chose to address the crowds in Latin and use an interpreter, even though patricians like himself were already capable of expressing themselves in Greek in this period. Thus, what Valerius Maximus calls for are real protective measures against a bilingualism that, in his eyes, gives Greek too important a place.

In 70 B.C., the decision Cicero made (and not without annoying his enemies) to address the Syracuse senate in Greek is one of many examples demonstrating how the old models Valerius Maximus invokes were no longer followed a century later. The emperor Tiberius was raised learning Greek and spoke it perfectly (he even used it when he wrote poems), but he refused to address the senate in this language, even to speak a few words, and he exhibited a haughty purism at the Hellenisms of cultivated Romans and the obvious excess of Greek borrowings in the Latin language. The same was true of the emperor Claudius.

Thus, in the last centuries of the Republic and in the first of the Empire, Rome's bilingualism was the general trend both privately and often publicly condemned by official figures. It is interesting to note that, in classical Latin, the adjective *bilinguis* is a pejorative qualification of the mixing of languages, and that, according to one of its meanings, it refers to a kind of duplicity, as if someone who speaks two languages could only be a deceitful rogue, defying the Roman requirement for straightforwardness. It can even refer to scandal-mongering and to lying, just like its heir in medieval French, *bilingue*. That reveals much about the mistrust, and the fascination, inspired by this Greek language learned at an early age. If Augustus encouraged Virgil and Titus Livius to write their founding works, it was primarily because he wanted poetry and history to have their pedigree in Rome, in order to counterbalance the influence of the great Greek works. According to him, Latin had to stop letting Greek serve as the principal lingua franca for the Mediterranean countries and the sole instrument of a prestigious culture.

Greek and the Roman Masses

Nevertheless, all the protective measures, all the fear and anxiety, were not necessary. Greek never penetrated beyond patrician society, because plebeians did not have the means to hire Greek-speaking tutors. Now, if only Greek had truly taken root in plebeian circles it would have been able to achieve a status powerful enough to rival Latin. In other words, an intruder language is solidly and deeply established only if it touches an entire community and not just its elite. Latin has enjoyed a brilliant and very long history in the West, while Greek is now the language of a little European country that was under the yoke of the Ottoman Empire for nearly four hundred years. This clearly demonstrates that the bilingualism of the Roman aristocracy in the classical period was only a short-lived episode. Greek's prestige never destroyed Latin's, even if it gave cultivated Romans inferiority complexes. And a language that keeps its prestige intact despite competition from another, even a very prestigious one, is not jeopardized in the least.

But when the loss of prestige occurs, other circumstances can heighten the grave risks that ensue, thus further reducing a language's capacity for resistance, if factors like the ones we have studied have already weakened that capacity. These are the circumstances we must now examine.

Some Circumstances "Favorable" to the Extinction of Languages

Among the circumstances involved in, though not directly causing, the disappearance of languages, we can list, first, defensive purism and the absence of standardization; second, the lack of a written script; and, finally, the fact of being a minority group.

PURISM AND THE ABSENCE OF STANDARDIZATION
The Perplexities of Purism
Exalting the Native Lexical Fund

An excessively purist and prescriptive attitude can accelerate the processes jeopardizing an ailing language. We can observe similar effects in apparently contradictory cases. In the one case, borrowings are rejected in favor of words from the local stock that have not been in use for a long time. Thus, in the threatened Celtic languages like Irish, certain elderly speakers use native terms that are completely archaic and unknown in place of words of English origin long since integrated and adopted by those who still speak the language. In the second case, this attitude is applied to grammar in the form of a touchy and stubborn attachment to outdated forms or constructions. Most notably, in the case of purists defending an archaic Nahuatl norm in parts of Mexico where the language is threatened by Spanish, we have seen (see chapter 6) that this is one of the signs of a language's obsolescence. Thus, those guarantors of good usage who, through artificially insisting on a stringent norm, try to convince themselves of their own competence without wanting to admit that it is cracking, are sometimes vilified by those who consider purism to be language's enemy.

The Perverse Effect of Refusing to Borrow: Renunciation

One other form of purism has a pernicious effect: the attitude of speakers who refuse to borrow foreign words to refer to global realities and modern technology, under the pretext that these borrowings distort the language. Obviously we should not ask speakers to be professional linguists. But this systematic rejection of a phenomenon like borrowing, natural and harmless enough when it is kept within certain limits, indicates an ignorance about what makes up the life of languages. This ignorance becomes pernicious when it produces the effect noted in other Nahuatl communities: without having the necessary terms at their disposal because the language has not created them, purists here consider borrowing Spanish terms impermissible within Nahuatl discourse, and thus simply renounce their own language and switch to Spanish!

The Circularities of the Purist Claim

Finally, we sometimes observe a strange circularity. Speakers begin by borrowing much more heavily from the prestigious language, and then they declare their own language impure, although they themselves provoked the implosion! According to evidence collected thirty years ago (Hill and Hill 1977), the speakers with the highest rate of borrowing from Spanish were also those who claimed that Nahuatl was so contaminated it humiliated them, and did not deserve to be preserved any longer!

Generalized attitudes of this kind tend to accelerate the disappearance of the ancestral language, whereas, precisely in those Aztec communities where Nahuatl is doing well, the speakers have assimilated Spanish borrowings and do not reproach themselves for using them when necessary.

The Dilemmas of Standardization

A surprising contradiction can be observed. The same ones who would rather renounce a language than introduce an excessive number of borrowings have no interest in doing precisely what would allow that number of borrowings to be reduced. The enterprise they so dismiss helped to fashion the vocabulary of numerous languages, among them French and more exotic examples such as Hungarian, Finnish, Turkish, Estonian, and many others (see Fodor and Hagège 1983–1994). This enterprise is a standardization, or the conscious action taken by experts, and supported, if not requested, by public authority, to adapt a language's vocabulary to developments in technology, information, and customs. Regulating languages in various periods of their history has often helped them adapt effectively to changes, as the study of those I have just mentioned, among others, clearly shows. In the area of vocabulary, reformers have often preferred national solutions (words derived from old roots and thus, in principle, familiar to natives) to international solutions (direct, and thus opaque, borrowings, even under a local guise).

That said, when a lack of standardization has eroded the powers of a language over a long period of time, it may be too late to intervene. The example of Celtic languages demonstrates this. Beginning in 1958, the Irish government promoted a written form, based on certain modern variants. Officials tried to give it genuine authority by introducing it into the school system on all levels and by using it in administrative procedures and in official documents whenever an Irish version was needed to accompany the English version. But this attempt does not seem to have slowed the decline of the Irish language, which has been continuing for more than a century and a half in the face of competition from English. That is because the Irish minority in the western counties who still have a natural command of their language use dialectical variants. The vital existence of these dialects is more real than any artificial creation.

That is even more true for Breton. Irish, at least, benefits from its official status in the country's constitution, which makes its promotion as the standard less illusory. But when the promoted supradialectical language has only regional status, the users of local variants then have even greater reasons for considering it artificial, and for not wanting to use it. The unified Breton that is being promoted has the merit of actually existing and clearly should allow for a renaissance of the language. But those who use dialects often remain suspicious of a constructed Breton that is nobody's mother tongue. Furthermore, it is important not to exaggerate the dialectical differences in Breton. Experience shows that all Bretons understand each other when they use their local dialects. Unifying Breton is a problem, certainly, but the lack of a shared norm is not the only reason for Breton's decline.

The marginal nature of a language's many dialects can discourage efforts at standardization, especially when the communities involved are confronting a language with vast regional or international diffusion and a powerful capacity for absorption. For example, even in the enclaves where they still exist, what can the Uralic, Altaic, and Siberian languages do, surrounded as they are by vast Russian domains? All attempts to extract a unified norm from the sharp dialectical contrasts that divide them are discouraged by their isolation and the lack of any educational or editorial policies expressing a shared cultural desire. Thus, barring happy reversals for which we see no signs, Enets (the Taymyr peninsula), Yukaghir (Yakutiya), Nivkh (Sakhalin Island), and many other languages seem destined for imminent extinction. We must repeat, however, that the absence of standardization is not in itself a sufficient cause, but, added to other causes, it aggravates the situation.

THE ABSENCE OF WRITING

Neither is the absence of writing, in itself, a direct cause of the extinction of a language. As important a role as writing plays in the history of civilization's languages, it still constitutes a later invention and an external facade that cannot be counted among languages' inherent properties. Possessing a written form has not prevented once prestigious and widespread languages from dying out, and, conversely, many pidgins exist in today's world, notably in Africa and Oceania, that are not written and are nevertheless useful enough means of communication to be in very good health and in no danger of disappearing any time soon.

That said, given two languages subject to the same risks of obsolescence, the one possessing a writing system will generally be better equipped to resist. Graphic notation is not a factor in a language's preservation or struggle to survive, but in most societies (though not all), it confers higher prestige, and, more important, it empowers a language to spread speech by reproducing it beyond the concrete situations of its exchange. The existence of a writing system allows for four other enterprises that also do much to strengthen languages: written literature, which helps to preserve it on physical media and does not rely, like an oral tradition, on memory alone; school education; the circulation of printed matter; and standardization. With regard to the last of these, let us recall an important point. It is because they lack writing systems that so many languages are called "dialects" by the masses. This term, which generally does not evoke the purely technical reality recognized by linguists, but a devalued, if not disdained, mode of expression, in turn affects the speakers themselves, and accentuates their disregard for their own language.

THE CONDITION OF MINORITY NATION
The Status of Minorities Among Homogeneous Nations

In certain societies, minorities are stigmatized, and, for a language, to be spoken by only a small number can reinforce other factors that place it in a fragile situation. This is especially true when the environment consists of a homogeneous community that is very conscious of its identity. The Thais are an illustration of this type of community. Their national pride was forged by five hundred years of unity based on previous domination by major groups, like the Mons and the Khmers. The Thais (at least those in Siam) were never colonized, by either an Asiatic people or a European country. Their system of monarchy and Theravadic Buddhism are, along with national consciousness, the pillars of Thai identity (see Bradley 1989). It follows that, despite the official recognition they are given, non-Thai minorities, descendants of populations that were conquered in the past or that remained peripheral, are regarded with hostility in Thailand, due to their very status as small, isolated groups. To escape their isolation, some have tried to assimilate through marriage. That is the case with the Ugong. The result is that their language is threatened with extinction.

A Sense of Identity Can Reduce the Effects of Small Numbers

Even when they live far from the great commercial tides that obliterate individual identity, it is difficult for little tribes to remain culturally and linguistically autonomous. That is even more true when they are exposed to the murderous greed of prospectors and merchants, as was the case with the Andoké of the Colombian Amazon (see above). Nevertheless, a strong sense of identity can make up for small numbers, and thus, no longer factor into the jeopardization of a language. Bayso, an eastern Cushitic language from southern Ethiopia, has for a thousand years resisted competition from the more widespread languages that surround it, although its number of speakers (five hundred in 1990) has always been small.

Likewise, we note an important difference between Hinoukh (northeastern Caucasus) and Negidal (a Tungusic language of the Khabarovsk region). Each of them has only about two hundred speakers. But the first relies on a strong sense of identity, which is not the case with the second. The Hinoukhs even offer proof that a powerful sense of identity can neutralize the effects of nonnative unions. Hinoukh men marry women from the neighboring village, where Dido is spoken, and Hinoukh women also leave the community to marry men of other ethnic groups (see Kibrik 1991, 259). Nevertheless, ethnic consciousness is so deeply rooted that it is not dissolved in these unions.

Thus, even in adverse circumstances, the will to survive and a passionate sense of identity can save a language from annihilation.

8. Taking Stock

Definitions and Criteria

ASSESSMENT OF THE NUMBER OF LANGUAGES CURRENTLY SPOKEN IN THE WORLD

Before establishing a tally for the death of languages, it is useful to have some idea of the number of those that are alive. This assessment can vary widely depending on the criteria used to decide what will be called a language. One of the reasons for the discrepancies is that if only languages are to be considered, then dialects ought to be excluded. Now, attributing one or the other of these two statuses to a given idiom varies depending on linguists, and not everyone agrees on the definition that seems the simplest: a language is one of the opposing dialects (at a given moment) that a political authority establishes, along with its power, in a certain place; if a written form exists, with an administrative and literary function, it will be put to the service of this dialect.

As this is not necessarily the definition all linguists use, they will not all produce the same figures, depending on the criteria they employ to decide if this or that idiom is a dialect or a language. Another reason for fluctuations in the figures proposed stems from the decision of whether to represent in the tally at least some languages whose survival over the short term, or even the medium term, is far from certain. A final reason, which is connected to the previous one, is the need, advocated by some, to include in the calculation only those languages spoken not only by adults, but also by children. In fact, a language known only to the adults and not to the children of a community must be considered on its way to extinction.

Taking into account these difficulties in arriving at a consensus, the assessments proposed by various linguists in the early 1990s range from forty-five hundred to six thousand languages. Five thousand could be considered a reasonable figure, and can be taken as the base to which the current losses in languages will be evaluated. Let us add that the number of languages spoken in the world probably experienced its height at the beginning of the sixteenth century, and began to decline in about this period, notably in the wake of European expansion and domination, and the accompanying brutalities, such as the conquest of South America by the Spanish, the recruitment of a servile labor force among the African peoples abducted from their villages, or other violent acts of comparable dimensions. For North America and Australia, this violence began a little later, but it lasted until the end of the nineteenth century, and resulted in just as disastrous effects for the languages it annihilated.

LINKS BETWEEN THE CONDITION OF THREATENED LANGUAGE AND VARIOUS PARAMETERS

Endangered Languages and Threatened Languages

We will call those languages for which there are many signs indicating an immediate threat of extinction "endangered languages." We will call "threatened languages" those that will be endangered in the foreseeable future, corresponding at best to a human life span. It is not always easy to maintain such a strict distinction, given the variety of situations and the rate of change, which is ever increasing with the current pace of events. But at least we can retain it as a general framework for clarifying our study. We will speak here of threatened languages as the larger category that includes the more extreme case of endangered languages.

The Link Between Threatened Languages and Underdevelopment, as Well as Between Threatened Languages and the Number of Languages

On the basis of figures established in 1990 (see Krauss 1992), we can note that the greatest concentrations of threatened languages are found in areas of the world where the conditions of underdevelopment dominate.

We can also note a correlation between the number of threatened languages and the number of languages overall, as if, at a certain threshold, this number prompts a struggle for survival, from which certain languages emerge as the victors and others as the vanquished.

The Link Between the Number of Languages and Underdevelopment

The majority of the 170 states that can be considered sovereign (not [politically] dependent on any other and constituting a legal entity to which international recognition is granted) have for their official language, whether exclusively or not, one of the following: English, French, Spanish, Arabic, Portuguese. In terms of the number of speakers, these are also among the most widely spoken in the world. In other words, the languages that are the most widespread are also those that belong to the most highly structured political entities.

According to a somewhat outdated evaluation (see Fishman 1968) that may now need to be revised upward, in linguistically homogeneous states the average gross national per capita income in the mid-1960s was at least $300, whereas in linguistically heterogeneous states this index showed low- to very-low-level figures, characteristic of underdeveloped states at that time and even more so today. The varying degrees of economic prosperity determine the varying degrees of prestige and, consequently, the emigration and immigration patterns. As I have noted, this situation has its effects on the survival or disappearance of the languages of poor ethnic groups.

Thus, a country's number of languages and its inhabitants' standard of living tend to be inversely proportional. This observation is not immaterial. In Papua New Guinea, precisely the world's richest country in languages, a longtime controversy has divided the partisans and adversaries of linguistic diversity (see Dixon 1991, 247). The partisans have emphasized that this diversity is healthy, since it enriches the number of different perspectives and thus helps to resolve individual, social, and technological problems. The adversaries argue that this profusion leads to inefficiency and has a divisive power. They see a direct correlation between underdevelopment and linguistic diversity. The government of Papua New Guinea has decided that preprimary education should be based on the vernacular languages. That is a good decision, but imagine the huge amount of materials it involves, and consequently the number of works still required on the Papuan languages, many of which have not yet even been described.

The Link Between the Health of Languages and the Number of Speakers

Of the count of something like five thousand languages that I established as the most likely total for the contemporary world, six hundred, that is, less than one eighth of that total, are spoken by more than one hundred thousand people. Inversely, five hundred are spoken by less than one hundred people. Moreover, 90 percent of the planet's languages are spoken by about 5 percent of the worldwide population. This is only slightly offset by cases like those of Hinoukh and Bayso (see end of chapter 7). Let us now examine two correlations that have general merit.

The Correlation Between Weak Demographic Volume and Poor Linguistic Health

A small number of speakers, especially if that number continues to decrease, can be considered one of the common, though not universal, signs of a language's decline and of the dangers threatening it. This has its own set of causes, which have been examined in chapter 7. The number of speakers is not always easy to assess, because in many ethnic groups with threatened cultures those who claim to be members are not necessarily all speakers of the native language. Thus, in 1989, about twenty-five hundred Itelmen were counted, among whom fourteen hundred lived in Kamchatka, their traditional territory (where their neighbors are just as rare and dispersed, and speak other languages in that same group, called "Paleo-Asiatic" or "Paleo-Siberian" by Russian researchers: Guiliak, Ket, Yukaghir, and Chukchi are all idioms that are themselves endangered); but more than 80 percent of the Itelmen indicate that Russian is their mother tongue, and today Itelmen is no longer spoken by more than two or three hundred people, all of whom are bilingual (Itelmen and Russian).

Putting aside this typical discrepancy between the totals for an ethnic group and for actual speakers, the important point is the correlation between the small number of users and the poor health of a language. If we allow ourselves a broad comparison of all the languages of the North American continent (Canada on the one hand, and the United States, including Alaska, on the other), we can note that the one showing the most vitality, the Navajo language, is also the one with the most speakers, about 140,000, even though it is far from certain that they all speak the language, or at least speak it as is normal for native speakers. But beyond that, Navajo itself is clearly in a more precarious situation than Nahuatl, and we are justified in correlating this fact with another numerical one: Nahuatl, which, as we have seen, does not show the same signs of good health throughout Mexico, nevertheless retains 1.4 million speakers at present.

The correlation goes still further. Quechua, Aymara, and Guarani are in healthier states than Nahuatl, and it happens that all three of them are spoken by a greater number than Nahuatl. In particular, Guarani, healthy for the moment, is known by three quarters of the population of present-day Paraguay — 2.5 million out of 3 million inhabitants. It is present as well, with smaller numbers of speakers, in southern Brazil and northeastern Argentina. In Chile, we must again mention Araucanian or Mapudungun, the language of the Mapuches, for which the number of speakers varies considerably according to sources and assessments — that is, between 150,000 and 1 million. Solidly established in this country, Mapuche is also energetically defended by its speakers, who do not all speak it nevertheless (Clairis 1991 proposes an optimistic assessment of 400,000). Thus, parallel reasoning would lead us to conclude that the weak demographic volume of a community is a facet of the general process by which its language becomes jeopardized.

However, as is often the case, when a language is not transmitted, a relatively high number of speakers will not compensate, despite the reassuring appearance it can produce. In Mexico, Purépecha (or Tarascan), which in the past was an important language (see chapter 7, "Decisions of the Conquerors and the Missionary Church"), is spoken in the state of Michoacán by some ninety thousand but is not being transmitted to children. At least, this is true in the Lake Pátzc-uaro region, in contrast to the mountains, which are nearly always more conservative and where monolingual children are found (see Chamoreau 1999). Purépecha must be considered a threatened language.

The Correlation Between the Number of Threatened Languages and the Number of Limited Communities

For a given region, this correlation reinforces the one just established between demographic significance and the health of the language. It is interesting to note here that certain groups who feel threatened by the very fact of their demographic weakness spontaneously resolve this problem by seeking to merge with a larger group. The consequences can be beneficial for their languages. Thus, in Guyana (the former British Guyana), the Mapidians, belonging to the Arawak family, and the Taruma, decimated by various catastrophes, placed themselves under the protection of the Waiwai, a more numerous Carib tribe. Within this new framework, they are in a position to preserve their language for many generations.

Using the Number of Speakers as a Discriminant

The statistics we have at our disposal regarding languages give information on the number of speakers, which is considered a sign — and a generally accurate one — of the health of a language, or, alternately, of the threat to its survival. Some systematize the value of this sign by calculating the index of vitality for a language, obtained by dividing the number of child speakers of that language by the number of child speakers of the dominant language of the country (a method used with regard to Mexico by T. Smith Stark 1995). Although these calculations can seem a little rigid in relationship to a fluid reality, the fact remains that the indexed value of the number of speakers is incontestable as far as children are concerned. That is why, when they exist, these figures will be used in what follows as indicators of the stage a given language seems to have reached. It is now useful for us to examine the elements in an assessment.

Numerical Data on the Extinction of Languages in Various Parts of the World

GENERAL DATA

Languages in Multilingual Countries

One group of twenty-two countries stands out with particular clarity because of the considerable number of languages that are spoken there, or that were still spoken there at the beginning of the 1990s (see Krauss 1992). Of these twenty-two, nine countries each possess more than 200 languages: Papua New Guinea has 850 and Indonesia has 670; then come Nigeria (410) and India (380); Cameroon follows (270), then Mexico (240), the Republic of the Congo (210), Australia (200), and Brazil (200). Thirteen other countries possess 100 to 160 languages each. These are, in decreasing number of languages, the Philippines, Russia, the United States, Malaysia, China, Sudan, Tanzania, Ethiopia, Chad, Vanuatu (formerly the New Hebrides), the Central African Republic, Burma, and Nepal.

Many of the numerous languages in the majority of these countries are threatened, and even endangered in many cases, according to the definitions given above. Actually, these languages present all, or nearly all, the characteristics studied as causes of extinction in the preceding chapter. The figures just mentioned are optimistic, because included in these calculations are languages that are not considered completely dead, given that the last studies done on them mention a single or a few old speakers. But it is quite probable that since 1992 many of these last speakers have died, taking with them the ability to utter the words of these languages. Furthermore, the lack of young speakers in these cases ought to eliminate such languages from consideration, if the adopted criteria are strictly applied.

Countries with a Single Dominant Language

Russia, China, Brazil, the United States, Australia, and Mexico appear in the preceding list, but we know that all these countries possess an official language that is heavily promoted by the means the political powers have at their disposal. Consequently, the threatened languages are those of numerous minorities. They do not benefit, of course, from any promotion meant to somehow compensate for users themselves voluntarily disowning their languages. All the other countries on that list — that is, sixteen of the twenty-two mentioned — also possess one or more official languages, but whether it originates with the former colonial power, or is the language of the economically and politically dominant community, one fact remains: in no case is it the vernacular language of an ethnic group with a population larger than that of all the other ethnic groups together. Nevertheless, in these sixteen countries, as in many others, the promotion of the language spoken by the group in power is just as formidable for the minority languages, particularly when the official language is not a foreign one and is not challenged by the other groups.

Thus endangered languages are subject not only to pressure from languages in perfect health that enjoy widespread and ever growing international use, but also to pressure from locally powerful languages, promoted through numerous means. The results of this situation are presented below.

Obviously we cannot provide a catalogue here of languages that have just died out, or are presently in danger of doing so. Let us mention only the most characteristic phenomena, from which we can draw a lesson that is more generally applicable.

Are the Extinct Languages All Truly Extinct?

In many cases, the situation seems completely clear: those who possessed the language have died without having ever transmitted it, and it is no longer heard anywhere, either in- or outside of the community. But even then, no one knows what is spoken within the privacy of the home. That is all the more reason not to rush to make funeral arrangements for languages that are obviously dying but not clearly and absolutely dead. Cholón, a language in the Quechua group from the Huallaga valley, on the eastern slopes of the Peruvian Andes, had been given up for dead when it was discovered to still be alive in a few family households (see Cerrón-Palomino 1987). That is why the following data must be read with all the nuances required by the complexity of the situations.

Africa

At least two hundred languages are in the process of dying out in Africa or have already disappeared as of this writing (July 2000). Certain families are particularly threatened, like those the linguists call Khoi and San, spoken in South Africa.

Tanzania by itself is an example that summarizes the phenomenon. Actually, it is the only African country where all the families of African languages with the largest numbers are represented. It is also a country where, throughout, the languages of small ethnic groups are in the process of dying. There is no absolutely reliable data on each particular situation, or information precise enough to tell us if a given language has already entirely disappeared, or, if it still exists, what its life expectancy might be. But one fact is certain: Swahili is dominant. Of course, the generalized bilingualism that characterizes this country is not perfect, and the native users of other languages do not always have absolute mastery over Swahili. But it is understood throughout. Let us recall that, among the privileged classes who formerly received a Western education, it has replaced the English of colonial times—not a cause for alarm. But beyond that, it exerts pressure on the other languages, which are very numerous. One of Tanzania's most famous men of politics, the former president J. Nyerere, declared in 1984 that the expansion of Swahili in Tanzania was a natural phenomenon. Swahili's pressure is all the more formidable because of its prestige as the great, and now official, African language, in addition to the fact that it enjoys a certain popularity due to its usefulness as a lingua franca, even among the small bilingual communities where it nevertheless puts other languages directly in danger.

As a result of this situation, we may consider that only four or five languages enjoy some regional prestige: Sukuma, Nyamwezi, Makonde, Shambala, and especially Masai. Earlier we saw the formidable and dangerous power of absorption that Masai has exerted or still exerts over the idioms of small ethnic groups. Also, languages exist in Tanzania that have "prestige" only on the local level. All the other languages have no prestige. As we might expect, the ethnic languages still valued by bilingual speakers are more threatened than those of monolingual speakers. Furthermore, for the idioms of small ethnic groups, no official support exists, through either an education policy or alphabetization. And nevertheless, a growing regional consciousness can be observed in this country. At least partially and temporarily, that could slow down the worrisome process of languages going extinct, which is already well advanced.

The Americas

Latin America

The situation varies greatly depending on idiom and region. In trying to establish a correlation between a language's degree of resistance and its number of users, we have seen that Nahuatl and, to an even greater extent, Quechua, Aymara, and especially Guarani possess a great number of speakers if they are compared to many other Amerindian languages. If they are taken all together, the languages that belong to the great Mayan family are spoken by an even larger mass of individuals. Guatemala alone counts more than six million of them, and significant numbers are found in the Mexican states of Yucatán, Quintana Roo, Chiapas, Tabasco, Campeche, and San Luís Potosí. We can note that the two least exposed Mayan languages, Yucatec (spoken on the Yucatán peninsula in Mexico) and Quiché (spoken in Guatemala), both have more than half a million speakers; Quiché might even have more than a million according to a 1993 census. Three other Mayan languages are used by speakers varying in number from .4 million to .7 million: Kekchi, Kakchiquel, and Mam.

We can hope that these diverse languages will continue in good health for a relatively long period. Nevertheless, they remain exposed to dangerous competition from Spanish, a situation that is even more true for the other Mayan languages. These languages are spoken by varying numbers of individuals depending on the populations—from a hundred to a hundred thousand—and four of them exist only in a single municipality. Children no longer learn them as first languages, or they are taught only in a few rural schools, or are continually losing speakers, especially those who are attracted to the cities and desert the rural communities, where languages are better preserved.

Still, we are speaking here of a language family that, for now, is relatively protected from serious losses. In general, this is the exception. As proof, we need only examine the Cariban family, which was healthy and abundantly represented before the arrival of the Spanish in the sixteenth century. Today, outside of Makushi, which has about fifteen thousand speakers, the Cariban languages all have less than one thousand. We do not know the fate of Matipú, Amapá, and Sikiana, which in 1990 had forty, thirty-seven, and thirty-three speakers, respectively. Wayana (French Guiana) speakers number in the few hundreds (see Launey, forthcoming).

Taking entire countries as our framework, and limiting ourselves to three examples, we will briefly examine the cases of Brazil, Mexico, and Colombia. Most of the some two hundred Indian languages of Brazil are spoken by very small communities, which does not bode well for those languages still in good health. Many of the languages of the Tupi family that used to be present all along the middle Amazon valley and in the state of Rondônia, near the Bolivian border, are probably dead today, especially Apiaká and Puruborá. Of the large Ge family, which once included a significant number of languages, only a very few members remain, and Nakrehé (Minas Gerais) and Pataxó (Bahía) are probably extinct at this moment, while Fulnió (Pernambuc), with four thousand speakers, is the only nonextinct Indian language in the northeast, which was once a veritable mosaic of idioms. The four languages of the Yanomami family, spoken in Roraima and also in Venezuelan territory across the border, have recently lost many speakers because of the violent intrusion of gold seekers (*garimpeiros*). Today, these tribes' languages, like their original and well-preserved cultures, are threatened.

Since the Spanish conquest of the Aztec capital, Tenochtitlán, in 1521, the Indians of the territory corresponding to present-day Mexico have suffered enormous cultural and human losses, in particular in the sixteenth, nineteenth, and twentieth centuries. The indigenous population of Mexico, some twenty-five million in 1519, had shrunk to one million by 1605! With regard to languages, it is quite probable that this erosion had begun in the fifteenth century, during the conquests carried out by the Aztecs themselves. More recently, in the twentieth century at least 130 more languages have become extinct in Mexico, belonging to all the linguistic families represented in that country.

In Colombia, apart from Spanish, which, as we might suspect, is firmly established throughout, and two Creoles, one with a Spanish lexical base in Palenque (Palenquero), and one with an English lexical base on the San Andrés y Providencia Islands, there exist sixty-five Indian languages. They are quite varied, given the geographical and climatic diversity of the country. Ten of these languages constitute isolates, as far as we know, and the other fifty-five are divided among twelve families. Some are significant in Central and South America—the Chibchan, Cariban, Arawakan, and Tupian families—and others are represented in Colombia alone—the Guahiboan, Huitotoan, Tucanoan families, etc. Of this great diversity of Colombian languages, as of 1995 five were dying and fifteen were endangered (see Landaburu 1995).

North America

Assessments of this continent vary from one author to another, and there are many gaps in the available information. Forty years ago (see Chafe 1962), in the United States (including Alaska) and Canada combined, there remained no more than 213 languages, as opposed to the 600 or 700 that existed at the beginning of the sixteenth century.

Of these 213, only 89 had speakers of all ages, from children to the elderly. Since 1962, at least 50 languages have died out, languages that were spoken by just one to ten older people at that time. We know the name of the last Cupeño speaker, who died in 1987 at the age of ninety-four in Pala, California. Thirty-five other languages that were used by just ten to one hundred speakers are certainly dying, and their deaths can be considered imminent.

Siberia

Many languages of small nomadic or sedentary groups dispersed across the reaches of central and southern Siberia are on the verge of extinction. This is true of Yugh (region of Krasnoyarsk) and of Kerek (region of the Bering Strait). The situation is hardly less perilous for Orok (Sakhalin), Ulch and Oroch (area of Khabarovsk). Alutor (northeast of Kamchatka) is seriously threatened, as well as other languages also belonging to the Siberian, Turkic, and Tungusic families, some of which were mentioned above. An illuminating case is the one of Evenki, the most important of the Tungusic languages, a branch of the Altaic family genetically linked to the Turkic and Mongol branches. The Evenki population was about thirty thousand in 1989, but among these trilingual people, who also speak Yakut and especially Russian, only 30 percent considered Evenki to be their first language. The situation is even worse for Udege, also Tungusic and closely related to Evenki: only 4 percent of the population possesses real competence in this language.

Andaman Languages

The languages of the Andaman Islands, located between southwest Burma and northwest Sumatra, cannot be linked with certitude to any known family. The natives numbered 460 in 1931. It may be that many of the languages belonging to the three groups, northern, central, and southern, are now extinct.

Southeast Asia: Tibeto-Burman, Austro-Asiatic/Mon-Khmer, Thai, Miao-Yao, Continental Austronesian, Japan

With regard to this vast group, we will consider only certain major points linked to the danger of extinction. This danger threatens the Muong, Palaung, Khmu, and Bahnar languages of Vietnam and Laos, very important from a comparative and historical perspective because they provide proof of the Austro-Asiatic origin of Vietnamese despite its being so deeply permeated with Chinese and Thai and their monosyllabic and tonal nature, which masks this origin (see Matisoff 1991). Other Austro-Asiatic languages belonging to the Mon-Khmer group, in the Pear subgroup, are on the way to extinction or already extinct in Thailand. In northern Japan, Ainu is dying.

Indonesia

The available information on this country, which, as we have seen, ranks among the richest in languages on the planet, is very spotty. A good fifteen languages died out in the twentieth century. Fifty-two of the 670 Indonesian languages have less than two hundred speakers, 121 have two hundred to one thousand speakers, and 200 count one thousand to ten thousand speakers.

Papua New Guinea

The country that is the world's richest in languages is also among those with the highest risks of extinction. There we find 130 languages spoken by less than two hundred individuals; 290 are spoken by less than one thousand people, and, among those that are spoken by more than a thousand, many are known only by adults. The pressure from Tok Pisin and Hiri Motu, the two pidgin languages spoken in the cities, particularly in Port-Moresby, the capital, have partly eliminated Koiari, spoken in a nearby region, and may have killed off Yimas, spoken in the lower Sepik River valley, even if the women are still attached to its use.

Australia

Australia is, without a doubt, the continent where the losses inflicted upon languages, as upon humans, have been the most rapid and the most violent. Two hundred years ago, it is likely that one to two million Aborigines lived there, speaking about two hundred fifty languages. More than fifty languages have disappeared since the arrival of Europeans. One hundred fifty others are dying at present. Of the remaining fifty, there exist a growing number, perhaps more than half (see Dixon 1991) that children under fifteen years old do not know. Only five to ten languages, the figure varying depending on the authors, are spoken by more than a thousand people. They are located especially in areas where whites entered later, and where they are still only partially established: northern territories, northern parts of south Australia, western Australia, and Queensland.

Philippines and Taiwan

In the Philippines, certain languages in the Indonesian family, like Tagalog, the official language along with English, or like Cebuano and Ilocano, are spoken by many millions and are not endangered. However, six languages in this family have less than two hundred speakers, and it is likely that three of these latter are now extinct. The indigenous languages of Taiwan, belonging to the Austronesian family, numbered at least thirty or so at the time the Dutch colonists arrived (1622). But on two occasions they were subject to Chinese domination: once in 1661, when Chinese opponents of the Manchu dynasty of the Ch'ing, which had established itself in Peking seventeen years earlier, left for Taiwan, driving out the Dutch, and setting about to make the population Chinese; the second time in 1949, when, according to a similar plan, the nationalist government of Chiang Kai-Shek, driven from the Chinese continent, came to establish itself in Taiwan. The result is that no more than ten native languages remain, and the situation of those spoken by less than two thousand people is quite precarious.

SPECIFIC CASES OF THE EXTINCTION OF LANGUAGES IN DIASPORA

Numerous Examples Throughout the World

We may note that none of the languages mentioned as cases of extinction in situ (in the places where the majority of their speakers live) belong to Europe (with the exception of the Celtic languages), or North Africa, the Near East, and western Asia. These are the lands where firmly established languages are spoken, or languages aided by international diffusion. Nevertheless, languages do not die only at home. They can also disappear in a diaspora. In chapter 6, we were able to see this in the cases of Hungarian in eastern Austria, the Albanian Arvanitika dialect in Greece, Bhojpuri in Trinidad, and Armenian in France.

On the Fate of French-Speaking Communities in Newfoundland and Ontario

Two striking examples involve French, found in places in North America with its English-speaking majority, where the absorption power is of course high. One is the peninsula of Port-au-Port, in the Canadian province of Newfoundland, where the Acadians came to settle between the mid-nineteenth century and the early twentieth century. In that period, the French-speaking population numbered two thousand, whereas now it is no more than one thousand at best, especially in the villages of Cap-Saint-Georges and La Grand'Terre. By 1980, two others, L'Anse-à-canards and Stephenville, no longer had any speakers other than underusers over fifty years old. The future of French in Newfoundland, the language of a tiny minority surrounded by English speakers the younger generations only want to imitate, seems bleak, barring some miracle. The second place where a French-speaking community is endangered is the city of Welland, in Ontario, close to Niagara Falls. About forty Franco-Canadian families from Quebec settled there after World War I, attracted by the development of the iron, steel, rubber, and textile industries. At the time of the 1981 census, they constituted 15.5 percent of the forty-five thousand inhabitants of the city. Nevertheless, the pressure from the Anglophone majority and its presence in all workplaces, continually augmented by mixed marriages, as well as the enormous pressure from the media, have resulted in the disaffection of the youngest community members with regard to French, despite the many measures that support it.

In all of North America today, only Quebec is capable of effectively defending, through law, the French language spoken on an island of six million people surrounded by a sea of over two hundred and fifty million English speakers. Whatever some of those latter may say, eager as they are to defend the freedom of language, the situation mirrors the one evoked by the famous expression attributed to Lacordaire: "Between the strong and the weak, it is freedom that oppresses, and the law that frees."

On the History of Norwegian in the United States

We have seen (chapter 6) an example of what happened to Finnish in the American environment, with regard to its linguistic structures. Norwegian offers another case. Beginning in 1825 and for part of the nineteenth century, more than a half-million Norwegians emigrated to the United States, seeking to make their living as farmers, essentially in the center of the northern part of the country: northern Illinois and Iowa, western Wisconsin and Minnesota, eastern South Dakota, and most of North Dakota, with a few more limited settlements in Nebraska, Montana, Washington, Oregon, and California. The Lutheran church and the population's solidarity created such strong ties that, at the end of the nineteenth century in some of these regions, you could travel across many farms without hearing any language other than Norwegian. But in the 1910s, the need to integrate the youngest community members into English-speaking society brought about a decline in the transmission of Norwegian. Norwegians believed they could give English a dominant place and continue to be Norwegians, engaged in typically Norwegian activities. Norwegian became continually more confined to use within the family. Because of the growing number of borrowings from English, which invaded the vocabulary more than the grammar, an American Norwegian developed. Among the 4,120,000 Americans who claimed to be of Norwegian origin for the 1980 U.S. census, it is doubtful that the 184,491 who declared themselves Norwegian speakers use it enough to ensure that the language is still truly alive among them (see Haugen 1989, 73).

ISLAND LANGUAGES, REGIONAL LANGUAGES, JEWISH LANGUAGES

We must consider separately cases of communities that have only recently been organized into states as well as others that have never been states but have long existed in isolation (languages of little coastal islands), or that have been victims for centuries of constant discrimination and persecution, either within formed states, or through their migrations and wanderings (regional languages, Jewish languages). The languages of these communities are not all equally threatened. But some of them are dying or are already dead.

Languages of Little Coastal Islands, or Dying Varieties of Languages in Good Health

Of course, it is hardly the case that all island languages are endangered. Consider British English, or Japanese, or Icelandic, or many other languages that are spoken in independent states long established and often with long histories of expansion. On the other hand, some languages exist on small coastal islands where situations can change and they suddenly find themselves endangered. That is the case on two islands off the Atlantic coast in the United States. One of them, Smith Island, belongs to the state of Maryland and is located in the Chesapeake Bay, six kilometers from the Delmarva peninsula. The other, Ocracoke Island, belonging to North Carolina, forms part of the chain of islands that border the entire northern coast of this state. These two islands, both of them populated by colonists who came from southern England in the middle of the seventeenth century, were, until recently, isolated from the mainland, to which no bridge links them even today. Specific and conservative forms of English developed there, in terms of both grammar and phonology.

These English dialects are disappearing, following an accelerating but separate process. On Smith Island, the disappearance is explained by that of the inhabitants themselves, numbering 700 in 1960 and 450 in 1990 (see Schilling-Estes and Wolfram 1999). The depopulation is due to the decline in traditional fishing occupations, essentially for crabs and oysters, and consequently, the exodus of islanders who are leaving to find work on the mainland. Moreover, their island is also sinking into the bay and may well become uninhabitable in a hundred years or so. On Ocracoke Island, tourism has replaced the traditional economy, also based on fishing. A growing number of mainlanders are building second homes on Ocracoke, and some are settling there and marrying islanders, all of which leads to the loss of the dialect's particularities and its fusion with mainland English. In contrast, the Smith Island dialect, which is disappearing only for the lack of speakers and not because it is under pressure from contact with another language, retains all its traits and remains unaltered. This shows us not only that some of the various forms of a language as healthy as Anglo-American can die out, but also that the reasons for this phenomenon can vary.

Regional Languages

The political consciousness of the Spanish Basques is not without effect on French Basques' efforts to preserve Basque in France. The same is true for Alsatian with regard to neighboring Germany, and for Catalan in France with regard to Spanish Catalonia. Corsica is well served by its traditional isolation as an island, and especially by the feeling of identity the originality of its language inspires. Long before the thousand years of strong Tuscan influence, Corsican had already developed a pre-Latin substratum and absorbed Roman archaisms belonging to the Tyrrhenian Basin. But the omnipresence of French and its symbolic importance in the history of the French nation are factors unfavorable to the development of regional languages, despite recent political change.

Jewish Languages

Jewish languages—that is, those languages that developed from languages used in the countries of the Diaspora—have shared the fate of Jewish communities themselves. Judeo-German (= Yiddish) was the language of the European Jews, the overwhelming majority of whom were exterminated between 1939 and 1945. It might seem as though the world expressed by Yiddish is "almost mythic" (see Szulmajster-Celnikier 1991, XI). Nevertheless, a kind of renaissance appears to be taking place (see chapter 11).

For Judeo-Spanish (= Judezmo), the situation is very precarious, and for the same reasons (see Séphiha 1977). North African Judeo-Arabic, in its three variants of Tunisian, Algerian, and Moroccan, was not transmitted by its last speakers. As with other Jewish languages, immigration to Israel, France, or the United States led to adopting the languages of these countries in daily life. The disappearance of traditional frameworks ruptured the natural conditions for maintaining the Jewish languages. The speakers who did not leave were elderly, for example, certain Judeo-Spanish users in the Balkans or Turkey. That is why all these languages are now dying out.

What Is Lost When Languages Die

After this quick but revealing trip across the territories of extinction, we might consider that all these disappearing languages simply share the fate of many other manifestations of human culture, leaving no place for tears and grief. Nevertheless, it may be useful to wonder what that means for our human heritage, what is lost when languages die. Without encompassing all of culture, languages are a fundamental component of it. The share of genius found in each one is large enough for the death of a great number of them to be a kind of catastrophe, and what disappears is lost from our universal stores of humanity.

LANGUAGE AND CULTURE
The Alibi of Adaptation

As we know, language is not the only component defining a culture. In the United States, for example, many communities of former immigrants retain their cooking habits, even if they have long been Americanized. The lack of anything resembling an American gastronomy as such comes to their aid here, and they can justly convince themselves that, in assimilating, they have not lost all that defined them. Moreover, the attachment to a community does not disappear with the loss of the language, as we can see in America among those who maintain the memory of their origins through organizations where descendants gather regularly to meet, as well as through university studies and research, or through historical and genealogical investigations.

But some go further. There are plenty of communities that switch languages under the pretext of the necessity to adapt to a new environment. They then try to convince themselves that losing one's language is not losing one's identity, and that by adopting the dominant idiom, they can truly be themselves, since they can make themselves understood more easily by the majority. As a matter of fact, they try to justify a renunciation motivated purely by economics. Is it necessary to stress that immigrant communities coming to make their fortunes in new countries are not exempt from hypocrisy when they use this alibi? In reality, the loss of language is the loss of the very instrument by which a culture expresses itself most directly. It is a serious loss in terms of maintaining an identity and the symbolic power that the use of a language grants that identity. In the Indian communities of North America today, it is the subject of a passionate debate. Some maintain that it is not necessary to speak the idiom of the tribe in order to participate in the dances with which that tribe identifies itself, or in social activities that are a part of ethnic culture. They can even conceive of discourse in English on traditional themes, maintaining that it is able to capture the important characteristics of vernacular discourse. There is reason to doubt this.

Verbal Activities and the Culture

A culture's verbal expressions have their origin in its history and go to the heart of its identity. "If you do not speak the language," said a woman belonging to the Oneida Iroquois tribe who had done ethnological research on her people, "you cannot understand the culture" (see Jocks 1998, 219). She was referring to ceremonies during which oratorical exchanges take place between the members of the tribe and belong to the primordial roots of the Iroquois culture. Furthermore, we have seen with regard to the Yaaku hunter-gatherers of Kenya and traditional societies in Australia that the disappearance of a lifestyle and customs leads to the death of the language. If language is not the only expression of a culture, it may embrace all the others, since it puts them all into words. Thus it retains a central place, and, in the long or the short run, its loss can mean the loss of the entire culture.

LANGUAGES AND THE HUMAN GENIUS
The Wonders of Initiatory Languages

In Australia, as in Africa, as in pre-Columbian America, there exist initiatory languages, that is, secret languages that are reserved only for the initiation periods of young men, that are taught to them during these periods, and, according to the tradition, that are not to be used afterward. One example is Damin, the language of initiation that existed in the past among the Lardil, a population of Mornington Island (in northern Queensland). It was learned in the advanced stage of the novitiate. The linguist to whom its existence was revealed in 1960 was able to gather only bits of it from very old men (see Hale 1992). Actually, only the men who had been initiated before the first decades of the twentieth century, that is, before the arrival of the Christian mission that then came to run the island could remember it. Because at that time, the priests, hostile to the animistic rituals and the sexual education that made up such initiations, forbade the practice, according to the general thinking of Christian missionaries, who (even if they had occasional misgivings), from Guinea to the Amazon, from Alaska to Patagonia, and from the sixteenth to the twenty-first century, destroyed and are destroying tribal cultures for being incompatible with the Gospel.

Damin is an invented language, as initiatory languages generally are. And what it reveals about invention is completely surprising. Phonetically, Damin contains sounds that are found only in one other part of the world, South Africa—that is, the clicks of the Bantu languages in the Nguni family and the Khoisan languages. These consonants are produced by inhaling, rather than exhaling, which is characteristic of all other languages. For the bilabials, for example, this produces sounds similar to the noise of kissing. Damin also contains sounds found in no other language in the world, notably an unvoiced ingressive lateral, or, in more familiar terms, an "l" consonant produced by swallowing air and without vibrating the voice. But it is Damin's vocabulary that is especially remarkable (the morphology and the syntax are those of Lardil). Damin was conceived to be learned in one day. That implies a reduced number of words, less than two hundred in all, and consequently a very high level of abstraction, allowing for the existence of terms from a very wide semantic spectrum: every Damin word must be able to cover a considerable number of meanings that, in any other language, would each be expressed by a different word.

That is why only two verbs exist for the very general meaning of "to act," one of which is used when the effect of the action is harmful, the other when it is not. All other semantic distinctions, that is, whatever other meanings all the verbs in other languages possess, transitive as well as intransitive, are deduced from context, since the action that either X alone exerts or that X exerts upon Y, can be conceived as a function of the meaning of X and of Y. Nevertheless, it is important for abstraction to be limited, because for a language to be able to function, expressive power must have a place in it. That is why Damin also contains certain semantic terms as precise as the corresponding Lardil terms, and, for example, one for bony fish, another for the homogeneous group of fish with cartilage (sharks and stingrays), and one more for the heterogeneous group of sea turtles and dugongs.

This sophisticated blend of abstraction and concern for the concrete assumes a whole body of subtle mental activities needed to construct a language assigned by tradition to specific ritual uses. Beyond the facts just cited, we know almost nothing about Damin; we know nothing of its past, or how it might have, or actually did, develop. But the little that we can glimpse of this language allows us to imagine what its disappearance represents in terms of the loss of precious material for the understanding of mental activities and for the cognitive sciences in general.

Five Ways of Running and of Being Seated

Certain languages express with absolutely striking precision the circumstances under which various movements are executed or various positions adopted, according to the identity and the number of participants. Thus, for the single verb "to run," in central Pomo, still known by a few old people living in reservations 160 kilometers north of San Francisco, we find five verbal forms that combine affixes and radicals in different ways. One means that the running is performed by a single individual; another that it is performed by many individuals; a third that the runner has four feet, and thus that it is literally a coyote, deer, or dog, or, metaphorically, an old person; a fourth that, instead of one, there are many runners of this last type; and a fifth that those referred to are a group of humans in a car. In this same language, five different verbs can be used to designate the act of sitting down. One case has to do with a single individual on a chair or a single bird on a branch; in another, with many individuals or birds; in a third, with an individual seated on the ground; in a fourth, with many in this position; and, in a fifth, with a container of water set down on a table (see Mithun 1998, as well as for the three following examples taken from Pomo).

We might consider this specificity in the description of actions or postures to be a luxury that can be dispensed with by modern Western civilizations, oriented toward efficiency and productivity. But first, nothing indicates that using such a language stands in the way of efficient action, and secondly, its disappearance marks the loss of a precious trace of human talent, as it manifests itself in the verbal reconstruction of the world.

The Division of Linguistic Work

In French we say *s'arrêter de cueillir* ("to stop gathering") (for fruits, etc.). The two elements of this construction are full verbs, even if it is true that in *il s'arrête de cueillir*, the second is in fact reduced to the status of verbal noun. The Pomo equivalent for *s'arrêter de cueil-*

lir is *sh-yé-w*, that is, word for word, *sh-* = PREFIX indicating the action of gathering + *yé* = verb "to stop" + *-w* = SUFFIX meaning the completion of action. In other words, whereas French handles the action of gathering with a verb, Pomo handles it with a prefix, and it is the action of stopping that it expresses with a verb. This Amerindian language reveals a possibility that Romance languages generally exclude, that is, entrusting the expression of full ideas, like "to gather," to grammatical tools such as prefixes. This phenomenon is not limited to Pomo: in Zuni, spoken by eight thousand people in a New Mexican pueblo as of 1990, and a language that must be considered threatened, a good third of the vocabulary is made up of elements that are distinguished from nouns by the fact that they are invariables, not taking the affix of singular or plural number. For this reason, these elements are called "particles" by language specialists. Belonging to this category are certain words expressing ideas that, in French, are nouns and adjectives, like *tepi*, "wild cat," *citta*, "mother" (as well as all the nouns of kinship), *shiwani*, "rainmaker," and *k'ayu*, "fresh."

The preceding illustrates the way in which, in central Pomo or Zuni, invariable word tools are assigned meanings that, in French or Spanish, are handled by verbs or nouns. These facts are quite specific, if they are seen in relation to the characteristics of many languages. Knowing about these phenomena allows us to expand the idea of the possibilities for constructing instruments of expression beyond the limited perspective derived from examining only well-described and healthy Western languages.

The Subtle Groupings of Meanings

The different meanings that a Francophone would never imagine handling with a single word appear logically related if we examine the way that a language can bring them together. That is the case with the three Pomo words *ba-yól*, *s-yól*, and *sh-yól*, meaning, respectively, "to suddenly introduce words into a song that one was in the process of humming," "to make one's biscuits go down (the throat) with coffee or tea," "to stir with a spoon." Ordinarily, a French speaker would not conceive of these three actions as related, as they seem, on the contrary, to have no relationship to each other. Whereas we can observe that, in Pomo, the radical *yól*, "to mix," appears in all three words. Understanding, moreover, that *ba-* means "orally," *s-* means "while sucking," and *sh-* means "while holding a handle," the three words mean literally "to mix orally," "to mix while sucking," and "to mix with an object having a handle."

Human communities construct their languages according to the associations their cultures establish between things. The same is true vice versa: the way words reflect these associations later leads the descendants to reestablish the same relationships between things. Thus, we see that, as compared with Western languages, Pomo embodies a completely original conception of objects. These are the sorts of treasures that are lost when languages die.

The Wealth of Means for Not Assuming

I use the term *mediaphoric* (see Hagège 1995), that is, referring (*phoric*) to an intermediary (*media*), for grammatical tools that many languages possess and that allow the speaker to attribute to others what he asserts, that is, by making known that he says it because of hearsay or deduction, or according to testimony other than his own. French does not possess any exclusive tool for that, but it offers a mediaphoric use of the conditional. For example, if the Evangelists had written in French, when in doubt, they might have wanted to use this mode. Thus, in Mark 9.2, for example, it might read, "Six days

later, Jesus *aurait pris* [is supposed to have taken] with him Peter and
James and John, and he *aurait conduits* [is supposed to have led] them
apart by themselves up a high mountain. He *aurait été* [is supposed
to have been] transfigured before them; his garments *seraient devenus*
[were supposed to have become] resplendent."

Certain languages have at their disposal a rich inventory of means
to mark that the speaker does not take responsibility for what he says.
Some are on the way to extinction. Here again, central Pomo provides a striking example. Besides the suffix *-ya*, indicating that what
is said results from knowledge through direct observation, there exist
at least four others that are mediaphoric — *-do, -d'o, -nme*, and *-ka* —
denoting, respectively, information gotten from a specific person,
knowledge through hearsay, awareness through the perception of a
sound indicating that there is no doubt about the event, and, finally,
supposition through logical deduction. The extinction of a language
possessing such rich means would certainly leave a serious gap in our
knowledge of the vast cognitive resources of human idioms.

The Lessons of Diversity
The Amerindian Example

Most European languages (see Hagège 1994) belong to one and the
same family, called, as we know, the Indo-European family. That is
a striking contrast with the Indian languages of North America, the
majority of which are endangered. These constitute a good fifty distinct families, perhaps even more than sixty, if we go by certain classifications (see Campbell and Mithun 1979). Some of these families
are limited to one example (a single language), like Zuni, cited above,
in sharp contrast with others, like Athapascan-Eyak-Tlingit, which
contains at least forty languages. Obviously, there have been attempts
to reduce this profusion by proposing groupings, for example, into

three large families (see Greenberg 1987), but these attempts have hardly met with general approval (see Campbell 1988).

The genetic diversity of Amerindian languages is coupled with just as remarkable a typological diversity. From the point of view of their structural traits, these languages differ even more among themselves than they do as a whole from Indo-European languages, taken as a whole. In some, the realities resulting from contact with foreigners were designated by the ingenious association of native words into complex ensembles, adapted to morphological habits. Thus, in the former easternmost language of the five tribes of the Iroquois Nation, Mohawk, a language in which most nouns come from verbal phrases, "school" literally means "one uses it to make oneself learn to know the words." A hundred other ways of expressing new realities and accommodating borrowings can be found in other endangered languages, even if we confine ourselves to a single Amerindian group.

If There Were Only English . . .

If no language other than English existed in the world, what would we know of how the human mind functions, as reflected through the structures of language, and what would we know of the fundamental principles of grammar? Assuredly, we would know much, because English, like any other language, illustrates a great number of those principles. But it is clear that there is much we would not know, because a far greater number of other principles are expressed in the immense diversity of human languages.

That is one of the scientific reasons why the death of languages cannot be viewed with indifference. The properties of language are the historical and social manifestations of the faculty of language.

If we confine ourselves to a single language, doing a very attentive and very in-depth study of it, we can discover what only one specific culture selected, through thousands of years of subtle development, as it constructed its modes of expression, usually in an unconscious or semiconscious way. From so limited a basis, it is impossible to derive the whole ensemble of universal traits that define a language. Some properties specific to English might be presented as universal, whereas English may lack others that are an integral part of the definition.

The Extinction of Languages and the Study of Linguistics

In the world of human languages, what is apparent in one place is concealed somewhere else. Thus, as in the example I gave above, what one language handles with a radical, the primary basis of a word, another language entrusts to a prefix or to a suffix, peripheral elements. What is a routine grammatical fact here is an exceptional phenomenon there. What one linguistic community deems worthy of naming, another ignores, denying it any direct access to the sayable.

The science of language and languages cannot be satisfied with being postulated on a monolingual foundation. It must, by all means, make use of all its materials, which are considerable. And it is precisely because languages die, or find themselves in danger of dying, that the study of linguistics is threatened by rhetorical drifts, encouraged by a dearth of concrete evidence. Thus, the decline in the diversity of languages is, in the long run, the decline of linguistics itself. It could even be a severe loss for the other human sciences. Because how can an idea of the mind's creative capacity be faithful and comprehensive if this evidence of its manifestations, witnessed nowhere else, is lost to the abyss?

Based on the number of languages in the state of obsolescence or in their death throes, the most pessimistic forecasts estimate probable losses at 90 percent by about the year 2100. That would be 4,500 out of 5,000 languages!

A comparison with zoological and botanical species can be made here. According to a recent study (see *Le Monde,* March 10, 2000), the rate of extinction among living species is a thousand to ten thousand times higher today than it was during the great geological periods of extinction. Contributors to this remarkable performance are intensive agriculture (less than 30 percent of plant species provide more than 90 percent of the food for the global population), massive and methodical (even if anarchical) deforestation, urbanization, and industrialization. The result is that a considerable proportion of the some 1,650,000 present-day species are in danger of immediate extinction, a figure that breaks down into 45,000 vertebrates, 990,000 invertebrates, and 360,000 plants. To give a few details, let us note that, of the 4,400 species of mammals, 326 (7.4 percent) are in danger, as are 231 (2.7 percent) of the 8,600 species of birds. Again, these figures are optimistic, and researchers producing them caution that if the problems of counting animals are taken into account, it would be more accurate to speak of 10 percent for mammals and 5 percent for birds. If things continue at the current rate, 25 percent of all animal species risk obliteration before 2025, and 50 percent before 2100, that is, at proportions approximately equal to those of languages.

However, if this tendency cannot be reversed, it is at least possible to slow its pace. Indeed, those states most aware of the immense danger have adopted or are adopting measures. The United Nations has more than forty international organizations for safeguarding nature. And in addition, private initiatives abound: there are more than three hundred associations for the protection of both the animal and the plant world.

The disappearance of languages is to be regarded as a serious blow to what has been called the "linguistic genome" of the human species (see Matisoff 1991, 220), or the legacy of linguistic genes represented by all the living and dead languages since the beginning of time. Can't anything be done to counteract this damage? Are the languages that still survive less worthy of protection than animal and plant species?

9. Factors in Preservation and the Struggle Against Disaster

The Factors in Preservation

A SENSE OF IDENTITY

The current attitude of a portion of Bretons, Scots, and Occitans, to take only these examples, can be considered something new. Just when the essential factors for abandoning these languages were closing in on the economic, social, and political levels, accompanied by the resulting loss of prestige, there was a resurgence of pride among the most aware. Pride is a factor that can counteract destructive forces. Those inheriting a tradition of humiliation can call it into question, and draw a heightened sense of identity from the very thing that made their ancestral language contemptible: its — or its speakers' — marginality.

An analogous phenomenon was found among the Australian Aborigines, despised by the whites, who were not content to have simply dispossessed them of their lands. The very languages that are, along with the cultures they express, the target of contempt, are often the object of renewed interest on the part of Aborigines, who abandoned them in order to adapt. That is because they allow them to assert their identity, especially in situations where they can also defy the authority of their adversaries, the white police, by using Aborigine idioms in front of them as secret languages (see Wurm 1991, 15). To be able to speak one's own language among one's own people, a language one's adversaries do not understand, is, of course, a reason to value it. Such a situation confers a feeling of superiority, stubbornly challenged by the oppressors' racist rejection. But this use of Aborigine languages to flout white authority is only one aspect of a general awakening among native Australians. In July 2000, the most determined of the Aborigines demanded recognition of the serious harm done to children forcibly torn from their families and their languages throughout almost all of the nineteenth century (see chapter 7).

The sense of identity is particularly strong in communities that have a solid structure, like certain tribes of the eastern slopes of the Andes, notably the Chuars (Ecuador), the Campas (Peru), and, more significant in terms of numbers, the Aymaras of Bolivia. It has even been reported that a leader of the Cogui tribe (an Arhuaco group of the Chibchan linguistic family, living in the midlands of the Sierra Nevada of Santa Marta in the county of Magdalena in Colombia), in his concern for preserving cultural identity and homogeneity, forbade that population from speaking Spanish (see Adelaar 1991, 51).

LIFE APART: HOME HABITAT, ISOLATION, RURAL COMMUNITIES

Native Habitat

The preservation of a native language seems favored by the speakers' attachment to their original territory. Conversely, the displacement, deportation, and resettlement of speakers away from their homeland have negative effects on the conservation of their languages. We saw above that the Cayuga survived better in the area of the American and Canadian Great Lakes, the original habitat of the Iroquois, especially in Ontario (*Ontario* is an Iroquois word meaning "beautiful [*oi*] lake [*ontar*]"). On the other hand, Cayuga is more threatened in Oklahoma, the state where the Indians of the "Five Nations" were originally deported (1834) and placed on reservations, to be joined later by other Indian peoples driven from their territories.

Likewise, in the former Soviet Union, voluntary or imposed displacement, and, in particular, resettlement on collective farms during the 1940s had harmful consequences for many populations' languages, notably Naukan and Nivkh, which owe their present survival only to remarkably strong ethnic consciousness. Until now, ethnic consciousness has almost neutralized the effects of another negative factor that affects Nganasan, that is, dispersion. On the other hand, even when the number of speakers is very low, many languages survive well in those regions where their speakers have lived for a long time, especially if those regions are mountainous and inaccessible. That is true, for example, for the languages of Daghestan (east of the Caucasus), for Bats in Georgia, and for the languages of Pamir (Yazgulami, Bartangi, and other Iranian languages).

The Choice of the Ghetto and Endogamy

A social choice can also achieve the same effects as isolation resulting from natural conditions. Third-generation Chinese-Americans living in the ghettos of districts that they alone populate ("Chinatowns") less often switch to English than those who live outside these places of voluntary segregation. Endogamy also constitutes a preservation factor, and is linked to the preceding one, since it is going outside the group that favors exogamy, and eventually puts the language in danger.

Rural Life
Removed from Major Routes and Rivers

Life within rural communities is also a factor in preserving languages. Again, this factor only really comes into play when those communities exist far removed from major routes. As has been noted (see Dixon 1998, 82), the majority of the indigenous languages that have been able to survive in the Amazon Basin belong to ethnic groups living quite far from major rivers. If they lived closer, they would be exposed to contact with larger communities, which are also the ones whose economic activity is based on the exploitation of hydrographic resources. In a different environment, the Nubians, who have continued to live rurally since 1960 when the construction of the Aswan Dam and the creation of Lake Nasser flooded their ancient territory and made them migrate a bit farther north, are not only still far removed from Cairo, but also a dozen kilometers from the banks of the Nile. Unlike urbanized Nubians, they attach much importance to conserving their language as a symbol of their ethnic identity, and could help to safeguard it, at least temporarily, against the prestige of Arabic and the total Arabization of a part of Nubian society (see chapter 7) that increasingly rejects Nubian. We will see further on, however, that one preservation factor that ought to work in favor of Nubian, religion, in fact constitutes another threat to it.

Preservation Through Sudden Prosperity:
Valle d'Aosta and the Southern Tyrol

The preceding discussion applies generally, but not universally. Under certain circumstances, renouncing rural life, rather than maintaining it, becomes a factor in preserving languages. Until the past few decades, the high valleys in the autonomous region of Valle d'Aosta, Italy, had a farming and herding economy. But the change to an economy based on skiing and tourism brought with it prosperity, and it became possible to finance a preschool program with trilingual education for children three to five years old. In this program, the Franco-Provençal dialect, whose overall situation is precarious, has its place beside Italian and French.

Likewise, the Ladin dialects, which, along with Swiss Grisons to the west, and Friulian to the east, constitute one the three fragile dialectical groups called Raeto-Romance, or Rhaetian dialects, have benefited from a surprising promotion. Nevertheless, the districts of southern Tyrol (in northern Italy) where one encounters these dialects are small and scattered: there are four valleys forming a cross around a mountainous massif in the Dolomites. But a flourishing tourist industry has developed there, centered on luxury skiing. Being largely international, this tourism has introduced not one single threatening language but many languages, which, moreover, cannot have a lasting effect, because it is tied up to a seasonal activity, the inhabitants remaining there by themselves during the other parts of the year, and in a certain state of isolation. It is not impossible that these factors have helped to strengthen the Ladin dialects, a trend observed now for some time.

India's Great and Minor Languages, and the Role of the Cities

In India, we find that it is urbanization, and not the promotion of rural life, that benefits many languages. Calcutta's role in the nineteenth century in the development of Bengali, and the role that Delhi played in the promotion of Hindi, have often been stressed (see Mahapatra 1991, 185–186). The state recognizes languages spoken in areas where there is at least one large city, and even if the argument is not made, this is very much the case for the nineteen named in the famous article VIII of the Constitution of the Indian Union. For some, like Telugu, Gujarati, Marathi, Assamese, and Punjabi, this fact meant the creation of new states endowed with political powers and each possessing a major urban center. And those centers became caldrons for the sometimes violent struggles for recognition directed against the federal government from the 1950s to the early 1970s.

Thus, the country went from having fourteen states and six territories in 1956, all defined, we should note, by linguistic bases, to having many more today (their number varies). For a long time, the situation was very tense in the far northeast, around Assam, on the high plateaus and in the Arakan Mountain Range. This zone borders, from south to north, various countries and provinces all equally multilingual: Bangladesh, Burma, Tibet. To the west, it meets the eastern edges of the Himalayas. Certain regions within it finally obtained New Delhi's recognition. Thus they constitute new political entities, once again defined according to the criteria of the dominant languages in the urban areas: the states of Manipur, Meghalaya, Nagaland, Mizoram, and Arunachal Pradesh. Languages belonging to the Tibeto-Burman family (like Garo and Manipuri) or to the Mon-Khmer family (Khasi, among others) are spoken in these places; the number of speakers varies, ranging from a few to a few hundred thousand, but all the languages are fragile. This official promotion strengthens them against the power of the languages that surround them: Bengali, Burmese, Assamese. As for the tribal languages in the rest of the country, spoken by impoverished if not destitute minorities, rural life is not a factor favorable to their promotion in the context of today's India.

Family cohesion and religious cohesion, which are often interdependent, certainly play a role as factors in maintaining languages. Both of them did much to preserve Norwegian in the United States for a long time until it was supplanted by the ever-growing omnipresence of English (see chapter 8). There is a logical relationship between these factors: religious cohesion gives more forcefulness to traditions, and one such tradition is the respect for elders, who are themselves the surest guarantors of the ancestral languages they have transmitted. Moreover, in the nineteenth century, religious cohesion led the Norwegians in the United States to close ranks around their Lutheran church, in haughty opposition to the many rival English-speaking Protestant persuasions.

The United States is rich with pertinent examples, and within that country the role played by religion can be observed insofar as only powerfully defended languages are capable of resisting the pressure of English, even if they are not completely immune to it. In central and southeastern Pennsylvania, as well as, more sporadically, in Ohio, Illinois, Indiana, Virginia, and West Virginia, there exist German communities, descending from those that were established in colonial times. Among all these speakers, German shows signs of major erosion, notably the confusion between the cases of declension, something we also find, admittedly, in various Rhenish dialects, among others, in Germany, but to a lesser degree. Now this decay is noticeably less pronounced among the German-Americans who are either Mennonites or Amish, sects that strictly observe their religion, especially the Amish. Even though surprising counterexamples exist (see Huffines 1989), we can deduce that religion has the power to contribute to the preservation of a language. It is even likely that if German was destined to disappear from daily use in Pennsylvania, it would be maintained in religious use.

However, in certain circumstances, religion can have exactly the opposite effect. For example, the Nubians of northern Egypt, who, as we have just seen, preserve what they can of their language in the isolated villages where they continue to live, are, paradoxically, caught in the grip of the Islamist revival taking place in Egypt as in other Islamic countries. Indeed, the language in which this revived faith is expressed, through growing attendance at mosques, is and can only be Arabic. Sermons are delivered in classical Arabic; Nubian children are rewarded for reciting verses from the Koran properly; Nubian women, often enthusiastic supporters of this religious revival, study Arabic in order to read the Koran and for Islamic practice in general. Nubian is absent from all these activities. It will be Islam's victim before long.

WRITING

In certain cultural environments, the fact of being written is an important promotional tool for a language. India illustrates this case very well. Formerly, the notation of the Prakrit languages through one or another variant of Brahmi writing, and then through Devanagari, constituted means for winning real national respect in each of the regions where they developed. But beyond that, at the present time, the languages recognized by the constitution and guaranteed survival are those that are written, as opposed to those of small ethnic groups, jeopardized by the absence of writing.

Nevertheless, here as in other cases, the situation is never simple. Writing can turn into a tool of oppression, insofar as its form is imposed from above and not chosen by the population. That is what happened in the Soviet Union when authorities brought Cyrillic writing into general use in the 1930s, after having promoted Latin writing during the 1920s. We know that the real intention behind this decision was to make languages and ethnic groups more Russian. That was clearly perceived by Russian intellectuals, like the linguist Polivanov, as well as those in the Turkish republics, from Uzbekistan to Kirghiztan, who took the risk of opposing this apparently harmless policy.

MONOLINGUALISM

I will not linger over this factor here. It is enough to recall that the ethnic languages with bilingual users are more threatened than those with monolingual users only. This fact, among others, can be illustrated by the various tribal languages of Tanzania, which are exposed to the tidal wave of Swahili speakers (see chapter 7).

MIXED LANGUAGES

Mixed languages is the name I will give those linguistic hybrids that result from contact between two languages whose systems totally merge. Thus it is not a case of code switching. It involves mixing at the level of the language's structure, not in the linear progression of the sentence where elements belong, alternatively, to one or the other of the two languages present. What is at stake here is a matter of the outcome of reciprocal influence, perhaps taking place over a long period of time. I will give a few illustrations here.

Communicating on Copper Island

Copper Island belongs to the little archipelago of the Commander Islands, located about ninety kilometers off the eastern coast of the Kamchatka peninsula, and 150 kilometers from Attu, the westernmost of the Aleutian Islands. A strange mixed language is spoken on this island (see Vakhtin 1998). About fifteen Aleuts were resettled on Copper Island by the Russian-American copper firm in 1812; again during the nineteenth century, many Aleut families from various neighboring islands were transported there, and in 1900 the total population was 253. These people were essentially Aleuts, who spoke their language and Russian, but also Russians and a few Eskimos and Kamchadals (inhabitants of Kamchatka). Now, the striking fact is that a mixed language developed here. To grasp its significance, we must compare the linguistic situation of Copper Island with that of neighboring Bering Island. On Bering, where a total of a few hundred Aleuts lived, the majority of the population switched to Russian, as in all of northeastern Russia. In 1990, Aleut survived only among about twenty elderly individuals. Thus, it is a language on the brink of extinction.

On the contrary, on Copper Island, during a century and a half of very close contact between the indigenous idiom and Russian, a hybrid language developed in which one says, for example, *axsa-**yit*** ("he dies"), *axsa-chaa-**yish*** ("you kill"), *sagyi-ggii-**yish*** ("you have a gun") or **ni**-*ayuu-**li*** ("they were not long"). In these phrases, we see that the verb endings are all Russian: **-yit** = third person singular present, **-yish** = second person singular present, and **-li** = plural for all persons past. Likewise, the mark of negation, **ni,** is Russian. On the other hand, all these words are from the Aleut language: the adjective-verb *ayuu* ("to be long") the verbal radical *axsa* ("to die") the factitive morpheme *-chaa-* (= "to make," as in "to make die," that is, "to kill"), the noun *sagyi* ("gun"), the auxiliary verb *-ggii,* which means "to possess" and indicates that one possesses what the noun preceding it expresses (here the noun is *sagyi* and, consequently, *sagyi-ggii* means "to possess a gun").

In other words, through affixation (prefixes and suffixes), the mixed language in question combines certain verb endings, negations, and other morphemes taken from Russian with radicals that belong to Aleut. The significance of this process comes from its rarity. We can easily convince ourselves of this by comparing the language of Copper Island to the language of Atka Island, located east of the Aleutians. In this language, the endings are native, and it is the radicals that are often borrowed, in this case from English, as in the phrase *fish-iʒa-xx* ("he usually goes fishing"), where the verbal radical *fish,* a borrowing, is followed by two Aleut morphemes, *iʒa,* which indicates habitual present, and *xx,* which is the verb ending for third-person singular.

We might wonder how it happens that the language of Copper Island is not a pidgin of Russian, that is, a language with a Russian vocabulary and reduced morphology. The reason seems to be that, here, the relationships are not unequal, as they were between slaves deported to the Caribbean plantations and their masters. On Copper Island, the Russians and the Aleuts were workers with the same status, and linguistic permeation was reciprocal. According to researchers who have studied this mixed language, the inhabitants are convinced that they speak Russian. And what is more, this language is thriving and does not seem threatened with extinction despite its small number of speakers. We can deduce from this that Aleut here is the beneficiary of a strange *salvation through hybridization.* For an Amerindian language of the great Siberian and Canadian north that is in danger of disappearing, the close symbiosis with Russian, brought about through that of two communities, Russian and Aleut, appears to be an unexpected, but effective, factor in its preservation.

Other Cases of Hybridization

There are other cases of intense hybridization. Ma'a, or Mbugu, is such an example. Spoken in northeast Tanzania, Mbugu is a language in the Cushitic family that borrowed from neighboring Bantu languages a great number of features for its morphology and syntax, even while essentially maintaining a Cushitic vocabulary. Another example is the language of a Gypsy group of Great Britain, which combines an English grammar with a Romany vocabulary. Still another is that of the "media lengua" spoken in Ecuador, which has a Quechua grammar and a Spanish lexis. A final example is that of Michif, a mixed language spoken on an Indian reservation close to a village called Lac La Biche and the lake of the same name, 220 kilometers northeast of Edmonton (Alberta, Canada), by a community of Cree and French half-breeds who came from Quebec at the beginning of the twentieth century. This hybrid language combines Cree (Algonquin) roots and a French grammar.

In none of these examples do we have to deal with the risk arising from a situation of intense contact, causing a language to lose some of its characteristics, as in the case of Dahalo abandoning its opposition between genders and its various marks of plural under pressure from Swahili (see chapter 6). Nor do I believe, as other authors do (see, for example, Myers-Scotton 1992), that borrowing a foreign morphology is the sign of a moribund state. I think this is even less true when a foreign lexis is borrowed and combined with a native grammatical base. Of course, hybridization is disruptive. Very composite languages like the ones just cited do not seem to be "normal" languages in the eyes of some. But it is the myopia of the present that distorts their vision. The history of languages contains many cases of borrowing on a vast scale. A language's struggle to adapt can result in its becoming mixed. Far from being a step toward death, it appears as the very image of life in the cases cited here, that is, a death deferred.

The Struggle Against Disaster

The maintenance of languages involves certain factors that help to prevent them from disappearing. But there are also concrete initiatives taken by societies to bring the languages created by their ancestors back from the brink of disaster. In this section I will examine, successively, school, officialization, the speakers' involvement, and the linguists' role.

SCHOOL

We have seen that English-speaking schools were a formidable factor in the extinction of other languages in the United States, Canada, and Australia. More generally, it is not a paradox to say that in all countries where one language dominates, the absence of schools where it is taught in certain isolated places gives the dominated language a chance, and may serve as an element — a negative element — that safeguards it. That becomes apparent, for example, in the areas of Thailand where minority languages resist the influence of Thai. Conversely, the creation of schools that teach the dominated language can be a decisive factor in saving it, even when it is on the point of disappearing. The history of Maori and that of Hawaiian attest to this. Success is less evident in the case of Irish and of the languages of Siberia.

The Rebirth of Maori

In 1867, the New Zealand government launched an education program in which English was the only language used. The success of this program was enhanced by missionaries who had been teaching the Maori people to read and write since 1835. By 1845, half the Maori population had copies of the New Testament. Literacy's effect on Maori was completely disastrous. Moreover, the language was scorned by the white population, and was on the way to being completely eradicated by English. Nevertheless, a national initiative took place in the 1970s yet apparently too late to save the gravely ill Maori language: of the three hundred thousand members of this nation, about a quarter still used their language, and children no longer learned it. The Maoris officially demanded the creation of schools that taught their vernacular idiom exclusively. By the end of the 1980s, six primary and secondary schools were created in which Maori was the principal language for instruction. Beginning in 1982, an immersion program was instituted into which thirteen thousand children were integrated in 1994. Then there were four hundred *kohanga reo*, or "language nests," where about six thousand children learned Maori. Thus, to some extent, this program is a success. There are certain circumstances in its favor. First, Maori is the only indigenous language of New Zealand today, and thus its promotion does not compete with other similar enterprises. Also, the Maori people have affirmed their desire to revitalize their language and not to let it disappear, insofar as it expresses values the white society has lost, according to them, and to which they are attached, among them tolerance and solidarity.

The Struggle for Hawaiian

Again, this involves a very recent endeavor. The example of Maori inspired members of the Hawaiian community, determined to do anything to save their language, teetering on the edge of the abyss. Because Hawaii is one of the fifty American states, it is easy to imagine what that means for a minority language, which, in its own land, Hawaiian is. Immersion programs for preschool-age children began as a private initiative, entrusted to a university professor. In 1987, the three programs that existed were recognized by the Hawaiian Department of Education and received state funding (see Zepeda and Hill 1991). Promoters even managed to obtain an exemption with regard to the purely pedagogical degrees that are required for teaching. The authorities really wanted to acknowledge the urgency and the difficulty of recruiting people simply capable of speaking to children and instructing them through dialogue, given the moribund state of the language. Nevertheless, there was an attempt to train teachers, so that instruction could be extended into higher grades, at least up to junior high school. Here an obstacle appeared that is common for languages threatened with extinction: the only natural speakers of Hawaiian were very old, few in number, and gradually dying out, as opposed to the ever-increasing number of children who needed instruction. To respond to this challenge, parents were invited to learn the language along with their children, and to try to speak it at home. Adult courses were offered. In 1987, about fifteen children between two and five years old spoke Hawaiian.

The Tribulations of Irish

I will not linger over this point, already treated elsewhere (see Hagège 1994, 242–245). I will only mention the existence of the *gaeltachtai*, that is, the zones, all located on the outskirts of the western counties (historic refuges of the Celts), where traditional lifestyles have preserved the use of Irish, and where it is the medium for instruction in the schools. These are the only living conservatories of this language. The combined effects of two factors render a true restoration more difficult: the British policy for eliminating Irish, conducted over several centuries beginning in the 1600s, and, of course, the universal prestige of English in the contemporary world.

The Languages of Siberia

For several years now, many Siberian languages have become the object of efforts to introduce them into the elementary school curriculum in areas where they are spoken. This is true of Yukaghir, Nivkh, Ulch, Selkup, and Ket. It is too early to know what results this policy will produce, applied to languages in very bad health, languages spoken by populations that are widely dispersed and have long been Russianized.

OFFICIALIZATION

Official Language and National Language: Regarding Luxemburgeois and Rhaetian

Official recognition by the state means, in fact, the inscription of a language into the constitution of that state. A language is considered official if the law supports it, if the state has the right to use it in diplomatic relations, and if any citizen is entitled to ask for it in court, services, etc. National languages are not necessarily official ones, even though they are granted de facto recognition. In Luxembourg, that is the case with Luxemburgeois, a middle German dialect of the Frankish group that is the language of the home, business, and the courts, and to which the inhabitants are attached as the very mark of their personality. They have not chosen to make it official, however, granting this status to French and assigning a significant cultural position to German. As for the whole constituting the Rhaetian dialects of the Grisons, a national language in Switzerland, it has recently become an official language, which involves financial backing by the canton and the Confederation (see Hagège 1994, 154–155). Many dominated languages, enjoying no status of national language, to say nothing of official language, have fought long battles for recognition. I noted earlier that in the Republic of India, this battle sometimes culminated in the recognition of a state or territory organized around a large urban center.

Faint Murmurings in North America

For any language whatsoever, other than English — and, in Quebec, French — to receive the status of official recognition in North America is obviously not conceivable in today's political and cultural context. That makes the recent and very isolated cases of two Canadian territories all the more significant. The Northwest Territories granted official status to the languages of Indian communities, along with English and French. The present condition of these languages remains to be seen. We can get some idea, knowing that another positive measure was taken not long ago by a second territory, the Yukon. Without granting official status to Indian languages, it simply declared their preservation to be an explicit goal.

Languages' Struggles for Recognition in Latin America

Latin America offers a very representative case of these struggles for recognition, conceived as a means of resisting Spanish and of not letting it replace native languages and drive them to extinction. Results have been mixed, as we shall see.

Nahuatl, Aymara, and Quechua at an Impasse

Taking into account only languages spoken by more than a million people, neither Nahuatl in Mexico, nor Aymara in Bolivia, Peru, and Ecuador, has obtained official status. In 1953, an academy with a largely symbolic role was created in Peru for Quechua, which experienced a brief period of glory in that same country when the military government of General J. Velasco Alvarado declared it the second official language along with Spanish in 1975. This was done by decree, with no preliminary work to promote or explain it and no means by which to apply it. The regime was toppled that same year, making the proclamation null and void.

This situation is worrisome. Nahuatl, Aymara, and Quechua may not seem threatened for the moment, if we consider the criterion of number of speakers (see chapter 8), but the worldwide audience for Spanish makes it a formidable rival for these languages, now as in the past. This is well understood by all those who struggled and continue to struggle for the official recognition of these languages in the countries where they have real demographic significance.

Guarani in Its Glory

Until now, Guarani has been the only victor in this battle. It was favored, of course, by a long history of promotion in the country where it is most widespread, Paraguay. This history is exemplary enough to warrant a brief review. Beginning in the mid-sixteenth century, the system of *encomienda* was established, or the division of Indians and their lands among Spanish colonists. Of course, this period is one of general interbreeding between the colonists, disappointed at encountering only Chaco's humidity and vipers along the route that was supposed to lead them to Peru's wealth of gold, and the subjugated and soon to be enslaved Indian population, thus forming the basis of Paraguayan society today. Moreover, colonists often knew Guarani. But they exploited the Indians and abuses multiplied, generating revolts, so that the Spanish crown, seeking a solution to the crisis, instituted the system of Reductions, or gathering Indians on large territories around an urban center, under the authority of missionaries (see Villagra-Batoux 1996, 183–218). There, the Indians were "reduced" vassals of the king, but also rescued from servitude by the priests, who, in order to more easily convert them, isolated them from the exploiters, that is, one segment of Spanish society. They were "invited" to cease being nomadic, pagans, "idlers." They were first under the charge of the Franciscans, beginning in 1575, and then the Jesuits, beginning in 1605.

It turns out that at the same moment, in the debate in European courts over what languages to use to Christianize populations, the Jesuits' position favored the "vernacularists" rather than the "Latinists." They were encouraged in this by King Philip II himself, who was more tolerant on this point than his father and recommended not forcing the Indians to abandon their languages for a brutally imposed Castilian. The consolidation of the Reductions, the close relationship between missionaries and Indians, and the needs of evangelism replacing bad treatment under the earlier regime had the effect of rendering mastery of Guarani indispensable and led to a linguistic policy quite different from the one that other Jesuits adopted in Mexico. Guarani soon occupied a place almost equal to that of Spanish in civilian life.

Remembering the cultural context of the period, marked by the past and by the history of Latin, that also meant access to writing, a situation all the more surprising as Castilian was considered to have robbed and also inherited from Latin the prestige of being written. Having fallen truly in love with Guarani, a beautiful and subtle language, the Jesuits gave it the literary dignity of a cultivated Indian idiom. In the end, they even made this "Guaraní Jesuítico" the only official language in the entire province. Under their regime, it remained the only language for instruction for all school subjects. Retaining the system of graphic transcription developed by the Dominican Luis de Bolaños, they performed the task of standardization for

Guarani, fixing an authorized form of the language among all the dialectical variants. As I said earlier, the lack of such standardization is detrimental and having it has ensured the solid status of so many European languages.

The golden age came to an end with the departure of the Jesuits, and a new period began at the end of the eighteenth century that resulted in a wholly new policy by the mid-nineteenth century: liberal mercantilism, concerned with opening Paraguay to modernity and to the means of production adopted by European capitalism, hastened to banish Guarani from secondary schools and to promote Spanish only. But a new twist in the lovely and dramatic fate of Guarani was its renaissance beginning in 1870, in reaction to the terrible war of the Triple alliance, an attempt at genocide against the population of this country by its neighbors in Argentina, Brazil, and Uruguay, all three of them nervous about Paraguay's economic progress and incited by Great Britain. To genocide was added an attempt at linguicide: a representative of U.S. interests recommended the extermination of the Guaranis and their "diabolical language" (Villagra-Batoux 1996, 276–277).

During most of the twentieth century, and notably under the military dictatorship that, following others, ruled the country from 1954 to 1989, Guarani experienced little of the glory it had known from 1575 to 1768, either in the schools or public life. That is why it makes sense to consider the events of 1992 a revolution as much as an achievement: article 140 of the new constitution declared Guarani the official language of Paraguay along with Spanish, while article 77 stipulated that bilingual education was obligatory. Two years later, the work of Consejo Asesor de la Reforma Educativa resulted in the introduction of bilingual education in all Paraguayan schools, making this country the only one in Latin America to date that gives such a status to an Amerindian language. Despite the large number of speakers, this new departure must be considered necessary to the struggle, because in the context of the modern world, all Amerindian languages, without exception, are exposed to the threat of extinction.

It is not inconsequential to add that in a country not far from Paraguay, Indian languages have not enjoyed the same privilege. Uruguay is a country without Indians, different in this way from all other Latin American countries, because the original populations were exterminated there, in particular the Charrúas, whom General Rivera lured into a deadly trap in 1831. Nevertheless, many traces of Indian languages remain, beginning with those that can be observed in the name itself, which is Guarani (in this language, *uruguá* means "snail" and *y,* "river"). Today there is some doubt that all Uruguayan languages are related to Guarani. Its presence in the toponymy could reflect the presence of a great number of Guaranis who left the Jesuit Reductions after the Jesuits were expelled (see Pi Hugarte 1998). But there is no doubt that there were many Indian hunting tribes whose languages disappeared with their speakers. Among them are Lule and Vilela, to which is sometimes added Charrúa, as well as an equally extinct language, Chaná, and all those for which no traces remain other than short vocabularies drawn up by missionaries.

THE INVOLVEMENT OF SPEAKERS

We must understand the involvement of speakers to mean both the attempts from outside to heighten speakers' awareness and the community's own spontaneous engagement in efforts to promote its threatened language. Thus the task of resuscitating or revitalizing a language is necessarily artificial, at least in part.

There are many programs for reviving languages throughout the world, thanks to the heightened awareness of the risks incurred by many of them. I will examine some examples from North America and Latin America here.

The United States and Canada
"U.S. English" and Indian Reactions

In North America, one of the continents where languages other than English are most threatened, heightened awareness among natives was favored to some extent by a very curious phenomenon. As we know, the United States does not have official language(s) (a tradition of "Anglo-Saxon pragmatism," as the gourmands of commonplaces like to say?), and English enjoys overwhelmingly dominant status only according to custom, not according to law. This was true at least until the mid-1980s. Actually, since then, a movement called "U.S. English," which began in 1983 with a (racist?) organization of parents hostile to immigration, has become active.

With supporters throughout the country, this movement is pushing the separate states to legalize English as the official language, while waiting for it to obtain this status at the national level. Its intention is explicitly stated: to prevent "the institutionalization of immigrant languages that compete with English." It turns out that one aspect of the U.S. English program presents the preservation of "native American languages" as "an intellectual obligation" referring to those languages that "are spoken nowhere else in the world" (see Zepeda and Hill 1991). But this aspect has gotten no publicity, by chance or by design, so, paradoxically, the Indian communities have focused on something else: they stress that by opposing financing for bilingual education, this movement threatens Amerindian languages.

That is how U.S. English has been the indirect force behind a flurry of initiatives taken by Indians in support of their languages, motivated by the fear of seeing English become the official language of the United States through a constitutional amendment. Of course, the U.S. English movement is not the only cause for this rash of activity. In any case, in 1990, the head representatives for the Sioux, Chippewa, Ute, Yaqui, Havasupai, Apache, and Navajo tribes, based on their legal status as sovereign nations having government-to-government relations with individual states as with federal U.S. authority, adopted linguistic measures according to which the Indian language is deemed the official language of the tribe, and English the second language. After various mishaps, the Indians succeeded in getting both chambers of Congress to pass the Native American Language Act, which guarantees the preservation, protection, and promotion of Native American languages (including those of Alaska, in addition to those of Hawaii and the Pacific islands [Micronesia] under U.S. administration), as well as the right to use them and develop their practice. The Canadian government has already taken similar measures.

The Revival of Mohawk

The principles thus recommended by official policy represent the ideal. Of course they ought to help save what is salvageable if they are applied. But it is useful to examine a few actual cases involving speakers defending their gravely threatened languages. I will begin with an Iroquois language belonging to a tribe whose contact with the whites dates back to the seventeenth century, Mohawk. The speakers of this language were known for their eloquence and their taste for verbal elegance. Nevertheless, Mohawk, like so many other North American languages, was almost never heard in public anymore at the beginning of the 1970s, and only the older speakers may have still used it in private. In 1972, the principal representatives of the Mohawk nation who lived in Quebec organized an educational system of immersion at Kahnawake, using manuals prepared by researchers (see "The Role of Linguists," below). The adults decided to speak Mohawk among themselves. Soon the children got used to seeing this language as something special belonging to their nation. Evidence showed that learning Mohawk was not an obstacle to learning English, or French, usually necessary in Quebec for finding work. It is true that there is still much to be done. But a psychological barrier was overcome, and the struggle to save this threatened language is well under way.

Hualapai and the Peach Springs Experiment

Another North American language, Hualapai, belonging to the Yuman group in the large Hoka-Sioux family, and formerly spoken in the lower Colorado valley, became the object of a bilingual education program beginning in 1975, meant to curb the alarming progress of its erosion. In the 1980s, the Peach Springs experiment, named for the town in northern Arizona on the southwest edge of the Grand Canyon where it took place, was cited everywhere among Indians in the United States. When the program was launched, nearly 50 percent of the Hualapai used English as their first language. The situation seems to have improved, but the continual decline in federal funding constitutes a negative factor, despite prodigious efforts and the devotion and competence of personnel (see Zepeda and Hill 1991, 146).

Guatemala, Nicaragua

We have seen that out of the twenty-some present-day languages in the Mayan family, only five, Yucatec, Quiché, Kekchi, Kakchiquel, and Mam, seem relatively healthy, with the number of speakers varying between four hundred thousand and one million. In order to strengthen and preserve all the others, for which the situation is much more precarious, the Mayans of Guatemala established an Academy of Mayan Languages after the civil war that ravaged this country in the early 1980s. The academy was officially recognized by the state in 1991. An alphabet valid for the whole family was developed and made legal through presidential decree. Other institutions also exist for the purpose of providing language training to the Mayan elite so that they can standardize the language.

One remarkable case is that of Rama in Nicaragua, a language in the Chibchan family spoken by about twenty-five people in the mid-1980s, and a victim of profound contempt among speakers themselves, in correlation with the switch to English under the influence of Moravian missionaries in the second half of the nineteenth century (see Craig 1992). After first promoting general education in Spanish, the Sandinista Revolution adapted to the demands of populations on the Atlantic coast, giving them autonomy. To this favorable but insufficient factor was added the involvement of speakers themselves and, in particular, one woman who, having fallen in love with Rama, devoted all her energy to saving it from extinction. And she was not even a native speaker!

THE ROLE OF LINGUISTS

Linguists, or at least those linguists who are interested in concrete languages throughout the world, are necessarily among those who cannot be indifferent about the death of languages. This phenomenon preoccupies them enough to have become a new theme within linguistic studies, and to have already been the focus of a great number of works and scholarly conferences. That is why the role that linguists can play in the struggle against the disaster of human languages going extinct in great numbers and throughout the world is certainly not negligible. This role is performed on two planes: actual linguistic work and working with populations of speakers, as we will now see.

The Ordinary Tasks of the Professional Linguist and Fieldwork
Scholarly Works

Like all science, linguistics proposes theoretical models. But it must also put them to the test, or else risk sterility. Certain linguists feed linguistic theory its own regurgitated ideas. Others, who are also professional linguists and thus theoreticians, practice and defend a linguistics of languages—both as prerequisite for and outcome of research into universal linguistic traits—as well as a linguistics of language.

That means confronting the realities of many languages, especially through work actually done in the field. And there, as in the place where the linguist withdraws to reflect and write, the ordinary tasks that await him are multiple. On the basis of elements gleaned from his informers, he must compile a phonology, a grammar, a dictionary, a collection of traditional tales, or more generally, the oral literature, all of which he must transcribe, when the language has no known writing system, according to a written form that he himself must establish, with the help of the most motivated of his informants. This orthographic aspect of his task clearly illuminates the importance of the service he is supposed to render. Because the spelling system that he develops, generally intended for scientific purposes, will note only what is distinctive among the sounds and not each detail of oral production. But it is often taken up by the informants as a model to respond to their own needs for writing.

The Urgency of the Struggle Against Time

The linguist who knows that a language is threatened is all the more motivated to make a description of it if it is spoken by many individuals of all ages. It is a painful and exhilarating task to gather from the lips of an old man the last phrases that he can still produce in a language that he does not easily agree to speak, because he has no natural interlocutors left with whom to share it. And often the linguist knows that, on his next visit, the old informer will no longer be there to transmit to him what he still remembers. The more isolated a threatened language is on the genetic level (that is, without related languages within a single linguistic family), and moreover, the more isolated it is on the typological level (that is, as the only example of the type of structure, phonological, grammatical, or lexical, that it illustrates), the more urgent it is to describe it before it dies.

But the description the linguist makes will serve not only science—though this dramatic fact would already be motive enough to act quickly. If linguists do not hasten to explore the many still unknown languages that are threatened with extinction, linguistics could very well be the only science to witness 50 to 90 percent of the material it works with disappear! Let us consider only one example of the tasks that remain to be done: out of some 670 Indonesian languages, and despite the numerous and good works produced by linguists in Leyden and other Dutch universities during the period when the country was a Dutch colony, only 6 percent are known in any satisfactory way. But in addition to this imperative for acting as quickly as possible, there is another: the linguist's work is often the only existing account of a language if he is the first to come to that place to study and describe it. Without him, a previously unknown and dying language would be lost to the abyss, and with it, the whole culture it expresses.

The Distinguished Calling of Testimony and Its Media: Books, Audio Recordings, Internet

That is why the work of the linguist takes on so much significance. It is the seed for a possible rebirth. In other words, if the linguist cannot save a seriously threatened language from extinction, he can provide the elements that can breathe new life into it, on the condition that a powerful desire is manifested for restoring it. Obviously, one could claim that the works of linguists turn dying languages into museum objects. But we must remember that besides the books he writes, any linguist, in principle, can also make audio recordings. Of course, such recordings are also material and may eventually deteriorate, but, whatever is said about them, they last quite a long time, and they can be invaluable for those determined to make use of them. Their number is increasing today thanks to a new outlet: Web sites on the Internet, about which I will speak at the end of this book.

The Role of Standardization

Linguists are often asked by those responsible for language policies, particularly in multilingual countries, to give their opinion or suggestions regarding the sometimes necessary work of finalizing and promoting a dialectical standard to cover widely dispersed dialects. It happens that such work favors the survival of a threatened language. Thus, the Khoekhoe languages, formerly called "Hottentot," of the Republic of South Africa and of Namibia, were reduced to nothing by two centuries of colonial politics, from the period (late seventeenth century) when the East Indian Company began to impose Dutch on the Africans, whose interesting languages with consonantal clicks (pronounced by ejecting the breath: see chapter 8) were considered by the colonists to be pure rumblings and hiccups uttered by savages.

Today, the only survivors in this linguistic family are Nama and Damara, which are very close to each other. Even though they are still spoken by some 125,000 speakers, they are in danger from the pressure of Afrikaans and English (see Haacke 1989). Only the actions of linguists in recommending standardization could help Nama to survive, the more widely distributed of the two languages, abandoned by many users with the notion that it has no prestige, because its kinship with Damara makes them appear as reflexes of an ancestor which is broken up into two similar languages, and thus it puts them in a bad position with regard to the job market.

The task of neology also often falls to the linguist. Whether speakers explicitly ask this of him or whether he himself feels it is necessary, he must propose new terms as a function of the adaptation needs of the vocabulary and of what he knows about the rules for forming words in the language he is studying. Linguists who go into distant countries to describe languages also find that sometimes political authorities invite them to contribute technical assistance to the work of building a modern terminology in many domains.

Action Among Speakers
Helping to Heighten Awareness

We will notice that, most of the time, speakers become aware of the danger their language is in only when it is too late for effective action. The linguist recognizes the signs of precariousness and of obsolescence (see chapter 6), and it is his duty to give the earliest possible warning to speakers regarding those processes he observes. Most linguists understand this and actively assist populations when they decide to develop bilingual education programs to save their languages. Thus the linguist helps them to respect and be proud of their languages.

One of the best ways to heighten awareness is quite simply to train professional linguists among the speakers. Again, this is a task many linguists perform, entrusting the continuation of the enterprise to well-trained informants when they leave the study site for good, and even when they plan to return again. These informants are better able to describe their languages, being native speakers themselves. The foreign linguist who pursues a scientific study intends to submit it to those who will judge it in his own country. Thus, he is concerned about academic promotion. But it is his duty to also be concerned about populations, and not only the native specialists to whom he has transmitted his technical expertise. That is why it is important for him to make readable the descriptions he compiles, at least to some extent, even if we must admit that he cannot avoid specialized terminology. Many field linguists who conduct their studies on threatened languages also leave the native speakers manuals they have compiled for helping to teach children. Thus, by a kind a paradox, the best informants provide the material, and the linguist, trained to interpret it and systemize it, offers it back as teaching material for the mass of native speakers in the process of forgetting their language! Often the speakers, who do not have the means to launch a program for reviving their threatened language, appreciate the linguist leaving a description meant to prevent it from being forgotten. That is the case, for example, with the Yimas of Papua New Guinea.

Helping with Resuscitation

In certain rare but proven cases, the action of linguists plays an important role in helping to resuscitate a language in escheat. Urat, a Papuan language of the province of eastern Sepik in New Guinea, was on the way to being abandoned in favor of Tok Pisin. But the linguists who did work in that area did so much to make Urat valuable again in the eyes of its users that it is experiencing a kind of renaissance. Another case is the one of Atacameño, formerly spoken in the desert region of the same name in northern Chile. Although not successfully reintroduced into daily usage, this language, which was dying out as early as the second half of the nineteenth century, was made respectable again by foreign researchers among its own users who had abandoned it for Spanish, to the point that, today, many natives can produce words and expressions if asked (see Adelaar 1991, 50). Unexpected concern coming from the outside has real power to spark the memory, because those who no longer believed in their language are so pleased by it.

The Mayans' Demands

One of the most interesting attitudes is that of the Mayans of Guatemala. Very aware of the cultural value of their heritage, very concerned with making themselves understood by specialists, a group of Mayans organized a workshop in Antigua in 1985 to address three explicit warnings to foreign linguists: not to contribute to the internal divisions of each Mayan language, not to isolate speakers while working on their own language, and not to monopolize linguistic methodology and knowledge without sharing with Mayan peoples. Four years later, in a new workshop, this same group affirmed that doing linguistics is essentially a political act, and that funding one linguistic study over another constitutes a political choice. The most determined member of this group openly declared (Cojtí-Cuxil 1990, 19) that the former reign of Spanish colonialism in Guatemala reduced Mayan languages to a subordinate status and condemned them to death, so that linguists can in no way pretend to be neutral or apolitical, and so they are faced with a choice: either active complicity with the colonial order, or engagement in favor of a new linguistic order that respects the rights of all communities.

A surprising detail involves the examples. The Mayans in this group hardly appreciate that the verbs meaning "to kill" or "to strike" appear in so many examples, and consider the linguist who gives these examples to offer a very negative image of their people as assassins and violent beings. Mayans who have received linguistic training nevertheless know very well that, in all human languages where one studies that phenomenon of grammar called transitivity, the notions of "to kill" and "to strike" present an important advantage: those who participate in these actions can equally be an "I," a "you," a "he," etc., and in singular as well as plural. This absence of grammatical restriction greatly facilitates the examination of sentences that are built upon a structure of pure transitivity; this last is one in which the agents (those who strike or kill) subject the patients (those who are struck or killed) to a process carried out to its end, this end even being, in one of the two cases, the suppression of the patient! It is syntactically revealing structures like these that really attract the attention of language specialists. Thus, is it odd to take such interest in the forms? Speakers do not easily accept the argument that this is the linguist's very vocation. Because for them, the language is primarily meant to produce meanings, appearing in actual situations, rather than in examples of grammar.

But the Mayans are not the only ones to think that. British readers are just as sensitive on this point: in the late 1970s (see Sampson 1980, 66 n. 1), the head of a respectable publishing house withdrew from the market all copies of a linguistics text on the eve of its publication. Actually, this work also illustrated the facts of transitivity with a great many examples in which Johns, Bills, and Marys had no other occupation except methodically massacring their entourage. The editor thus feared that readers bearing these very common names would be tempted to take legal action to obtain compensation for attributing to them the ignoble behavior of serial killers. We can understand why the linguist is embarrassed by such attitudes, if even the speakers of languages not at all threatened are opposed to the diabolical image given of them, in their opinion, by a linguistic tract that had no such intention at all.

We cannot evade the problem posed to linguists by demands like those of the Mayans. Linguists are trained in scientific rigor, in concern for an "objective" examination of the facts, in rejecting any subjective or normative position, in the study of models of sentences that give the most faithful image possible of the way a language functions, including with respect to the relationship between the verb and its subject, as well as its possible object. And nevertheless, it remains true that the demands of populations directly affected by their work cannot be ignored. The best they can do is to provide them with all the tools they demand, show them great attention, and, in their interests, do the most thorough work possible.

THE DESIRE AMONG SPEAKERS TO ABANDON THEIR LANGUAGE
A Solo in Another Key

Faced with the concert of voices warning of dangers, another, almost opposite, opinion arises, and it is probably not so isolated. According to this opinion (see Ladefoged 1992), it is paternalistic to want to make speakers return to their languages when they have opted for disowning them, and it is not up to linguists to thwart the choices of the speakers. In fact, to my knowledge, no linguist has ever exerted direct pressure to compel speakers of a dying language to readopt it. And in any case, the impossibility of such behavior is so obvious that even mentioning it seems ridiculous. In chapter 7, I analyzed the causes of languages' extinction, and it ought to be apparent that those who cease speaking their language are not acting from whim. They are led to this by the pressure of events, or they do it, or believe they do it, by free choice. It is true that, for their descendants, using a language that was not spoken by their ancestors seems a given. This is the world they are born into, and, about the one where the ancestral language ruled, they know only what they have been told. But on the other hand, a good portion of those who experience the change perceive it as a bad thing. A great number of positive reactions to the work of linguists attest to this.

Defending Political or Economic Motivations

I have heard adversaries of Indian languages in the United States — whom I cannot cite by name because these were anonymous encounters while traveling and on assignment — maintain that the tribes claiming to promote their languages, which they do not use anymore, are not motivated by purely cultural concerns. According to this opinion, the demand for linguistic restoration, far from being sincere, might really be simply a noble flag veiling economic claims, like the possession of a territory concealing rich underground resources. The same adversaries claim that defending the language may hide political aims, like the administrative autonomy of a region inhabited by this or that ethnic group. I do not have the means to verify such claims. If it should turn out that there is some truth to them, it is not clear how linguistic promotion could suffer from having been used as a pretext, provided that it is successful. Moreover, the death of Indian languages in America is closely linked to the violent expulsion of native tribes from their traditional territories over the course of the nineteenth century. Reclaiming these territories can work only in favor of Indian languages.

Freedom of Choice

It is absolutely true that those who abandon a language which, in their opinion, lacks prestige, value on the job market, and future perspectives for their children often make this decision as a matter of free choice, and no coercion whatever is involved. "Is it any more humane," asks G. Mounin (1992, 157), "to try to artificially save nonviable languages than it is to try to sustain a life through heroic surgical interventions when the patient's diagnosis is hopeless?" It goes without saying that the essential factor is the will of the speakers. But this will is itself a result. It is a result of the economic and social causes analyzed in chapter 7, which are not willed by those whose languages are affected.

We can certainly admit that the death of languages is a phenomenon as natural as that of cultures. But we must also understand that in losing its language, a society loses a lot, and that those whose vocation it is to describe languages see in their death the death of precious evidence of human creativity. That is enough to make it legitimate to struggle against this phenomenon, insofar as it is possible to do so, not blindly, of course, not through artificial excesses, but also not without strength.

Part III. LANGUAGES AND RESURRECTION

10. Hebrew — From Life to Death and From Death to Life

The Language of the Hebrews in Ancient Israel

A LANGUAGE THAT, FOR MORE THAN THREE THOUSAND YEARS, HAS BEEN CALLED "HEBREW"

The Hebrew that we now call "Biblical" as opposed to modern Hebrew, also called "Israeli" Hebrew, was a spoken language for a considerable period of time. A spoken language here means a language that not only existed as a system, but also possessed the essential dimension that F. de Saussure called parole (see chapter 3). It is often hard to imagine that ancient languages could have been the means of daily communication. This difficulty is greatly eased here, because the language spoken today in the state of Israel, where it has official status, is designated by the same name as the one spoken on the same soil about . . . thirty centuries ago. The same is true of its speakers, the Hebrews, inhabitants of the Hebrew state. On the other hand, the peoples associated with those Hebrews disappeared thousands of years ago, lost to the abyss of time. Or rather, those peoples exist only in the notes about them found in ancient history textbooks or in scholarly studies published by archeologists. We are speaking of the peoples of early antiquity, the Assyrians, the Babylonians, the Akkadians, and many others still, the evidence of their lives lying in the dust of archeological digs. Hebrew is thus closely tied to the Hebrews, and it has remained so indefinitely, despite a death that might have seemed endless, since the Hebrews were the contemporaries of nations and states long since disappeared.

PRE-BIBLICAL HEBREW

I will not linger here on details that are easy to find in specialized works. Suffice it to say that, within the Hamito-Semitic family, Hebrew belongs to the western branch, whose northern part, Canaanite, the mother of Hebrew, also includes Moabite, Phoenician, and others, all extinct since time immemorial. The beginnings of Hebrew are thus the very modest ones of a Semitic language among other Semitic languages, used in a scant territory by a limited number of speakers. It has had ample opportunity to disappear altogether and for good. And despite what was thought and written in retrospect by learned worshippers of the mythic uniqueness of Hebrew as a sacred language, there was nothing inevitable about it becoming what it became, except the fact of being linked so closely to the special fate of a small and stiff-necked nation.

There exists no written corpus of pre-Biblical Hebrew, that is, the period between the twentieth and the twelfth century B.C. But we possess many hundreds of toponyms and isolated words, transcribed in Akkadian and Egyptian syllabaries and clearly belonging to a stage of Hebrew close to Canaanite. It is sometimes called Amorite, from the Akkadian word *amurru*, "west," by which the Akkadians, who were originally located in the east of the Semitic domain, designated the western branch. Other important evidence of pre-Biblical Hebrew dates back to the beginning of the fourteenth century B.C. These are documents recently discovered three hundred kilometers from Cairo, the glosses of Tell el'Amarna, that is, some eighty translations in Hebrew attached to letters addressed by the pharaohs Amenophis III and Amenophis IV to their legates or allies in Canaan. Apparently, the Hebrew-speaking scribe noted in the margins the exact Hebrew translations of Akkadian terms when he was not sure of their meanings.

These documents reveal an archaic form of Hebrew that possessed, in particular, the marks of declension for nouns (almost absent from Biblical Hebrew), a more elaborate system of expressing the dual than found in later Hebrew (where the plural extends to many nouns formerly liable to take on a dual form), and more varied conjugations than those of Biblical Hebrew. Thus, Hebrew seems to have lived a very long history.

BIBLICAL HEBREW, LIKE ANY OTHER LANGUAGE: CONTINUITY, CHANGES, DIALECTS, BORROWINGS
The Golden Age of Biblical Hebrew

The composition of the books that constitute the major monument of ancient Hebrew, that is, the Bible itself, extends over a significant period of time, but we may assume that, except for the Song of Deborah (Judges 5), probably going back to before the year 1000 B.C., the majority was written beginning in the second half of the ninth century B.C. The classical age of biblical literature lasted until the end of the seventh century B.C.: it was then that the fundamental text, the Pentateuch, was fixed, the books of Joshua, Judges, Samuel, and Kings were written, and the prophecies of Amos, Hosea, and the first chapters of Isaiah collected. As for the more recent Biblical texts, they appeared no later than the sixth century B.C. The language in which all this was written reflects current usage for the Hebrews, but the literary form of it. The Hebrews used the spoken variant of this language itself. The Bible bears witness to this fact in many spots, for example, when the Aramaean Laban and the Hebrew Jacob seal a pact, made concrete by a monument defining linguistic territories. Another passage is the one in which spies, dispatched to Jericho by Joshua before the city is taken and the land of Canaan conquered, converse without difficulty with Rahab. Still another passage occurs when the Gibeonites easily make themselves understood by Joshua.

Historical Development, Dialectical Diversification, Borrowings

Thus, for at least eight centuries, and no doubt much longer, Hebrew was a spoken language in the fullest sense of the word. That does not mean, especially given so much time, that Hebrew did not experience many changes, like any language, as well as the corollaries to these changes, that is, dialectical differentiations between territories. One in particular developed very early and became more pronounced by the split in Solomon's realm at the time of his death in 931 B.C., a split brought on by the deep-rooted antagonism between northern and southern tribes that resulted in two monarchies being respectively established in these two zones, that is, Judah (with Jerusalem) and Israel. Often-cited biblical evidence for dialectical differentiations in Hebrew is found in Judges 12:6, where, during the course of the war that sets them against each other, the Ephraimites, recognized at the Jordan River crossing by the people of Gilead simply by their pronunciation of *s* instead of *sh* at the beginning of the word *sibboleth*, are slain one-by-one by the latter. During the long life of Hebrew, another phenomenon influences the evolution of its form and the division into distinct dialects, a phenomenon completely natural to a living language: borrowing from neighboring languages, that is, Akkadian (and, through Akkadian, Sumerian), Pharaonic Egyptian, and also, although to a much lesser extent than in a later phase of Hebrew's fate, Aramaic.

Hebrew was not only spoken, it was also written. For that, it used an outgrowth of the system that the Assyrians adopted about seven centuries before Christ, that is, the square Aramaic alphabet that replaced the hieroglyphic writing system in cuneiforms they had abandoned. The Aramaic alphabet noted only consonants, two of which (*w* and *y*) were nevertheless used often to represent the long vowels *u* and *i*, in addition to their consonantal use. This is the alphabet that is used today, resorting only in particular cases (in the whole biblical text, as well as when there is some ambiguity) to the notations for short vowels established in the ninth and tenth centuries A.D., at the same time as various other phonetic signs, by the Massorets of the Tiberian school in order to guide the cantillation of the sacred texts and prayers. Current orthography multiplies even these *matres lectionis,* that is, these "mothers of reading," so that the waw (*w*) and the yod (*y*) are used when they note vowels, since they make the reading of an old Semitic language easier in which, as in Arabic, it is not customary to write the vowels.

THE BEGINNING OF THE END: BABYLONIAN EXILE AND ITS LINGUISTIC CONSEQUENCES
The Taking of Jerusalem and Exile

We will briefly review some well-known historical facts, the consequences of which are clearly essential to the fate of Hebrew. Too weak to achieve political independence in the face of the conflict that set its two powerful neighbors against each other, the realm of Judah oscillated dangerously between an Egyptian and a Babylonian alliance. In 600 B.C., Jehoiakim thought he could take advantage of a Babylonian setback by revolting against the tutelage of Nebuchadnezzar II. The latter retaliated by marching on Jerusalem, which he took in 597 B.C.

The royal family, the aristocracy, the priests, and the wealthy property owners of Judah were taken away as captives to Babylon. Ten years later, King Zedekiah, who attempted to raise a coalition against the Babylonians, was crushed by them, and this time Jerusalem was razed, the temple was destroyed, and a new deportation followed (see Briant 1996, 56).

Returning from Captivity in the Company . . . of Aramaic

Now the language that reigned in Babylonia was no longer Akkadian. Its two forms, Assyrian in the north and Babylonian in the south, were in the process of being eclipsed by Aramaic, despite the brilliance of Nebuchadnezzar II's reign. The trend toward Aramaic continued after the taking of Babylon in 539 B.C. by Cyrus the Great's Persian troops, whom the population, tired of Nabonidus's impieties, probably welcomed as liberators. But most importantly, Cyrus, having formed an alliance with the God of Israel, according to the *Deutero-Isaiah*, issued a decree shortly after his victory over the Babylonians. He ordered the return of the Judeans to their fatherland, the rebuilding of the Jerusalem temple, and the restitution of gold and silver utensils that had been taken by Nebuchadnezzar. Beginning in 538 B.C., the first convoy of exiles returned to Jerusalem, at the expense of the Babylonian Jews. In 520 B.C., at the beginning of the reign of Darius I, a new contingent returned from captivity. We know about these facts through the biblical book of Ezra (1 and 6:2–12), named after the priest and sacrificer who succeeded Nehemiah.

Nehemiah was promoted to governor of Judea in the middle of the fifth century B.C. by Artaxerxes I. Nehemiah raised the wall of Jerusalem again, and carried out important reforms. Ezra continued his work, and they both played prominent roles in the history of Judaism as restorers of the religion and authors of the definitive form of Mosaic law, as the current Pentateuch records it. Ezra's restoration also attempted to expand the use of the Hebrew language to the detriment of Aramaic. But this was in vain. Actually, the sixty years in captivity had increased Aramaic's presence even more among the Hebrews, where it had been present for a long time before they lost their independence. The Babylonian exiles had returned to Jerusalem in the company of Aramaic.

Aramaic's Fortune

The Persian victors did not attempt to impose their language upon the vast territories they conquered. Paradoxically, the reign of Aramaic was so well established that those who took over were not tempted to replace it with anything: from Sardes to the Iranian plateau, from Egypt to Babylonia, and even in Persepolis, the satrapic chancelleries had no choice but to resort to local scribes, and among these scribes, the lingua franca in a multilingual situation was Aramaic almost everywhere. The Persians could not communicate directly in Persian with all their citizens. Achaemenid offices were thus obliged to lean on the elite and local traditions (see Briant 1996, 88).

How strange and brilliant is the destiny of Aramaic. A language close to Canaanite, together they form one of the two northern branches of the western Semitic languages. Even though it was a language of the vanquished, that is, of the Aramaic realms that Sargon destroyed at the end of the eighth century B.C., a century later, having supplanted Akkadian, it became the language of interactions throughout the Assyrian empire, its conqueror! Originally nomads and merchants of the vast areas north of Arabia as far as Syria-Palestine and Babylonia, the Aramaeans, who spread everywhere throughout the Near East, became officials and civil servants for the Akkadians. Later, they did the same for the Persian empire, to the point that one could speak of an "Aramaic empire" despite dialectical differentiations, an empire that borrowed its share of administrative vocabulary from Persian, it is true. Thus, Aramaic long dominated a large part of the Near East as the language of power, even though it no longer had any political authority, not to mention its own Aramaic state!

POST-EXILE HEBREW AND THE INFLUENCE OF ARAMAIC
Hebrew and Aramaic

Any attentive observer could note the resemblance between Hebrew and Aramaic. "*Vicina est Chaldaeorum lingua sermoni hebraico,*" Saint Jerome wrote in the fourth century A.D. Adopting the Aramaic alphabet to transcribe Hebrew heightened this impression of closeness. The system of sounds presented clear similarities as well as noticeable differences. The vocabulary sprang from identical roots, and phonetic correspondences, when they were not identical, were consistent enough to strike the ear of a knowledgeable speaker and often to allow any minimally adept candidate for bilingualism to guess the Aramaic word from the Hebrew word, and vice versa. The forms of conjugation and personal pronouns revealed many resemblances between the languages. In many cases, it is hard to determine if the formal and semantic relationship between a Hebrew word and an Aramaic word is due to a borrowing or shared origin. Since Aramaic was a neighboring language that had become the lingua franca of a powerful empire, this closeness between the two idioms was probably a factor that increased Aramaic's pressure in the capital city, to which the Jewish elite found themselves deported.

The Pressure of Aramaic

Actually, long before their exile, the Hebrews in the north and northeast of their territory had already been in close contact with Aramaic, the vernacular language for many neighboring populations. Archeology reveals the presence of Aramaic in Palestine itself as early as the ninth century B.C. (see Hadas-Lebel 1976, 95). In 721 B.C., the Assyrians' conquest of Samaria, the capital of the realm of Israel, had led to the arrival of an Aramaic-speaking population to replace a portion of the Israelites, victims of a first exile in the Assyrian empire before the one that struck Judah in 597 B.C. In 701 B.C., delegates from Hezekiah, held in Jerusalem by Sennacherib, king of Assur, had addressed the Assyrian general in Aramaic to negotiate ransom payment.

It was not only the Jewish elite deported to Babylonia who soon acquired total use of Aramaic, the unofficial official language of the empire, to the point that the Hebrew of the exile prophets, like Ezekiel, is riddled with Aramaic influences. Beyond that, the masses remaining in Judea offered only weak resistance to the strong pressure of Aramaic, spoken by a large population. The Bible echoes this situation: "half of their children speak in Ashdod [= Aramaic] and they cannot speak in Judean" (Nehemiah 13:24).

Post-Exile Biblical Literature; Hebrew Spoken After the Return from Captivity and the Restoration

We know that parts of chapters 4 (6–8, 18) and 7 (12–26) in the book of Ezra, as well as chapters 2, 4–7, and 28 in the book of Daniel, are written in Aramaic. But the Hebrew of the post-exile books of the Bible, which can be called late Biblical Hebrew, is itself permeated with Aramaic elements. Generally we classify as post-exile literature the parts of the Bible recording or commenting on events following the captivity and return: the books of Haggai and Zachariah, prophets of the restoration, as well as the prophetic books of Daniel, Joel, Obadiah, Jonah, Malachia, and the end of Isaiah (chapters 55–66), but also the historical books of Ruth, Ezra, Nehemiah, Esther, Chronicles, and, finally, the poetic books of Song of Solomon, Qoheleth (= Ecclesiastes), Job, Proverbs, and most of Psalms (see Hadas-Lebel 1976, 95). One criterion all these books share, as compared with earlier parts of the Bible, is that they are written by authors for whom Biblical Hebrew does not seem to be the spoken language. Thus, we find in Esther and in Jonah a clear attempt to compensate for the influx of new terms by the overzealous imitation of the syntax and style of earlier Hebrew. The same is true, although to a lesser extent, for the book of Nehemiah, as well as for the books of Ezra and Daniel.

It is interesting to compare the text of Chronicles with the passages from the books of Samuel and Kings that it directly follows: it is in the differences between Chronicles and these two books that we can detect the effort to adapt to speakers who no longer use the Hebrew of the great classical books. This shows how far the spoken language has probably evolved. Ecclesiastes and Song of Solomon also seem to reflect popular Hebrew in the period following the exile, as well as Aramaic's influence, which is a characteristic of the new form of Hebrew. Not only can we observe numerous borrowings from the vocabulary, but the very word order in the sentence is altered according to the Aramaic model, which itself serves as an intermediary for introducing into Hebrew Akkadian words that Aramaic borrowed, as well as a few Persian words.

MISHNAIC HEBREW

A Stage in the History of Spoken Hebrew

The facts here are well known and well studied (see, for example, Segal 1927 and Hadas-Lebel 1976). I will repeat only that, following post-exile Hebrew, the Hebrew called Mishnaic is named for the Mishnah (from *shanah*, "to repeat" [speech, for oral transmission]), the large collection of commentaries, devoted to the ways of applying the written Law. The first components of the Mishnah date far back, certainly to at least the third century B.C. The choice and organization of the texts, attributed to Juda HaNassi, date from the end of the second century B.C., as does the fixed version that served as the basis for new commentaries compiled — in Aramaic — in the two great spiritual monuments of Judaism, that is, the Babylonian and the Jerusalem Talmud. It is likely that, at least in Judea if not in Galilee, Mishnaic Hebrew was the vernacular language. We can infer this from details in the post-exile books. Thus it represents another stage in the historical development that begins with Biblical Hebrew and continues through post-exile Hebrew. Nevertheless, rather than the successor of Biblical Hebrew properly speaking, which is a literary language, Mishnaic Hebrew must be considered heir to the form of the language the Hebrews spoke before the Babylonian exile.

Religious reverence for Biblical Hebrew and general ignorance about the natural development of languages made rabbis and Jewish scholars long believe that Mishnaic Hebrew was an invention of the Talmudists, not corresponding to any language actually in use. Of course, not everyone shared that opinion. For example, the great Spanish philosopher and doctor of the twelfth century, Maimonides, in his *Commentary on the Mishnah*, affirms that Mishnaic Hebrew was very much a spoken language. But he was an exception, and the theory of Mishnaic Hebrew's artificiality was for a long time the authoritative one.

We can consider only one of the counterarguments here: Biblical Hebrew offers two forms for the first person singular pronoun (not interchangeable, actually, if the facts are carefully examined): *anokhi* and *ani.* The second becomes dominant in later Biblical Hebrew; it is used exclusively in Mishnaic Hebrew. If Mishnaic Hebrew was an artificial language, by what criterion would the rabbis have decided to retain only one of the two forms? Thus it is difficult to maintain that Mishnaic Hebrew was not a spoken language. We can be certain, however, that it was not the only language spoken. Aramaic was spoken at least as much among the Hebrews, not without consequences for the form of the Hebrew language.

The Mishnaic Language, Aramaicized Form of Hebrew

The long and continual contact between the two languages had the effect of allowing Aramaicisms to flourish in Mishnaic Hebrew. Vocabulary borrowings are numerous, or else, in some cases, a word or a meaning rarely used in the Bible was reactivated if Aramaic possessed commonly used equivalents. In morphology, Mishnaic Hebrew certainly did not go so far as to adopt that peculiarity typical of Aramaic that consists of placing the article after the noun. Nevertheless, according to the Aramaic model (but with words uniquely native), it created two grammatical instruments almost unknown in Biblical Hebrew: first, *she,* a relative pronoun and subordinate conjunction that replaced the *asher* of Biblical Hebrew; and second, *shel,* a connective equivalent to the English *of,* as in *the book of the child,* and made up, according to a transparent formulation, of *she* ("which") and *l(e)* ("[is] to/of"), that is, *the book of the child = the book which is the child's.* This connective *shel* must have prospered in Hebrew's long history; today it is one of the most common grammatical tools in Israeli Hebrew.

WHEN DID HEBREW STOP BEING SPOKEN?

This question is no less complex than the question of Latin's demise (see chapter 5). I will try to answer it with those means at our disposal.

In What Language Did Yehoshua of Nazareth (= Jesus) Express Himself?

In the first century A.D., was Mishnaic Hebrew still spoken? Had the language that served the Hebrews since the Babylonian exile at least, over nearly five and a half centuries, been replaced? Didn't a great number of the Hebrews henceforth speak Aramaic? Did they still speak Hebrew in Judea, where Jewish life had returned to its course after the captivity? And, in any case, hadn't the provinces located farther north, Samaria and Galilee, been repopulated by Aramaic-speaking communities after the deportation to Babylonia and before 100 B.C., when Galilee was reabsorbed into the Hasmonean realm and allowed to become Jewish again? In what language did Yehoshua of Nazareth speak? Today it is agreed that he spoke in Aramaic. The texts seem to state this clearly: the words uttered during the miracles (Mark 5:41 and 7:34), and likewise the invocation to God at the moment when the crucified one is about to die (Mark 15:34), are reported by the evangelists in Aramaic. To this evidence is added that of liturgical practice, that is, the targums, or commentaries, spoken in Aramaic during synagogue readings. But we do not know the age of this practice or if, in Palestine, it was meant for the faithful in regions where only Aramaic was spoken or for Babylonian communities established in Jerusalem, rather than for Judeans who no longer knew Hebrew.

The First Century A.D.: Mishnaic Hebrew-Aramaic Bilingualism Among the Majority of Hebrews; Mishnaic Hebrew-Aramaic-Greek Trilingualism Among the Urbanized Elite

Bilingualism of the Masses

That is why it is most likely that a bilingual situation ruled in Judea in the first century A.D.: Aramaic-Hebrew, at least for the great majority of the population. And this situation probably dated back to the last third of the sixth century B.C. It must have lasted until the beginning of the second century A.D. (see below with regard to Bar Kokhba). Aramaic aside, it is clear that what was spoken was an evolved form of Mishnaic Hebrew, as compared with what was spoken five centuries earlier following the exile. Yehoshua of Nazareth, like most Jews of his time, most likely spoke such Hebrew, as well as Aramaic. This man, who was not without culture, may even have spoken a third language too, then present in Palestine.

The Hellenization of the Elite and Trilingualism

Actually, the most educated of the Hebrews were quite Hellenized and knew Greek. Of course, at first, that is, after Alexander's conquest of the Persian empire and the death of Darius III in 330 B.C., religious barriers had kept the Hebrews relatively isolated from the Greek world. But the Hellenization of pagan peoples surrounding Jewish territory on all sides finally spread to the Jews, too, where at least the elite were in constant contact with Greek settlers brought to Samaria by Alexander much earlier. Loathing for gymnasium practices in light of traditional Judaism had given way in the cities to adopting certain Greek customs linked to the life of theater and athletics. Among the Hebrews of higher society, a good knowledge of Greek became common, and even some familiarity with Greek rhetoric, traces of which we find in the Mishnah. This collection contains more than five hundred Greek words. As for the Jerusalem Talmud, according to recent estimates, it contains up to eleven hundred of them. Mishnaic Hebrew borrows heavily from the Greek, and a portion of these phonetically Hebraicized Greek words have been retained in Israeli Hebrew. Just to give a few examples: *avir* ("air"), *teatron* ("theater"), *dugma* ("example").

The Maccabees' Brief Surge of Anti-Hellenism

Nevertheless, it is true that, from 167 to 134 B.C., the Maccabees revolted against the Hellenization policy of the Seleucid king of Syria, Antiochus IV Epiphanes, who wanted to impose Greek culture on his states, among them Palestine. For the Jews, that meant participating in the religious rituals of Hellenism. Adopting them together with the Greek language that expressed them meant renouncing monotheism and the Mosaic law. Revealingly, the Maccabees associated defending the Torah with promoting Biblical Hebrew. In about the same period, the Essens adopted the same ideal. Their purist language came to light with the discovery of the so-called Dead Sea Scrolls in 1947–1956, found in the Qumran caves in the Judean desert.

Still, in the struggle between a return to the sources and modernist temptations, the latter often win. Once they obtained national independence, the friends of Hellenism took control again under the kings of the next (sacerdotal!) dynasty, the Hasmoneans, who loved to adopt Greek names, just like many affluent Jews, who, moreover, often used the Greek version of the Bible (the Septuagint). The movement only became stronger under Roman domination, Latin thus remaining isolated as the language of the foreign power, and in this epoch and context, paradoxically, Romanization appearing on many fronts as an instrument of Hellenization. We can understand the reasons for this (see chapter 8).

Judeo-Aramaic

Thus, in the first century A.D., at least a part of the Hebrew population was trilingual. And among those who did not know Greek, especially present in the cities, the majority were bilingual. The Aramaic spoken by the Jews, which could be called Judeo-Aramaic, coincides neither with the principal dialects then present among Aramaic populations nor with the Aramaic of the empire that Achaemenian authority had promoted and that still existed in the Roman period. It was a Hebraicized Aramaic in its phonetics as well as in certain aspects of its syntax. Tradition considers Aramaic or, more precisely, its Hebraicized form, as a language belonging to the Jews, and thus views it with sympathy and respect. Nevertheless, this favorable opinion is not unanimous. Some cannot forget that the moment that Aramaic was superimposed on Hebrew—six centuries before it would supplant it—corresponds to a tragic episode in Jewish history, the exile. Thus, the Talmud of Babylon (Baba Qama treatise, 82) attributes the following quote to a compiler of the Mishnah, Juda HaNassi (see above), who was born during the revolt of Bar Kokhba: "Of what use to us is the language of the Syrians in the land of Israel? Either the sacred language, or Greek!"

The Destruction of the Second Temple and
the Beginning of the Dispersion

The tactlessness of Roman authority, and harassment linked to imperialism under Titus in a Palestine divided into three parts since the death of Herod provoked a nationalist and messianic uprising in A.D. 66 that resulted in the first Jewish war, ending tragically, as we know, for Judea. Admittedly, the Zealots, the last resisting Jews, still held the Romans in check in the fortress of Masada until A.D. 73. But we can easily imagine how the destruction of the second temple in A.D. 70 by Titus's legions, putting an end to the existence of a state that had embodied a passion for independence, was a serious blow for the Hebraic language, at the same time as it signaled the dispersion of the Hebrews (in the sense that this term is commonly used, even though there were other dispersions earlier, like the two exiles from Israel and Judah). Despite the defeat of 70 A.D., as the oppressed Jews set out on their long and irreversible journey, their language briefly regained its value as the tongue that expressed the fate of their nation. We are speaking of the second Jewish war, that is, the episode of Bar Kokhba.

The Revolt of Bar Kokhba and the Last Known
Words Belonging to Living Mishnaic Hebrew

Mishnaic Hebrew and Aramaic in the School of Yabneh

During the siege of Jerusalem in A.D. 70, a highly respected rabbi, Rabbi Johanan ben Zakkai, had managed to persuade Titus to create a school in Yabneh, near the coast, where the Jewish people, scattered but sustained by faith and spiritual vigor, rebuilt a sort of national and religious center, directed by a patriarch, head of the Jewish community in Palestine, and soon recognized by the Romans. Other communities formed in Babylonia and Alexandria. Mishnaic Hebrew and Judeo-Aramaic continued to thrive there as expressions of Jewish existence. But less than thirty-five years after the fall of Jerusalem and the destruction of the second temple, all these centers rose up against Roman oppression.

The Revolt of Bar Kokhba and the Letters in Hebrew

Violent repression could not prevent a revolt from breaking out once again in Palestine in 132, during Emperor Hadrian's reign, led by Simon Bar Kokhba. With the support of the rabbis, Bar Kokhba proclaimed the restoration of independence and the Jewish state, promoted the Hebrew language, freed numerous cities, and even began to mint coins. Excavations done at Wadi Murrabaat in the Judean desert southeast of Jerusalem in 1952 brought to light many legal actions contemporary with the second Jewish war. Five of them are in Hebrew; all the others are in Aramaic. But a dozen letters from this same period were also discovered, all written in Hebrew, two of them by the head of the insurrection. Fifteen letters by Bar Kokhba were discovered in Nahal Bever (Israel) in 1960, five of which were composed in Hebrew, eight in Aramaic, and two in Greek.

Whatever the reasons for this choice, the fact remains that Bar Kokhba and the Jewish nationalists of his staff knew how to read and write in three languages, and Hebrew was still used. It was even common everyday Hebrew, detailing a chief's instructions to his lieutenants on various concrete aspects of the operations under way. Nevertheless, it is interesting that the language of these documents is less Aramaicized than usual, demonstrating an effort to move closer to the classical norm of Hebrew. It is possible that we must see this phenomenon in relationship to the strong messianic undercurrents of the insurrection, divinely inspired, according to a famous rabbi, Rabbi Aqiba (killed during this war).

The Talmud, Aramaic, and the End of Mishnaic Hebrew

Bar Kokhba's revolt was finally crushed in A.D. 135. The Jews were then cruelly persecuted and banished from Jerusalem. Persecution ceased under Hadrian's successors. Supported by the moral authority of the patriarch of Yabneh, the doctors of the Law continued to compile religious works. But henceforth they did so in Aramaic. The same was true in Mesopotamia, which, under the authority of an exilarch, became the center for Judaic spiritual life after the Christianization of the Roman Empire by Constantine in 325. In subjugated Palestine, the Christianization was followed by persecution of the Jews and finally by the abolition of the patriarchate by Theodosius II in A.D. 415. In order to keep religious teachings alive, the scholars deemed it necessary to devote themselves to studying commentaries on the Law through a careful comparative examination of the formulations of all the rules. A long period of intense work followed, lasting until the sixth century A.D. And the language in which they wrote this learned and pious book — called the Talmud (*talmud tora* = "study of the law") — was quite naturally Aramaic. Hebrew ceased to exist as a spoken language. It had ceded its place to Aramaic, notably because of the concentration of Aramaic-speaking Jews in Jerusalem from the eastern diaspora (see Segal 1927, Introduction).

In the Jerusalem Talmud, which takes up the problem of languages many times (thus, in the Pe'ah treatise, 1, the study of Greek literature is authorized, although with reservations), it is clear that Hebrew is considered a sacred language, for liturgical use only, and is not spoken in daily life (see especially Sota treatise). Here, of course, one means Biblical Hebrew. But with the collapse of Bar Kokhba's revolt, Mishnaic Hebrew itself had become a literary language, its oral use in constant decline. Throughout the history of Israel we can see that maintaining or reclaiming a spoken Hebrew, in any stage of its evolution, has always been closely linked to maintaining political independence, that is, to the struggle for Jewish identity and national recognition. Here, the disappearance of the ancestral language goes hand in hand with the loss of the state.

Jewish Languages, the Death of Hebrew in Oral Use, and Its Preservation in Literature

ARAMAIC, THE BIRTH OF JEWISH LANGUAGES, AND THE STATUS OF HEBREW IN THE DIASPORA

The Decline of Aramaic Beginning in the Eighth Century, and Its Survival Today, After Three Thousand Years of Resisting Death

Following the Arab conquest at the beginning of the seventh century A.D., the status of Aramaic in Palestine, as well as in Syria and Mesopotamia, was turned on its head. The Hebrews were not alone in gradually abandoning it, since, according to an irreversible trend, the same thing happened among numerous populations that had it as their mother tongue or used it as a lingua franca. Thus, at least insofar as its Western dialects are concerned, Aramaic began a phase of decline that staggers the imagination when you consider its prestige in the East for more than thirteen centuries.

Nevertheless, although it does not present that exceptional scenario—Hebrew's alone—of a dead idiom coming back to life, the history of Aramaic is no less unique. This language, along with Chinese, is one of the oldest still alive (if we exclude Coptic, which is no longer used orally, and Greek, which has undergone significant changes), and continues to be spoken today in two places. First, by about two hundred thousand people in the mountain regions that form the eastern extremities of its northern domain. There called eastern neo-Aramaic, or neo-Syriac, this group of dialects has been preserved, though greatly transformed of course, among Uniate, Nestorian, and Jacobite communities in the district of Tur'Abdin in Iraq, and around the lake of Urmia in Persia. Second, a western neo-Aramaic still exists in three Syrian villages in the Anti-Lebanon mountains, thirty kilometers northeast of Damascus.

Jewish Languages in the Countries of the Levant After the Arab Conquest

In Palestine, Mesopotamia, and Egypt, after the Arab conquest (seventh century A.D.), the Jews continued to live according to their Law and customs, but Arabic, imposing itself more and more in their daily existence, finally replaced Aramaic as well as Greek, where it was in use.

Jewish Languages in Europe and the Maghreb
Jewish Languages in Africa, Spain, and Other Countries of the Diaspora

The Jewish communities, scattered throughout Gaul, Germania, and Iberia, where Jews fled after the destruction of the second temple, joined those established in these territories at the end of the Roman Republic, and even in Rome. In Rome the Jews, who dominated the important sea trade of grains and olive oil with Africa (Tunisia today), owned homes in the area of Mount Coelius, between the Coliseum and the Appian Way (see Hagège 2003, 306). Hebrew remained the religious language of all the Diaspora, but, for nearly nineteen centuries, the Jews ceased to speak it. They adopted the languages of the "host" countries. Later, the communities expelled by the Catholic kings of Castille and Aragon in 1492 did likewise. Forced into exile and flight due to the Inquisition, the Jews in Spain, and those later in Portugal, found refuge in various places: North Africa, Holland, southern France, Italy, Bosnia, Greece, and Turkey. In some of these countries they retained their Judeo-Spanish language (Judezmo).

Judeo-Languages

Judezmo is one of the specific languages, called Jewish languages or Judeo-languages, that were formed in most of the countries of the *galut* (Diaspora). These languages are studied as a special chapter in linguistics, since they are of interest as illustrations of the hybridization phenomenon: all of them, actually, are composed of the local language or the language adopted in exile as the base, but with a more or less significant lexical contribution of Hebrew and, to some extent, Aramaic. Today these languages are in a precarious situation (see chapter 8). The Hebraic contributions found in all of them attest to the powerful fascination of Hebrew. Long after it disappeared as a living language, it continued to exert its hold through borrowings, facilitated by continual contact with the biblical texts among the more religious Jews.

Besides the Jewish languages, calque languages even developed, the works of devout literati. One or another of the languages of the Diaspora provide their vocabulary, while the syntax and morphology are modeled on Hebrew, with astonishing results. The Judeo-Spanish calque, or Ladino, is a well-known example of this. We are not talking about Judezmo, a spoken language, but about the Hebraicized Spanish — not spoken though transmitted orally — of the Bibles used by the Jews after their expulsion from Spain. The rabbis' goal in transferring the Hebrew text onto a Gentile language was, here as always, to prevent the holy language from falling irrevocably into obscurity among Jews threatened with losing their Judaism, who no longer spoke anything other than the idioms of the various nations.

Latin and Continuity / Hebrew and Rupture

To put into relief, on the one hand, all these efforts by rabbis to maintain at least a trace of Hebrew, and, on the other hand, the way in which Judeo-languages are constituted and the materials upon which they are built, we must recognize a completely exceptional phenomenon for which we find no examples in the history of Romance languages or of Greek. In those cases, there really is continuity. French or Spanish, even while no longer being Latin, are products of Latin's evolution. Modern Greek is a product of the evolution of ancient Greek, even though the distance between them is important. On the contrary, in the case of Hebrew, the dramatic events that began with the Babylonian exile and that continued, 667 years later, with the destruction of the second temple, resulted in an interruption in the life process. The chain was broken. Hebrew (spoken Hebrew) disappeared. Other languages replaced it. Its liturgical use further increased its inaccessibility as a language of prestige. It was not even partially present through heirs. It was impossible to imagine how it could be revived . . .

MEDIEVAL HEBREW

Biblical Hebrew, Mishnaic Hebrew, Medieval Hebrew, Modern Hebrew

What the tradition calls medieval Hebrew cannot be considered a new stage in the history of Hebrew without confusing the oral reality of languages with the somewhat artificial nature of their literary use. The Hebrew of biblical times possessed a spoken form as well as a written one. Mishnaic Hebrew was also as much a spoken language as a written one, even if the last stages of its oral use did not allow the integration of the many innovations by Jewish authors throughout the centuries, as a living language usually does. Finally, Israeli Hebrew, a contemporary language, is as much spoken as written. On the contrary, medieval Hebrew exists only as a written language. It is a purely bookish idiom in which the literati, even while establishing the Bible and the Mishnah as models to imitate, introduced many scientific or poetic words. These words corresponded to no living reality, to no spontaneous speech, but were meant only to satisfy stylistic and aesthetic needs, often through imitating languages of the Diaspora, Spanish, Arabic, German, etc. The literary genre called *piyyut*, which designated religious poems in a mannered style, is the chief illustration of this activity. But the literati wrote treatises in prose as well: works of geography, philosophy, grammar, and science. These works will spark unexpected interest: they will be used in the methodical enterprise to be discussed later.

Hebrew in the Literature of the Diaspora
Until the Eighteenth Century

Tradition applies the notion of medieval Hebrew not only to the language of Jewish authors in the Middle Ages, but also to that of subsequent eras, up to the nineteenth century. To add to this inaccuracy is another problem: even though we are speaking of a purely written language and hence one that is less susceptible to evolution, the authors' styles, varying with the periods, offer quite a wide range, making it difficult to apply a single qualifier, especially "medieval."

After A.D. 70, Hebraic literature was scattered throughout many centers, among them Babylonia, Alexandria, Antioch, Athens, and Rome. Here certain names become famous, including the renegade historian Flavius Josephus and the philosopher Philo Judaeus. Much later, authors in the Islamic world — in Kairouan, Fez, Granada, and Cairo — wrote not only in Arabic but also in Hebrew. They produced works that would restore the language of the Bible, either by studying its sounds, like Judah ben David Hayyuj in the tenth century A.D., or by using it as material for lavish poems, like Judah Halevi in the twelfth century A.D., or for philosophical or grammatical treatises, like Avicebron (ibn Gabirol) and Abraham ibn Ezra, respectively, also of that same century, or again for esoteric works, like the Portuguese cabalist Isaac Abravanel of the fifteenth century.

Only a few names are cited here, as the point of this chapter is not to create an inventory, but to recognize certain milestones in the fate of Hebrew. The one under discussion here is famous for being an illustrious period for Hebrew as a literary language. In both Arabic and Hebrew, authors expressed their talent within the basically tolerant cultural framework of the Arab countries of the East and, above all, for nearly eight centuries until the Catholic reconquest, they participated in the intellectual and religious brilliance of Islamic Spain. This is the first golden age for Hebraic literature and language after the dispersion. But we cannot speak of a renaissance. Hebrew is still only a written language.

Hebrew and the Haskalah

Haskalah (from *sekhel*, "intelligence," "mind") is the name specialists give to the Jewish equivalent of what the West calls the Enlightenment, that is, a flourishing of brilliant thinkers, called (from the same root) *maskilim*. Through the late eighteenth and the nineteenth centuries, these thinkers, inspired by German, French, and English philosophers from earlier generations, furthered a renaissance of Jewish culture by striving to open it up to the values of European civilization without betraying the historic traditions of Judaism. Understandably, the question of the Hebrew language particularly captured the minds of the *maskilim*. M. Mendelssohn, and especially his friends, joined with N. H. Wessely to found the first Hebraic literary periodical, *Ha-me'assef* ("The Anthologist") in 1784. They drew inspiration from M. H. Luzzatto, whose early eighteenth century work had given Hebraic poetry a renewed beauty it had not known since the Spanish golden age. They proposed adapting Hebrew to modern times in order to make it an instrument capable of expressing secular knowledge.

They intended to reduce the sacred aura surrounding the venerable language of the Bible, precisely to allow it to "revive," at least in writing, by enabling it to express more than religious and liturgical realities. But paradoxically, in rejecting the *pilpul* (sophistry) of rabbinical argumentation, they embraced the pure language of the prophets. Nevertheless, the *maskilim* were not just imitators of biblical style, like the fifth century A.D. imitators of Virgil's Latin, Claudian, or Saint-Avit, or, much later in France, the authors of Latin poetical works, J.-B. Santeul in the late seventeenth century or M. de Polignac in the early eighteenth. On the contrary, the *maskilim* wanted to modernize the Hebrew lexicon. But they restricted themselves to the Bible, with its obviously limited vocabulary, even though Mishnaic Hebrew could have provided fodder for neology. Lacking a sufficient number of words given this limited corpus, the *maskilim* invented a great number of compound expressions, unwieldy enough to make us smile today, as will be described below. The stiff manner of these well-intentioned men is derisively called *melitsa* ("[style that cultivates the] figure of rhetoric").

At least the *maskilim* demonstrated an essential principle, even if their application of it was clumsy: by constructing new words, it is possible to adapt a very old language, long fallen out of oral use, to modern realities. As we shall see, this lesson will not be forgotten, even though for the *maskilim*, the revival of Hebrew was not an end in itself (see Zuckermann 2003).

Written Hebrew Beginning in the Mid-Nineteenth Century

The *maskilim* had emulators in many countries of the Diaspora, and especially in Russia. Many writers used their talents to produce works celebrating the high points of ancient Jewish history. In the mid-nineteenth century, the Hebraic press was represented by many titles, and, at the end of that same century, one writer, M. L. Lilienblum, advocated a national renaissance. Others, like Mendele Moykher-Sforim, often considered the father of modern Hebraic literature, dared to tackle realities less flattering than ancient Israel, that is, the sad and picturesque life of the central European ghettos. The *maskilim* had wanted to disassociate themselves from such realities, which, in their eyes, symbolized backwardness and poverty. A whole host of remarkable writers then appeared, mostly with Russian or Ukrainian backgrounds, like S. Tchernikhovsky and especially H. N. Bialik, who enriched written Hebrew with powerful works in which the language, full of neologisms, reveals rare creativity.

Neither did the heirs to the *Haskalah* hesitate to denounce anti-Semitic oppression, and this denunciation was directly and logically linked to demands for national independence, although their inevitable consequences for the language were still not perceived. It is out of this rich soil that the ideology of Zionism grew, initially conceived as a doctrine of liberation for the Jewish people. The Zionists were hardly unanimous in considering Hebrew, hypothetically revived, as the necessary language for the Jews. It is particularly revealing that

T. Herzl, author of *The Jewish State*, the famous 1869 book that established the Zionist doctrine, only envisioned a multilingual solution, on the Swiss model, in which Hebrew did not play a part.

Hebrew: No Longer Living but Not Dead

We can understand the attitude of one faction of the Zionists, faced with the problem of language. Hebrew had not been spoken since the third century A.D. From this perspective, it could be said to be dead. But there is speech and there is language (*parole* and *langue;* see chapter 3). What is more, Hebrew was far from being dead in the sense that Sumerian or Akkadian were. It had long fallen out of ordinary use, no longer found its way into *parole*, but, nevertheless, Hebrew was hardly a petrified language, deprived of all life. A striking indication of its very special status is how new words and phrases never stopped being created in Hebrew, from the Middle Ages to the twentieth century, including the *Haskalah*. This neological creativity is explained by the fact that Hebrew required innovations, precisely because it so successfully functioned as a language of written exchange, not only between rabbis, but also between merchants (see Turniansky 1994, 420–421). Is it necessary to point out that it was used for bookkeeping, and over a very long time?

Hebrew would benefit from the new ideas of the late nineteenth century. In 1880, Lilienblum founded the "Lovers of Zion" movement, and among its followers were M. M. Dolitzki, N. H. Imber, D. Frischmann, and N. Sokolow, as well as writers, poets, literary critics, and journalists. It was closely connected to the socialist theories that flourished in central and eastern Europe at the end of the nineteenth century, and its followers created an intellectual atmosphere favorable to a crazy idea that no one until then had explicitly defended, even if some people dreamed of it without daring to imagine that implementing it was even possible: the rebirth of Hebrew. Thus all that was lacking was someone to make the dream a reality. This person existed. He listened. He read. He gathered information. He took part. He was ready to intervene. His name was Eliezer Ben-Yehuda.

The Resurrection of Hebrew

The resurrection of Hebrew is linked to the name of Ben-Yehuda. But we will see that the facts are not so simple and that there were others as well who played essential roles. We will also see how this man encountered deep hostility among certain Jewish circles.

BEN-YEHUDA'S INTUITION

Sacred Tranquillity and Profane Ferment

In 1858, when Eliezer Perelman, who would later take the name for which he became known, was born in Luzhky, Lithuania, the country was governed by functionaries of the czar. Thus Russian was one of the languages with which the child soon had contact, the others being Lithuanian, probably, and, of course, Yiddish, his mother tongue. He read Biblical Hebrew and Aramaic early, not only because he had a very quick mind and was burning with curiosity, but also because his uncle, who provided for his education, sent him to a Polotsk Talmudic school (now in Belorussia). The adolescent then retreated into the study of sacred texts and the maze of rabbinical interpretations. He even dreamed of making his own contribution to the scholarly exegeses, when he made an important acquaintance: he met a progressive rabbi. That was how a profane world opened to him, a world of secular Jewish authors and the literary, political, and social themes about which they wrote. He began to read these works voraciously.

But when his uncle learned that Eliezer was no longer content with the hermeneutics of the Talmud, he indignantly sent him packing (see Zananiri 1978, 4).

This early episode in Ben-Yehuda's life already reveals the choices he would be led to later on. Subsequent episodes are no less revealing. Welcomed into a family that favored assimilation as a means for the Jews to enlarge their field of possibilities, he then left to go to the governmental high school in Dünaburg (now Daugavpils, in Latvia), where, in an urban environment very different from the Polotsk yeshiva, he met other Jews pursuing a wide variety of paths, but he also met Christians.

The Jewish People, Hebrew, and National Independence: A Constant for a Thousand Years

Ben-Yehuda dreamed at one time of pursuing his studies at the University of Saint-Petersburg, and of becoming a professor, so that some day he could help emancipate young minds from submission to the oppressive power of the czar. But he soon became aware that, whether it was a matter of religious studies or profane literature, the environment in which he had grown up and the personality that he had developed made him entirely different from ordinary Russians. He was a Jew, who encountered and had to resolve problems specific to Jews. Thus, even while he shared the Russian intelligentsia's indignation during the Turkish-Bulgarian war in 1878, Ben-Yehuda, recently turned twenty, made a sudden discovery. The Jews needed the principle of emancipation that the intelligentsia wanted applied to oppressed peoples, the means to become free from foreign and usually burdensome authority. Since democracies fully approved and even encouraged the Greek, Armenian, and Bulgarian struggles for unity and independence since the early nineteenth century, why wouldn't they approve the Jewish struggle?

This intuition, which came to him in this same period, would guide his whole life. But restoring the nation could not be the only thing at stake. Restoring the language was intimately bound to it. And Ben-Yehuda took that step that others could not bring themselves to take because of their conception of the written language. By doing so, Ben-Yehuda was simply subscribing to the age-old logic of Jewish history. We saw it earlier with regard to the restoration of Nehemiah and Ezra, we saw it once again with the revolt of the Maccabees, and we saw it while reviewing the events that marked the Bar Kokhba insurrection. Always and everywhere among the children of Israel, attachment to Hebrew is linked to national independence or, if it is lacking, to the project of restoring it. Always and everywhere, the loss of freedom, or even worse, slavery, is accompanied or followed by forgetting Hebrew, and dispersion completes the work of weapons by killing the language. That was the situation after the destruction of the first temple, Solomon's temple, which incarnated the splendor of Judah. That was the situation once again when the second temple was destroyed in turn. This is Israel's fate: the language follows the nation; it dies with it. Thus, they can be reborn only jointly. Ben-Yehuda's Zionism was linguistic because it was political.

Thus, the link between restoring the nation and restoring the language was an early obsession for Ben-Yehuda. But this is not specific to Jews. In other cultures, the actions taken by restorers of the state have demonstrated the same link. After the Catholic kings came to complete their reconquest after the fall of the emirate of Cordoba in 1492, A. de Nebrija only reflected the monarchs' ideology when he wrote in his *Castilian Grammar*, published at that same time: "always, language accompanies power."

But what is peculiar in Ben-Yehuda's case is that restoring Hebrew, if it is associated with national identity and linked to a land, did not yet openly postulate political independence. The most pressing concern was the language. Ben-Yehuda was a Zionist. But, because he died in 1922, he could never know about the state of Israel. We can only guess that if he had been alive at the time of its creation, he would have considered it integral to the continuity of Jewish history. Nevertheless, let us add here a related consideration: Ben-Yehuda was interested in the Arabic language, and he recommended that many words be borrowed from it. He was intimately familiar with the great Jewish works of the golden age that were nurtured in Islamic countries opened to the flourishing of Jewish culture in the Middle Ages. We can presume that the modern methods of dealing with Arab populations in Palestine would have been hard for him to accept. But that is another argument.

BEGINNING TO TAKE ACTION BEFORE DEPARTING
The Stay in Paris and the Appeal

Ben-Yehuda conceived great plans in the springtime of his life. He was not yet twenty-one when he composed his *Appeal* to the Jewish people. The circumstances that pushed him were most unusual. He was in Paris, where he had come with the express intent to study medicine. Looking for great examples, he also encountered illustrious figures with their share of age and renown, like Victor Hugo. But he was disappointed by his reception among leading Jews, to whom he revealed his projects and who saw in him only a dreamer from the ghetto, like one of those meteors as quick to illuminate the night as to disappear. Now, at this time a dramatic episode would hasten the course of his life. In the cafés with his friends, where he remade the world and one day spoke in Hebrew for the first time, his only nourishment, besides his grandiose dreams, was a cup of tea. Worn out by overwork and poverty, he was diagnosed with tuberculosis, which resulted in the university not allowing him to proceed with his plans (G. Zuckermann, personal communication). He therefore began to study the principles for the formation of states. Renan's courses at the Collège de France on the transcendence of reason made an impression on him, as well as the meaning of the public good and the ideal of justice and social peace that he found in Gambetta, where he saw a model to follow, a sort of secular republic of the ancient Hebrew prophets. But there was no known cure for tuberculosis at the time, and the doctors did not hide their diagnosis from him. Ben-Yehuda thus decided he would not die before delivering his message to the world, the message contained in his *Appeal*. This piece was accepted by Smolenski, the editor of the Jewish Viennese monthly journal *Ha-Shahar*, generally inspired by the same ideas as the Haskalah in trying to help Jewish readers see the importance of being informed as well as increasing the number of devotees to the Hebrew language. Like his contemporaries, Smolenski could not go so far as to conceive the necessity, or even the possibility, of making Hebrew the spoken language of a restored Jewish nation. But he had an open mind, and he allowed Ben-Yehuda, then an unknown student, to express ideas that he "did not entirely share." The *Appeal* was published in 1879 under the title "An Important Question." This was the first act in the resurrection of Hebrew.

The Letter to Smolenski: 1880

Ben-Yehuda wrote an open letter to Smolenski from Algeria, where he had gone in hopes of recovering his health as well as to hear the Sephardic pronunciation of Hebrew, the only one faithful to the ancient language, unlike the Ashkenazic pronunciation of European

Jews. Smolenski published this letter in his journal in 1880. The main passage, where he exposes his credo, reads thus:

> Why have you arrived at the conclusion that Hebrew is a dead language, that it is useless for the arts and sciences, that it is only valuable for "subjects that touch upon the existence of Israel"? If I did not believe in the redemption of the Jewish people, I would have rejected Hebrew as a useless hindrance. I would have admitted that the Maskilim of Berlin were right in saying that Hebrew was only of interest as a bridge to the enlightenment. Having lost all hope of redemption, they could see no other use for this language. Because, sir, allow me to ask you what Hebrew can mean for a man who ceases to be Hebrew. What more does it represent for him than Latin or Greek? Why should he learn Hebrew or read its renaissance literature?
>
> It is insane to proclaim in loud voices, "Let us preserve Hebrew for fear that we will perish!" Hebrew can only exist if we make the nation revive and return it to the country of its ancestors. That is the only way to carry out this redemption that is never-ending. Without this solution we are lost, lost forever.
>
> [. . .] There is hardly any doubt that the Jewish religion will be able to survive, even in a foreign land. It will change its look according to the spirit of the time and place, and its destiny will be that of other religions. But the nation? The nation will only be able to live on its own soil, and it is on that land that it will regain its youth and that it will bear magnificent fruit, as in the past.

Ben-Yehuda's convictions are clear. It is useless to comment upon them further. Today, the debates over the legitimacy of Hebrew in the state of Israel are no longer debates over ideas. What came about responds to what he wished for, even though, in his time, it was only a matter of a visionary's dream. What would human history be like if, once in a while, here and there, beings of such stature did not exist?

Ben-Yehuda and the Linguistic Projects of Jews in His Time
The Attitude of European Jews in the Eighteenth Century, Faced with the Existence of Two Languages: One Written and One Spoken

Despite their lavish efforts to adapt Hebrew to express the realities of their times, none of the writers and theoreticians of the *Haskalah* had dreamed of reviving it as a spoken language. To understand this attitude, it is helpful to imagine the cultural framework within which they lived: Christian Europe in the classical age. Even though national languages asserted themselves in the form of literary monuments from the late Middle Ages on, Latin remained the language of learned culture, and it retained a part of the prestige that its status as the only written language had long earned it. So it was not shocking, even at the end of the eighteenth century, to make use of a literary language distinct from the spoken one. In the case of Hebrew, three considerations were added to this general attitude among the educated: first, the antiquity of its age of glory, biblical times; second, the fact that its status was one of a sacred language; and finally, the absence of a place to use it in terms of a national life — in Jewish thought, the notion of such a place was linked with the idea of living Hebrew.

The status of Hebrew in relationship to Yiddish does not exactly reflect that classical idea of an opposition between the written and the spoken, because Hebrew had an entirely different function from Latin. Until the late eighteenth century, the Jews of central and eastern Europe were accustomed to the opposition between the sacred language, never used in oral exchange, and Yiddish, which, for the most part, served this latter function, even though it had also long been used in written works. This was not enough, however, for the Jewish reformers of the eighteenth century to see Yiddish as a language of the future. They turned their backs on it.

The Glory of Yiddish in the Nineteenth Century

The ideas of the classical age regarding Yiddish would later be challenged. Its restoration and newly acquired literary dignity were significant events in the second half of the nineteenth century. Thus, becoming a fully legitimate written language, it burst upon the scene in all domains: prose, poetry, drama, essays, etc. In 1908, at the conference of Czernowitz, it was recognized by the Jewish elite of central Europe.

The Risks of Fracture: The Secularization of the Sacred Language in the Face of Yiddish Literary Conquests, or Central and Eastern European Jews in Possession of Two Languages of Identity

The rabbis used Yiddish to provide commentary to the masses, who no longer understood Hebrew, though they wrote their religious texts in the sacred language. But when Yiddish began to dominate literature more powerfully than ever before, Jewish communities found they had two written languages at their disposal. Actually, at the very moment when Yiddish achieved real literary promotion, a crop of remarkable writers who used Hebrew also appeared. They used it even more than those writers of the Spanish golden age who had also written in Arabic. And most importantly, contrary to this other group, they dealt with profane subjects (essentially novels, drama, and poetry). Those Jewish writers of the second half of the nineteenth century, a few names of whom I cited earlier, thus succeeded at a venture almost without precedent in Jewish culture: the secularization of the sacred language. From then on, a competition was established between Yiddish and Hebrew, both of which had become languages of Jewish literature.

The same Jews who, in the preceding epoch, had heralded the romantic doctrine of a single national language in which the soul of a people is expressed (see Fishman 1994, 432) now arrived at the cultural scene with two languages of identity!

Ben-Yehuda's Choice

This is the very epoch of Ben-Yehuda's prime. Even though buoyed by a powerful current, he alone would bring plans to their logical conclusion. Of course, the many Zionists and socialists whom he had read and encountered loved and respected Hebrew. They preferred it over Yiddish for use in their publications, trying hard, for the most part, to imitate the prophets and advocating it as the purist norm. But in the event of a return to Zion, the language that seemed the obvious choice was the one all central and eastern European Jews spoke in their everyday lives: Yiddish. Furthermore, Yiddish was promoted by those who, in the last years of the nineteenth century, had founded the Bund, the socialist workers party in Lithuania, Poland, and Russia, later linked to the Mensheviks (minority revolutionaries in Russia), and preoccupied, not with the national rights of the Jewish people, but rather with the struggle against anti-Semitism and the means for winning full citizenship for Jews in their respective countries. That said, Yiddish did not just have friends. It prompted reservations as well, echoing those of the time of the *Haskalah*. As the language of the ghetto, it appeared to some as the humiliating symbol of a tradition of poverty and oppression. Still others sometimes promoted it and sometimes rejected it. Faced with these antagonisms and renunciations, at least Ben-Yehuda proposed a clear solution, even if it seemed utopian.

To carry out the project clearly described in his letter to Smolenski, Ben-Yehuda emigrated to Palestine in 1881. From then on, his work took five precise directions (see Hadas-Lebel 1980a): the adoption of the Hebrew language in the home, journalism, teaching, the dictionary, the Language Committee.

The Beginnings: Hebrew at Home, Journalism

The First Hebrew-Speaking Family of the Modern World

Ben-Yehuda founded the first Hebrew-speaking family of the modern world, having made the decision to raise his children — by his wife from Polotsk — speaking Hebrew. Not content with simply putting his ideas into practice in his own private life, he also launched appeals to the local population as well as to the Diaspora, encouraging everyone to speak Hebrew at home. Nevertheless, plenty of sarcastic remarks were made, as well as warnings; someone once said to him, "If you only speak a dead language to your children, you will make them idiots!" But he remained deaf to such reproaches.

The effort to persuade families to raise their children hearing Hebrew from the cradle up did not produce convincing results. Even according to Ben-Yehuda, ten years after his immigration only four families in Jerusalem used Hebrew exclusively. According to the *Hashkafa* newspaper (no. 19), there were ten such families in 1900. In 1930, Y. Klausner, who had come from Odessa to join forces with Ben-Yehuda, could still write, "The majority of those who arrive in

Palestine do not make Hebrew their own customary language, the language of their home and their life." Perhaps such a judgment was a little pessimistic at that time. Whatever the case, it was in the following decade, and especially after 1945, that Hebrew became the standard language for all the Jews in Palestine.

Journalism

If Ben-Yehuda was able to launch his appeals in favor of Hebrew at home, it was thanks to his second activity: journalism. He founded a newspaper almost singlehandedly, supervising its printing and distributing it himself, at the price of exhaustion. Other newspapers would follow, and they would all experience many ups and downs. Ben-Yehuda used the press not only to promote the use of Hebrew, but also to make his neological creations known.

The Continuation of the Action in Palestine: The Teaching of Hebrew (in Hebrew) in Preschool as an Essential Factor in the Rebirth of the Language

Ben-Yehuda's journalism did not produce all the expected results, due to the lack of means and of time. On the other hand, teaching had a powerful effect, both short-term and long-term. However, the credit does not go to Ben-Yehuda alone. Actually, he was recruited by an Israelite Alliance school where he remained loyal to the director through attacks by parents who denounced the secularization of Hebrew. But he fell sick after three months and had to abandon the enterprise.

But his method of direct teaching, which consisted of speaking Hebrew only, was subsequently applied by a number of excellent teachers who believed in his work, had followed him for a long time, and asked to be part of this crazy experiment. They compiled manuals and used them in classes. In 1889, kindergartens were created where only Hebrew was spoken (see Masson 1983, 455). This must be considered a decisive moment in the history of the rebirth of Hebrew. Because until then, the only ones speaking it were adults who, despite their enthusiasm and their willingness, had been formulating their thoughts in another language since childhood. Henceforth, beings at the beginning of their lives learned to express their first thoughts in Hebrew. Only in this way did Hebrew enter onto the path that could lead to its becoming a language like any other.

The Stage After Action in Palestine: The Great Dictionary of the Ancient and Modern Hebrew Language
A Work Not Surpassed Even Today

The most important work in the eyes of Ben-Yehuda, and to which he devoted the greatest part of his activity in Palestine, was not completely without precedents. Even if we do not go back to the Egyptian Saadia ben Yosef, *gaon* (head) of a great Syrian school of translators and the founder of the Hebraic grammarian tradition, and who compiled lexicographical works in the early tenth century A.D., we can at least recall that, in the nineteenth century, biblical or Talmudic dictionaries and lexicons had been published, none of which encompassed an especially large period. The only one that did, and whose author we can consider a true precursor to Ben-Yehuda, was a work published in Germany. M. Schulbaum, a translator of German poetry and scientific treatises into Hebrew, began work in 1880 on the *Complete General Neo-Hebrew-German Dictionary* to resolve the considerable difficulties involved in this task. He drew the material for his dictionary from a vast corpus, taking into account Yiddish (permeated with Hebrew) as well as Biblical Hebrew. He rejected the complex periphrases of the *maskilim,* and recommended drawing inspiration from other Semitic languages to renew the lexis of the language from the inside, poorly adapted as it was for expressing acts and objects of everyday existence, because, he said, "almost everything is missing in Hebrew."

Ben-Yehuda no doubt was aware of Schulbaum's dictionary. Also noting Hebrew's inadequacy when it came to expressing things from modern and daily life, he began to publish glossaries of everyday terms from various domains. But soon he understood that despite his lack of training in lexicography, it was necessary for him to undertake much more extensive studies, beginning from as broad a base of materials as possible, in order to attain true knowledge of words' meanings and development. Thus, using a method comparable to Schulbaum's, he covered all of Hebrew literature, from the Bible to the works of classical authors, modern and contemporary, and including the Mishnah, the two Talmuds, exegetical books, collections of poetry, philosophy, grammar, the Kabbalah, medieval writings, and Hebraic borrowings from all levels in Jewish languages. It was a Herculean task.

Ben-Yehuda only mildly appreciated the biblical pastiches of the *Haskalah.* But he devoted much attention to the Talmudic period, and particularly to the Mishnaic language, in which he quite rightly recognized the most recently attested state of spoken Hebrew. He fostered a great esteem for the Spanish golden age, and he drew from Arabic, as the Jewish authors of this period had done. He also took an interest in the writings of the Karaites, that community of believers who, contesting the obligatory nature of the Mishnah and the Gemara, outgrowths of oral commentaries, and recognizing the authority of the written Law only, carefully studied the text of the Torah.

Thus Ben-Yehuda did not examine just Hebrew, but also the

Judeo-languages, successive forms of Hebraicized Aramaic, and other idioms as well. It is fortunate for Hebrew that Ben-Yehuda was not a linguist, because only an amateur would be foolhardy or oblivious enough to launch into such a venture. A professional linguist not only would have believed it impossible to bring Hebrew back to life, but, to meet such a challenge, would have done anything to avoid pitting himself against the task to which Ben-Yehuda sacrificed his already compromised health.

To accomplish this task, Ben-Yehuda was not content with working in the Jerusalem libraries. He visited a great number of libraries in cities worldwide in order to consult the works his research required. The dictionary became a veritable thesaurus. According to H. N. Bialik, even though Ben-Yehuda covered only a hundredth of the total material, he read or examined forty thousand works, and copied five hundred thousand citations, working eighteen hours a day. To find the necessary funds, he received much help from his second wife (the sister of his first wife, who died), who paid visits to various philanthropists and scholars, from whom she solicited financial support and recommendations. The fifth volume, which concluded on page three thousand, appeared shortly before Ben-Yehuda's death. The proofs of the next two volumes, prepared in the author's lifetime, were corrected by his disciples. The last eleven, from the sixth to the sixteenth, were respectfully prepared by a team of students and friends.

For each entry, Ben-Yehuda's *Dictionary* contained a translation into German, Russian, French, and English, as well as an indication of the corresponding Arabic root. Moreover, the author marked his own creations with a sign in order to leave the reader free to accept or reject them. The work is hardly flawless, and many errors and omissions have been brought to light, not surprising given that Ben-Yehuda managed almost singlehandedly, or with collaborators responsible for purely technical tasks, an endeavor that probably required a large team. That said, the work is without equal even today. Despite modern methods, no comparable dictionary has ever been carried through to completion.

The Personal Contributions of Ben-Yehuda, Inventor of Words

In Israeli Hebrew as in other languages, the words forged by writers beloved by the public compete with the neologisms of scholars. Five hundred words today may be attributable to H. N. Bialik, whereas Ben-Yehuda is credited with about three hundred words, out of which eighty to ninety were accepted by native speakers, according to G. Zuckermann (personal communication). Ben-Yehuda did not make any mighty claims about being a great designer of new words. He wished that at least a portion of his creations would be integrated enough so that everyone would forget that he had fathered them. He avoided invention when other solutions were possible. With all the moderation of a learned man, quite well-informed for someone practically self-taught in lexicography, he applied the principles that many other language reformers have applied, in Hungarian, Finnish, Amharic, Turkish, Mongolian, Chinese, Korean, or other languages (see Hagège 1983): to resort to a term with a foreign origin (or, in the particular case of Hebrew, to a Hebraicized Aramaic term) only when none of the successive layers of the history of the language could provide a native term; to create terms — if no other course of action was available — only on the basis of attested roots, or at least present in a genetically related language, which, in the case of Hebrew, means Aramaic or Arabic; to introduce a word only if it is indispensable (filling a gap in the lexis) and well formed (respecting the structural rules of the morphology).

Thus, Ben-Yehuda replaced the very awkward compound words Hebrew owed to the *maskilim* with the lighter words vital to contemporary language: in place of *beyt-'okhel* (= "house-[to] eat") for "restaurant," *sefer-milim* (= "book-[of]words," a calque of the German Wörterbuch) for "dictionary," *ish-tsava* ("man-[of the]army") for "soldier," he created, respectively, *mis'ada* (prefix *mi-* of place name on a root meaning "to take a meal"), *milon* (a term formed on the radical of *mila*, "word," not made plural *milim*, but broadened with the suffix *-on*), and *xayal* (on a root meaning "strength"). Sometimes Ben-Yehuda gave a profane meaning to religious words from the Bible. Among the terms that he borrowed from biblical Aramaic, we find *ktiv* ("spelling"), and from Talmudic Aramaic, *hitnagdut* ("opposition") and *'adish* ("indifferent"). And using Arabic as a model, which derives *huwiyya* ("identity") from *huwa* ("he"), he formed *zehut* ("identity") on the demonstrative *zeh* ("this").

The Last Aspect of the Action in Palestine: The Language Committee; The Rebirth of Hebrew as a Collective Work

Ben-Yehuda did not work entirely alone — far from it, in fact. In 1904, after one fruitless attempt, he created a Language Committee (often called Language Council), whose works would span half a century. One of his reasons for this decision is easy to understand. After the initial major difficulties of trying to implant Hebrew in Palestine, many teachers had been recruited by Hebraic schools, in full expansion since the first years of the twentieth century. They began to resolve the phonetic and lexical problems their teaching presented according to their own individual choices. Ben-Yehuda and his friends decided that an advisory authority capable of responding to the concerns of the teachers had become necessary. The size of the Language Committee grew from seven original members to eleven in 1910. Its task was to publish lists of words, as well as to make sure that a certain standard was respected, as happens in a period of linguistic ferment, and all the more so because it was not a matter of an ordinary language, but of a dead language that had been exhumed from a very ancient past.

From all parts of Palestine, abundant letters reached the Committee, whose meetings, monthly at first, became weekly in 1912, the date when it was recognized as the highest authority in matters of the Hebrew language. Teachers proposed their terminological innovations, and the Committee gave its opinion. This type of collaboration played an essential role in the resurrection of Hebrew. Here, that resurrection appeared in the full light of what it was: a collective work. This is not at all a matter of denying Ben-Yehuda credit, whose perseverance and devotion to the cause must be admired. But we cannot forget that the enterprise of restoring Hebrew could not have succeeded without two elements, the first of which was mentioned earlier, that is, the action of kindergarten teachers, and the second being this vast consultation among a single people who constructed, or reconstructed, a language through the concerted participation of each member, and under pressure from concrete problems posed by everyday expression.

The consultations of the Committee were not limited to teachers. Individuals who were interested in the construction of the language also sent many questions and made many proposals. And the action of the Committee was only the most prominent; there were many other exchanges outside of these proceedings. Many promoters of the language wrote in newspapers, which all included an extensive column on linguistics. Some pioneers considered themselves no less competent than Ben-Yehuda, and for many words there were many proposals; discussion, but also individual whim and often habit, finally decided among them. Certain words established by usage were born under these circumstances, with most users never knowing who invented them, the inventor sometimes being a dispersed body participating in the neological enthusiasm.

Thus, some terms as common today as *yaroq* ("green") or *mishqa-faim* ("glasses") are owed to Ch. L. Hazzan of Grodno (see Klausner 1935). At least in these cases, there is information regarding the circumstances of their appearance. But as strange as it seems, for most neologisms, we know neither the source nor the context of their origin (see Masson 1983). For most well-studied languages, we do not know anymore than we find in specialized works: the history of the word, the forms of its introduction. Could there be better proof of the collective nature of the enterprise? And isn't the success of a new word measured especially by how well integrated into common usage it is, so that most people do not know its etymology and hardly wonder about it?

In 1953, the Language Committee had to become the Academy of the Hebrew Language, and the creation of words was integrated into academic programs. Many scholars, among them Aba Bendavid, a well-known grammarian, subsequently built upon the work of the first constructors. Nevertheless, the resurrection of Israeli Hebrew was never a truly planned work. Proposals surfaced here and there. The Committee had been founded precisely to address this cheerful anarchy that coexisted, without contradiction, with the serious effort of individuals resolved to bring their many-thousand-year-old sacred language back to life. No doubt Hebrew would have remained permanently dead if its resurrection had been a skillfully and meticulously orchestrated enterprise. In reality, it was a work of passion: Zionist passion, nationalist passion, the passion of revolt against anti-Semitic persecution. That is the whole meaning of the wild project to revive Hebrew. But the passion was clearly collective. The promoters' voluntarism could succeed only because it coincided with the aspirations of an entire community.

Adversaries and Detractors

The Struggle Against Other Languages, Among Them German

Ben-Yehuda did not have to contend with just poor health and penni-lessness. He had to face open competition from other languages, and the political authorities that backed them. Because the Istanbul court pushed the teaching of Turkish, Saint Petersburg financed the ex-pansion of Russian, and most importantly, Berlin maintained many German schools under the auspices of a Jewish aid society, Hilfs-verein der Juden (in this period, Germany, or really Prussia, looked favorably upon the Jews . . .). In fact, Berlin prepared to dominate a Turkey in full decline by working its way into its Palestine province in particular, where Wilhelm II, pursuing a policy of nationalist af-firmation on many fronts, granted his support to Herzl, not without reservations.

Supported by striking teachers and students, Ben-Yehuda struggled to prevent the opening of technical schools where German would be the only language. He ultimately prevailed. There was a time when it would not have taken much for German to supplant Hebrew in Palestine. But history decided otherwise. The outcome of World War I, which resulted in the Turkish collapse and the Prussian defeat, cost the German language its prominence. Destiny served Ben-Yehuda's designs.

Denunciation by the Devout

Ben-Yehuda also had to struggle against the orthodox Jews of Pales-tine, for whom the return of the people of Israel to the Holy Land could occur only through the coming of the Messiah. They also con-sidered it sacrilegious to teach Hebrew as a living language. The same Jews who threw stones at the Alliance school where Ben-Yehuda briefly taught Hebrew did not approve of diverting young Talmudists from their study of the sacred texts to work the land in the settlement colonies. Resolved to stop him, these censors worked so hard that they succeeded in getting Ben-Yehuda incarcerated under the completely false pretext of an offensive article that he had supposedly written. He was quickly released.

More disturbing was the condemnation of Ben-Yehuda's work by an eminent Kabbalah specialist, G. Scholem, the author most notably of a book well known among modern Kabbalists (see Scholem 1962). In a letter from December 1926 to F. Rosenzweig, published sixty years later, we can read (see Mosès 1985):

> The initiators of the Hebrew renaissance movement had a blind, semifanatical faith in the miraculous power of that language. This was lucky for them. Because if they had been gifted with clairvoyance, they would never have had the fiendish courage to resuscitate a language doomed to become an Esperanto [. . .]. As for us, fear grips us when in a discussion we are suddenly struck by a religious term used indiscriminately [. . .]. This language is rife with catastrophes to come [. . .]. In truth, it is our children, those who know no other language [. . .] who will have to pay the price of these encounters that we have prepared for them, without having asked them, without being asked ourselves. The day will come when the language will turn against those who speak it [. . .]. On that day, will we have young people capable of facing the revolt of a sacred language? [. . .] The names haunt our sentences; writers or journalists play with them, pretending to believe or to make God believe, that none of that matters. And nevertheless, in this debased and spectral language, the power of the sacred often

seems to speak to us. Because the names have a life of their own [. . .].

Among Hebrew words, all those that are not neologisms [. . .] are charged with meaning to the point of exploding. A generation like ours, which reclaims the most fertile part of our tradition, by which I mean its language, cannot exist without tradition. When the time comes that the power buried in the depths of the Hebrew language manifests itself anew, [. . .] our people will find themselves once again confronted with this sacred tradition [. . .]. Then, they will have to submit or disappear. Because at the heart of this language in which we never cease evoking God in a thousand ways—thus, in some way making him come back into the reality of our life—, God himself, in his turn, will not remain silent. But this inescapable revolution of the language, in which the Voice will make itself heard once again, is the only subject never addressed in this country. Because those who have set about to resuscitate the Hebrew language do not believe in the reality of the judgment to which they have subjected us all. Pray to the heavens that the rashness that has led us down this apocalyptic road does not result in our downfall.

The Divorce Between Linguists and Philosophers of Religion as to What a Language Is

The debate raised by this text is certainly significant for at least two reasons. In the first place, the text clearly reflects the rabbinical tradition's vision of Hebrew; this vision was the cause of violent denunciations that Ben-Yehuda had to face from the religious community. In the second place, these lines shed light on the different conceptions of what a language is and, more specifically, on the divorce between linguists and philosophers of religion, to say nothing of the insurmountable difficulty this second group sometimes has in trying to understand the first group's work. We have seen that Ben-Yehuda was born and received his early education in a religious environment, as did most eastern European Jews who participated in the Zionist movement. The very inspiration of this movement, at least for those who saw no other possible seat for it than Palestine, could not be totally exempt from religious implications, and included here were thinkers who, at the end of the nineteenth century, confined themselves to claiming national recognition for the Jewish people according to the model of other oppressed peoples. Nevertheless, what inspired Ben-Yehuda's choice of Hebrew and adherence from his first allies and then from a growing number of Jews was nothing other than the very history of Israel since earliest times: a history in which, as I have stressed, the restoration of the nation implies the restoration of the language.

From then on, even though he was not a linguist, Ben-Yehuda adopted an attitude close to the one a linguist would have adopted, if there were a linguist capable of believing in such an enterprise and carrying it out. The point of departure for Ben-Yehuda was nationalistic and religious, of course. But his end point was a conception of the language as an instrument of communication above all else. In his eyes, the resurrection of Hebrew could only be that of the national language of the Jews, the only thing conceivable in the historical and cultural context of a Palestine facing a language so completely dispersed as it was. It followed quite naturally that this language must be adapted to the modern age. The reformers of many other languages, in the past and especially in the twentieth century, after many decolonized countries won their independence, had no other objective but this (see Hagège, 1983). However, the position taken by orthodox rabbis and by G. Scholem in the cited text is based on an ancient tradition according to which Hebrew is a sacred language, this fact constituting an absolute impediment to any oral use. If it had not been dead for seventeen centuries, during which time its only use was liturgical, perhaps it would have been more difficult for the religious community to regard it as sacred.

It cannot be overlooked that, in biblical times, the language of the Torah had a perfectly vital spoken variant. And through its successive states as a language that changed, as all human languages do, it was used by the Hebrews for entire centuries in the preexile history. Thus, it is not necessarily sacrilegious to have fashioned a spoken Hebrew in the modern and contemporary period. So the question posed here is whether G. Scholem was right to think that modernizing Hebrew altered its powers of religious evocation. I will attempt to respond to that question below.

Ben-Yehuda's Ultimate Fulfillment

It is reported that Ben-Yehuda had the habit of saying, "Everything needs its lunatic," in reference to the madness he embraced. At least he was able to see his crazy idea become reasonable fact: about ten months after the Balfour Declaration, which, on November 2, 1917, informed the world that the British government looked favorably upon "the establishment in Palestine of a national home for the Jewish people," Hebrew was declared an official language, with Arabic and English, in Palestine. This was on August 31, 1918. At that very moment, the dream was no longer a dream. Ben-Yehuda would have no more opportunities for joyful tears, nor would his contemporaries have time to benefit from more of his mad ideas. He died of exhaustion at an age when men of the same mettle can still accomplish many great things: he was sixty-four years old.

A Few Distinctive Characteristics of Israeli Hebrew

A UNIQUE ENTERPRISE IN THE HISTORY OF LANGUAGES

The Voluntarism of Pioneers and the Affirmation of Identity

As we have seen, Zionism is inscribed within the framework of central and eastern European nationalism at the end of the nineteenth century. Ben-Yehuda gets credit for convincing people of an essential fact: if the second component of the concept of a nation is the language, the other being the territory, that language could only be Hebrew. In fact, many Zionists were all the more willing to admit, even if in itself the idea seemed crazy, the choice of any one language for the Jews—Russian, for example, instead of German, etc.—would have encountered opposition from the speakers or the partisans of another language. But since it was necessary to revive Hebrew, it could only be a matter of a voluntarist enterprise, completely practical, natural, and spontaneous, Hebrew having disappeared eons ago. Furthermore, if the pioneers understood that in reconstituting this language they could not avoid borrowing from others, they were nonetheless convinced that Hebrew had to assert its presence as much as possible, since their cultural identity defined itself by the very choice that they had made.

A Spoken Language Constructed from a Group of Written Languages

Among many others, Israeli Hebrew possesses one astonishing characteristic: it is a spoken language fabricated from a written language. In all other cases, the reverse process takes place. Of course, Israeli Hebrew is also written, but Hebrew, in all phases of its history, never stopped being written. What is revolutionary is precisely that, after such a long time, its status as a living, spoken language returned.

That fact goes against all evidence. The Romance languages are the products — the natural and unconstructed products — of vulgar Latin, which was a spoken language; and it is precisely when they accommodate writing that they assert themselves as full-fledged languages (see chapter 5). Neo-Norwegian was constructed beginning from spoken dialects of western Norwegian (see chapter 11). Similarly inspired by nationalism, Atatürk wanted to construct a modern Turkish vocabulary as remote as possible from the Ottoman norm, teeming with Arabic-Persian borrowings. He demanded especially that the Turkish languages spoken by the eastern nomads be used as sources. The Prakrit languages are the various forms that succeeded Sanskrit, a written language, at the beginning of middle Indian. Far from being an oral reconstruction of a written state, literary Arabic, a Semitic language like Hebrew, and representing the norm in all Arab countries, is, on the contrary, a language that in principle is only written. The many Arabic dialects, only oral, are not, as some believe, historical outgrowths; neither are they reconstructions, but living legacies. There are countless other examples.

But there is more. Not only is Israeli Hebrew a spoken language reconstructed from the written. It is a language reconstructed from many written languages, not just one. Biblical Hebrew and Mishnaic Hebrew are fairly different from each other, to say nothing of the differences between medieval Hebrew, a written language exclusively, and the Aramaic of the Talmud. Ben-Yehuda, like many other promoters of the language, established the practice of calling upon all these corpora at once, and the dearth of sources faced with the immensity of the expressible was one more reason encouraging them to do this.

Revival Rather Than Renaissance

To simplify things, we speak of the rebirth of Hebrew. But the preceding discussion makes it clear that this term is not absolutely correct. Because "renaissance" would imply that Hebrew took up its evolution as a living language exactly where death had interrupted it. And furthermore, to cause an organism be reborn implies that a single organism is dead. In reality, Israeli Hebrew is the revived form of many languages. The most surprising thing is that such a challenge to natural evolution and, to put it bluntly, such an artificial creation, was able to succeed.

HEBREW AS BASE AND AS DOMINANT MODEL
Fidelity to Hebrew

As soon as the pioneers had created a new Hebraic language according to the dictates of their will, faithfulness to the various levels of Hebrew as the basis for construction, at least in all those cases where such fidelity could be maintained, became a radical necessity. That is how the word formation processes typical of Semitic languages like Hebrew were all preserved. These processes, which are called templates, begin with a root that usually has three consonants and consist of varying the vowels and prefixing, inserting, or suffixing various elements to obtain nouns, adjectives, verbs, etc. The opposition between masculine and feminine was retained as well, even in those words that were borrowed from Hebrew by Yiddish, the mother tongue of many of the pioneers, and had switched into neuter, like *dalut* ("poverty"), *hitlahavut* ("enthusiasm") (in Yiddish, *dales, islayves*). The introduction of new templates was rejected, even when they were directly inspired by the structure of already attested templates. The existing templates were heavily exploited, or reactivated if they had lost their productivity over the course of Hebrew's history.

One of the most productive today is the template with the prefix *hit-* and the vowels *a* and then *e*, often formed from a noun. Illustrated by the Mishnaic Hebrew *hit-maʒel* ("to have good luck") (*maʒel* = luck), this schema corresponds to French verbs that are pronominal or reciprocal in meaning. We find, for example, *hityaded* ("to strike up a friendship") (based on *yadid*, "friend"), *hitmaʒreax* ("to orient oneself") (based on *miʒrax*, "orient"), and also many verbs with foreign bases that, through this template, assume a completely Hebraic appearance: *hitgaletsh* ("to slide") (based on the Yiddish *glitsh*, "slide"), *hitrandevu* ("they had a rendezvous") (jocular Israeli slangism), *hiʒdangef* ("to stroll along Dizengof boulevard") (a well-known avenue in Tel-Aviv; note that, in this verb, where we can see a complicit wink as in many Israeli words, the consonants *d* and *ʒ* are reversed, and the *t* of the prefix *hit-* disappears, because Hebrew does not allow *-tdʒ-* or *-dʒ-* in succession).

Many of the classical processes used for forming nouns were readopted. One of them consists of creating acronyms by inserting a vowel *a* between the consonants obtained through abbreviation. For a long time, this process was even used for shortening patronyms. Thus, the traditional Hebrew name of the philosopher called Maimonides by Westerners is Rambam, because he was called Rabbi Moche ben Maimon. Likewise, in the modern language, acronyms were formed that have become common nouns, like *tsahal* (*tsava* ["army"] + *hagana* ["defense"] + *l'israel* ["of Israel"]), the name of the Israeli army.

Thus, in many cases, the construction of the language, marked by Zionist ideology, appeared cautious with regard to what was not specifically Hebrew in structure. Especially in the earliest times, to speak Hebrew was to transmit a message, as in any language, but it was also something more: it was to participate in a great work of revival, all the more assured of success if the rules of Biblical Hebrew were strictly followed, to which could be added the rules of Mishnaic Hebrew for the less rigid.

Making the Borrowings Hebrew

One result of this loyalty, whenever possible, to the classical age of Hebrew was the rejection of all elements belonging to national languages. This rejection involved only the area of grammar, that is, of grammatical tools, like prepositions or conjunctions. In the area of vocabulary, initially only those words were introduced that were found simultaneously and in analogous forms in various European languages, in which case they were considered international, and accepted, but not without Hebraic packaging.

Thus, many verbs were formed on foreign roots, but by integrating them into a Hebraic structure, one that presents a vowel *i* after the first consonant (or as the first letter), and a vowel *e* after the central consonant or the two central consonants. Based on the model of Biblical and Mishnaic Hebrew, we see verbs like *ibben* ("to petrify"), *diyyer* ("to put into a sheepfold"), *pirkes* ("to beautify"), *ligleg* ("to scoff at"), *gimgem* ("to stutter"), etc.; verbs of the same type with modern Hebraic roots, like *inyen* ("to interest"), *ixʒev* ("to disappoint"), *kiyef* ("to lead the good life") (from *kef* ["good times"], borrowed from Arabic); and verbs like those where the root is an international word but where the template is Hebraicized, such as *pider* ("to powder"), *bilef* ("to bluff"), *tilfen* ("to telephone"), *pitrel* ("to patrol"), *kitleg* ("to catalogue"), *hipnet* ("to hypnotize"), etc. In all of these we can recognize the English or French, or, more generally, international, words.

Ideology Can Shape a Language

What the above facts seem to prove is that a conscious ideology can succeed in deliberately leaving its mark on a language. We know this, of course, because of the many cases when it was necessary to build a vocabulary adapted to the modern period, and language reformers often preferred national solutions to international borrowings. But nowhere is the action so radical as in Israeli Hebrew, a language refashioned on a vast scale by pioneers driven by a certain ideal (see Masson 1986).

This is even more true for the hard kernel of the language, that is, the grammar. Passive conjugations, which are morphologically complex, were maintained, as in general was the system of verbs. With the noun, the mark of the dual number (sometimes considered a linguistic trait of archaic societies, attentive to small numbers, where objects may appear in pairs) was sometimes preserved as well. Also retained was a grammatical word, *'et*, indicating that a definite noun is the object of a transitive verb. This gives rise to a surprising phenomenon for which the history of languages offers very few examples. The debate over retaining or abandoning the preposition *'et*, since it is a matter of pure syntax, is the kind of issue supposedly reserved for professional linguists alone. In Israel, however, it became the subject of long controversies, in which one of the founders of the state of Israel, Prime Minister D. Ben-Gurion himself, took a position (see Hagège 1993c, 34–35).

Israeli Hebrew and Esperanto

The Baltic and Russian-Polish borders were among the select territories for innovative thinkers, used to the ideas of freedom that marked the eastern European intelligentsia at the end of the nineteenth century. The inventor of Esperanto, L. Zamenhof, was born in 1859, roughly two years after Ben-Yehuda, in the northeastern part of Poland. Bialystok, his hometown, was subject to Russian control, and Jews formed the majority. It was located a few hundred kilometers from Luzhky as well as Polotsk. One cannot help being struck by the similarity between Ben-Yehuda's insane desire to resuscitate the only common language possible among all the dispersed Jews, and the desire Zamenhof nurtured in this same period, as did other men of peace in Europe, to destroy the barriers created, he believed, by the multiplicity of languages. The idealistic adoption of a language whose usage obeys no ulterior motive (economic, political, etc.) assumes adherence to an internationalist ethic. That is the point the two projects had in common. But that adoption also assumes (see Hagège 1983, 19–20) a symbolic power rooted in a history. Only Hebrew responds to this second requirement, which obviously resulted from the fact that it involved a single nation, and not the entire world, as Esperanto did.

What is more, there is an essential difference between the two enterprises, even if the invention of an international language and the revival of a dead language have points in common. Even though it was very much inspired by Latin, Zamenhof created Esperanto completely from bits and pieces, from the Romance languages, the Slavic languages, etc. Ben-Yehuda did not re-create Hebrew all by himself, as we have seen. Moreover, he used existing materials, even if the synthesis he made of them was partly artificial, and his neologisms follow attested Hebraic schemas.

THE WESTERN NATURE OF ISRAELI HEBREW

Despite their attachment to the classical forms of Hebrew, the constructors of Israeli Hebrew could not prevent it from also taking on aspects of western languages. That becomes apparent in relationship to Jewish languages, as well as various other ways, a few of which I will examine below.

The Role of European Jews: The Prestige of European Languages and Judeo-Aramaic, the Lack of Prestige for Sephardic Languages: Judeo-Spanish and Judeo-Arabic Dialects
Pressure from Russian and Yiddish, the Languages of the Ashkenazim

One surprising fact is that Judeo-Spanish and the various forms of Judeo-Arabic provided nearly no elements for the Israeli Hebrew vocabulary. Arabic provided many such elements, but, on the other hand, we find only a few Arabic morphological elements in modern Hebrew grammar (if, for instance, the colloquial adjective template *ma-ú*: Zuckermann 2003, 251). The majority of the pioneers who fashioned Hebrew were European Jews (*Ashkenazim* in Hebrew). They introduced a great number of words common to Russian, German, English, and French, usually in their Russian form, because, along with Yiddish, and for some, Polish and German, Russian was the original language for many among them, beginning with Ben-Yehuda, and also for many of the great writers, like H. N. Bialik. The influence of Russian was thus very important in the first stages of re-creating Hebrew. That is why we find in Israeli Hebrew *obyekt*, *keramika, galateria* ("novelty items"), *tsenzura* ("censor"), etc. (see Masson 1976). The presence of Yiddish is also very significant, even though, as the language of the central European ghettos, it was considered by some of the pioneers to lack all prestige.

As for the western Jews (*Sephardim* in Hebrew, from *Sepharad* ["Spain"]), they constituted only a small number before 1948, and those who immigrated afterward were never very numerous.

Judezmo did not have the prestige of the northern European languages. As for Arabic, it was appreciated by Ben-Yehuda and other promoters only in its literary form. Ben-Yehuda saw it as a source for lexical borrowings but not for morphological models. And after 1948, promoters had even less use for it as the language of the adversaries, or for all the unprestigious dialects of immigrants from Yemen and North Africa with their own traditional cultures. For all these reasons, Israeli Hebrew appears clearly as a creation of the Ashkenazim. Among the many neological processes on which Yiddish humor left its mark, one in particular consists of repeating a word by adding, before the repeated part, a prefix of derision *m-* or *shm-*, as in *igen-migen* ("Israeli of Hungarian origin") (because *igen* = "yes" in Hungarian), *um-shmum*, the pejorative designation for the UN (from its acronym in Hebrew: *um*).

The Status of Judeo-Aramaic

It is paradoxical that Judeo-Aramaic, which Ben-Yehuda and other reconstructors of modern Hebrew drew from abundantly, is a language of prestige in their eyes, since it is an Eastern language and, worse, it belonged to the persecutors of former times, those Babylonians who had adopted it as the common idiom long before the destruction of the first temple and the deportation of the Judea elite. In some way, those grave events, and the ones that followed, turned Aramaic into a Jewish language, or at least, into a language of the Jews, as I have written above. And nevertheless, Israeli Hebrew, which drew so many vocabulary words from it, did not borrow any, or hardly any, elements or processes of word formation from it, introducing only complete, unparsed Aramaic words.

The Pronunciation of Israeli Hebrew: Officially Sephardic, but in Practice Ashkenazic

As its promoters wished, the official pronunciation of Hebrew is faithful to what it probably was in the past: it is modeled on the pronunciation of Sephardic communities of northern or eastern Africa. Like Arabic, it possesses guttural consonants, articulated in the areas of the pharynx and the larynx. But in practice, because the first Zionist immigrants at the end of the nineteenth century used Yiddish, which does not possess these sounds, they are not part of standard pronunciation. One of them, the *h* (found in the Arabic name Muhammad), is pronounced like the *ch* in the German *machen*, although Hebrew possesses this sound anyway, distinct from the *h*. A loss in the range of possibilities results.

The Expression of Affectivity: Diminutives, the Deficiencies of Hebrew, and the Pressure from European Jewish Languages

Borrowing formative elements for words from languages other than Hebrew was avoided when possible by the pioneers. But sometimes it was necessary. There are reports that the first leaders of the Israeli state, in moments of anger, insulted each other in Yiddish. At first, Yiddish was also used in intimate conversation, as if the expression of passions could be conceived only in the language learned in childhood (see chapter 7, regarding Greek among the Roman patricians). That is even more true when the language one must use is largely artificial, since it was reconstituted by an act of will. Moreover, Hebrew was experienced as transcendent, through the transcendence of the Bible in the eyes of the Palestinian pioneers. But there is an area where a second reason also comes into play. That is the area of diminutives and what linguists call hypocoristics, that is, words marked by affectivity, mocking or tender, that the oral registers of all human languages possess. The language of the Bible, perhaps because it is a literary text, is almost entirely devoid of them. On the other hand, Yiddish and Russian are filled with them. Thus, Israeli Hebrew borrowed diminutive suffixes from these languages. One of them is *-tshik*, which can have an affectionate, mocking, or pejorative meaning: we find it in *bakhurtshik, khamortshik, khayaltshik, khamudtshik, shamentshik,* and *askantshik,* meaning, respectively, "little fellow," "little ass" (actually, an affectionate term!), "little soldier," "little treasure," "little fat man," "political schemer," diminutives of *bakhur, khamor, khayal, khamud* ("beloved"), *shamen* ("fat"), *askan* ("dealer, macher"). Another affective and diminutive suffix is *-le,* as in *abale* ("little papa"), *yaldale* ("little child"), *khamudale* ("cutie, beloved [feminine]"), etc.

Also, through the intermediary of Yiddish, Russian provided a productive suffix *-nik,* which, added to Hebraic or, more rarely, foreign radicals, or abbreviations or various expressions, loses its affective implication to designate the originators of numerous activities: *igudnik* ("member of a union"), *yudalefnik* ("sixth-grade student") (designated by the letters *yud* and *alef*), *xelavirnik* ("aviator"), *klumnik* ("good for nothing") (*klum* = "nothing"), *kedainik* ("opportunist") (*kedai* = "it's worth the trouble"), *olraitnik* ("a good type") (English "all right"), *phudnik* ("bore with a Ph.D.") (to describe researchers who show off their knowledge and their degrees). We can note the tone of derision (others speak of Jewish humor) inherent in these words. We can also note that among the expressive formations cited above, the last five belong to colloquial language. Given not only its limited means, but also what it symbolized, it was difficult for Hebrew to provide such material all by itself.

The Expression of Identity Through the
Accentuation of Words

Hebrew is a language with a tonic accent on the last syllable, whereas Yiddish tends to stress the next-to-last syllable. Thus, in neither of these languages is there argument over where to place the accent for the same word. But contention arises in Israeli Hebrew, a phenomenon quite specific to it because it is a hybrid language. In fact, the pioneers began to use Yiddish accentuation for words referring to realities that were typically Israeli, and thus linked to the cultural world of the Yiddish speakers. On the other hand, they pronounced these same words with Hebraic accentuation, that is, stressing the final syllable, when they referred to more general realities. That is why, for example, *habimá* ("stage") is opposed to *habíma* ("Theater of the Bima"), or *hatikvá* ("hope") and *hatíkva* ("Israeli hymn [containing this word])" (see Hagège and Haudricourt 1978, 152). For those who worship Hebrew, this natural intrusion of habits of articulation linked to the languages of the diaspora still constitutes an "infraction."

The Massive Influx of Nominal Compounds

Biblical and Mishnaic Hebrew have many derived words (= words formed with prefixes and suffixes), but do not offer much opportunity for nominal compounds, like the French *garde-malade* ("home nurse"), *lave-vaisselle* ("dishwasher"), *faux-semblant* ("pretense"), *ex-mari* ("ex-husband"), etc. We find hardly any such words in the Bible. Thus, the promoters of Hebrew felt this process to be modern, both in structure and in the meaning of the words it allows for. Aware of its usefulness in the neological enterprise, and knowing that it was accepted in most European languages, they created a considerable number of compounds, usually by calquing those of German, Russian, French, and English. By way of illustration, we can cite *ramkol* ("loudspeaker") (*ram* ["loud"] + *kol* ["voice"]), *shmartaf* ("babysitter") (*shamar* ["to look after"] + *taf* ["child"]), *du mashmaut* ("ambiguity") (*du* ["two"] + *mashmaut* ["meaning"]), *rakével* ("cableway") (condensation of *rakévet* ["railway"] and *kével* ["cable"]), *tapuẓ* ("orange") (portmanteau blending of *tapuakh* ["apple"] and *ẓahav* ["gold"]; a creation of Y. Avinéri), *beyn-memshalti* ("intergovernmental") (*beyn* ["between"] + *memshala(t)* ["government"] and -*i* adjectival suffix), *al-enoshi* ("superhuman") (*al* ["super"] + *enoshi* ["human"]), *parat-moshe-rabénu* ("ladybug") (parat ["calf of"] + *moshe* ["Moses"] + *rabénu* ["our master"], because the Russian *boẓhja korovka* ["little calf of God"] could be only partially calqued without committing outright blasphemy, which would have horrified the pioneers).

The implicit association between nominal compounds and modernity or Westernization in Hebrew today is still obvious from the fact that manufacturers and merchants use them abundantly for designating their products.

Liberties Taken with Meaning: Israeli Hebrew, a Semitic Language According to Its Morphology and a European Language According to Its Semantic Calques
The Manipulation of Meaning and the Disruption of the System of Concepts

In reality, the attachment to ancient Hebrew involves, above all else, the forms: inherited words, the structures of nouns, verbs, and adjectives faithfully preserved. But on the level of meaning, Israeli Hebrew reflects an image of manipulation that may explain the hostility of conservative rabbis. It is this rashness, to use G. Scholem's word, that inspired his somber prophecies in the text cited above.

For a linguist, it hardly matters. Languages are used to communicate, no matter what means they employ toward this end. Human action upon languages is a universal phenomenon (see Hagège 1983), and the success of the enterprise of resurrecting Hebrew, in forms so different from those we find elsewhere, is really something to marvel at. It is true that it includes many cases of very pronounced semantic changes that, moreover, were decreed and not produced by natural evolution as in other languages. The calques from European languages produce combinations that would have had no meaning in ancient Hebrew, like *nekuda meta* ("in neutral," "at a standstill") or *shirat ha-barbur* ("swan song"). But beyond that, classical meanings were diverted in order to translate notions absent from the ancient texts because the corresponding objects themselves were absent. Thus, *katsran, totakh, kinor,* and *psanter* have switched, respectively, from their ancient meanings — "succinct person," "club," "zither," and "ancient harp" — to "stenographer," "gun" or "cannon," "violin," and "piano."

Moreover, the relational system of the concepts of classical Hebrew (Mishnaic as well as Biblical) was disrupted. One example can demonstrate this. The verb *khana* is used in the Biblical language to indicate that the Hebrews stopped in the desert or at an encampment (Exodus 13:20; Numbers 33). This verb was chosen to form the word *takhana* by prefixing *ta-*, according to a classical pattern. It refers to a station as stopping place. But because the word with this meaning is used in languages like English and French in combination with many other words to refer to all kinds of stations, by transfer, such words were formed in Hebrew (see Rosen 1970, 97 s.): *takhanat shidur* ("transmitting station") (*shidur* = "emission"), *takhanat délek* ("service station") (*délek* = "fuel"), *takhanat 'ezra rishona* ("first aid station"), etc. Thus, the semantic networks of Hebrew were reorganized on the model of European languages.

Paronymic Calques and Wordplays

The creation of new words through wordplay is not exclusive to Israeli Hebrew. To translate the French and English words *élément/ element*, the promoters of Hungarian created the term *elem*, which has the dual advantage of resembling both these two words and the purely Hungarian word *elő* ("what is in front"). To render *école* and *school*, the creators of modern Turkish formed *okul*, which immediately evokes *oku* (*-mak*, by adding the suffix for the infinitive), meaning "to read" (let alone that the *-l* of *okul* could be analyzed as deriving from *-la*, a Turkish locative suffix, as recalled to me by G. Zuckermann). Estonian's great reformer, J. Aavik, invented from French and English *crime*, the word *roim* ("crime"), which had the advantage of resembling a term belonging to a sister language, the Finnish word *rikos*, with the same meaning (see Hagège 1983, 51, 57).

We can see how the process works. With the implicit smile that accompanies some of the very serious, but also playful, operations performed upon the weave of languages, the neology inventors took advantage of happy accidents. Certain words in their languages were found to have forms and meanings resembling those of words from the model languages. In Hebrew, there are many paronymic calques of this kind. One of them is *ilit* ("elite"), cleverly resembling *ili*, the Hebrew word meaning "superior." Another example is *déme* ("simulacrum"), which resembles both the English *dummy*, with the same meaning, and the Hebrew verb *dama*, "to seem": cf. *mitan déme* ("dummy bomb"), *totakh déme* ("dummy cannon"), *bitsuréy déme* ("dummy fortifications"), *mivkhan déme* ("dummy examination"), *trufat déme* ("placebo").

The Secularization of Religious Terms

Giving secular meanings to words borrowed by the neology creators from an ancient and prestigious stage of a language is hardly unique to Hebrew. To mention only one example, modern Hindi has given to the Sanskrit words *urja* ("power"), *rajpath* ("royal way"), and *akashvani* ("voices of the gods") the respective meanings of "energy" (in the technical sense), "highway," and "Indian radio." In Hebrew, a great number of terms from the religious vocabulary changed meaning through a process of secularization (see Hadas-Lebel 1980b). This dialectical relationship between the sacred and the profane is hardly a recent phenomenon in the history of Hebrew. It goes back to at least the Middle Ages.

But in the twentieth century, it experienced an unprecedented expansion, because in choosing to fight for the revival of the Biblical language, the promoters established the sacred within the everyday, if we evaluate this action according to the perspective of Judaism. The political vocabulary in particular was enriched by these means. *Torah*, the venerable term that refers to the Law of Moses as revealed by the Pentateuch, can be used today in the sense of a "political doctrine" of any kind. *Herem*, which means "object of a curse" in the Bible, now takes the meaning of "embargo" or "boycott." *Keneset*, a Mishnaic Hebrew word meaning "assembly of the faithful," was adopted to designate the Israeli parliament, as we know. *Minyan*, another Mishnaic term that designated (and still designates among practicing Jews) the minimum number of ten men needed to recite a prayer in public, has been specialized to the secular meaning of "quorum." *Sar* and *nasi*, today meaning "minister" and "president," respectively, referred in antiquity to religious functions and ranks. *Qorban* ("sacrifice on the altar"), in Biblical Hebrew, has taken the modern meaning of "victim (of war, or sometimes of an accident)."

G. Scholem would have considered all these adaptations as so many sacrilegious diversions.

The Fate of Hebrew

Two relatively recent phenomena are affecting Hebrew today, and they could not have been anticipated by those who re-created it in the heroic era. These are diglossia and Americanization.

DIGLOSSIA, OR MISTAKES AND LIFE

By diglossia we mean (see Hagège 1996a, 253–255) the linked existence of two usages, one of which is a form more usually written and the other a form more usually spoken of the same language (see chapter 5 regarding the specific case of Arabic). Current dictionaries make almost no mention of a significant phenomenon in contemporary Hebrew: the increasing development of a spoken language from which I have cited a few examples above. For a portion of Israeli society, it constitutes a slang very far removed from the written norm. The differences between this written norm and the spoken language even affect the form of personal pronouns, the expression of possession, and the negation of verbs. The spoken language is more analytical than the written language, in that way extending a difference that goes far back, since this is also what separates Biblical Hebrew from its later stages. The gap could thus be explained in part by the heterogeneity of the sources that the promoters of modern Hebrew used.

The relationship between present-day speakers who are at least forty years old and Hebrew can no longer resemble the pioneers' relationship to it. It is one no longer of veneration, but of daily usage. For today's generations, Hebrew is not a sacred object. It is their language. The astonishing success of linguistic voluntarism generated the very forces opposed to the purism it quite naturally professed during the years of gestation. That being the case, the normative condemnation of spoken forms, banished, by certain purists today, as so many deviations, could very well be a mistake. It is because Hebrew has once more become a living language that it is open to "faulty" turns of phrase. A dead language is recognized especially by the fact that one does not have the right to make mistakes in it. That is why today's spoken Hebrew could provide the forms for an evolution, to be recognized in the very innovations it proposes.

If a new language should arise from this evolution, would that be reason enough to say that, despite everything, Ben-Yehuda's dream remained a dream, that the Hebrew he thought he had restored was only a chimera? Alternatively, one could say that the pioneers gave this revived language a true existence, that is, an actual linguistic life, since they reconstructed an object capable of changing, even though the heterogeneity of the sources makes it very much a chimera, in the sense of a slightly monstrous imaginary object. Furthermore, this new product resulting from everyday communication is now achieving literary status, since in their works certain writers choose a style close to the spoken language. This is a kind of revolution, because the Hebrew of writers from the Middle Ages to the early twentieth century was used as a reference and was integrated into Ben-Yehuda's corpus. Thus, the choices of writers tend to constitute a kind of surety, and the usage they encourage could one day appear as the norm for Hebrew.

THE TIDAL WAVE OF ANGLOPHONIA

Two reasons can explain, without justifying, the contemporary invasion of English in the Israeli state. First, Hebrew is an unknown language (except among certain Jews of the Diaspora) outside of

Israel's borders. Second, the privileged relationship with the United States, and the conviction held by many Israelis of unfailing American support for their unfortunate confrontation with the Arab world give English a very strong position. Supported by omnipresent audiovisual means, notably by films in their original versions, Anglo-American has won for itself the status of a cultural language, henceforth capable of rivaling Hebrew in more than one domain.

Despite these disturbing signs, one fact remains: just as the Hebrews, since ancient biblical times, have asserted themselves as a distinct nation, so too was their language revived in the twentieth century, unlike any other dead language.

Nevertheless, the renaissance of Hebrew should not be a unique phenomenon. Of course, it is often difficult to find will, collective passion, and persistence so united, or the very specific circumstances born of such extended persecution and desire for freedom. It remains true nonetheless that the rebirth of a dead language is not impossible, provided there is cross-fertilization with the revivalists' mother tongue. Hebrew provides proof of this, and even if immense desire and a bit of madness are necessary, its example is available to all those who will not tolerate the death of languages.

11. New Languages, Creoles, Promotions

Rebirths, New Languages, Creoles, Promotions

LOCAL RENAISSANCES

Since they are not a matter of rebirths in the strict sense, I will not revisit those courageous efforts by a few enthusiasts who refuse to sit by and watch their languages disappear. In this regard, I have already mentioned, in chapter 9, Maori, Hawaiian, Mohawk, Hualapai, Rama, Urat, and Atacameño. At least in the case of Maori, it seems that, so far, these efforts are successful.

The proven cases of dead or dying languages that come back to life can be distinguished from Hebrew in that none of them involve the language of an established and independent state. Until now, as far as I know, only Hebrew has become a state language, through an exhumation that followed a very long silence. That is why I will speak of local renaissances in the cases known to me. These include Cornish, Scottish Gaelic, and Yiddish.

PERSEVERANCE IN CORNWALL

Cornish, which, along with Breton and Welsh, belongs to the so-called Brythonic branch of the Celtic languages, was driven back to the farthest reaches of Cornwall by the advancing Saxons, who distanced it from its two cousins, cutting it off from Welsh and isolating it from Breton. In the sixteenth century, Cornish was a victim of the Reformation and began an irreversible decline. It had almost completely died out by about 1800. It had fallen out of usage in most of its former territory for at least a century: according to the evidence we have, N. Boson, who tried to revive it at the end of the seventeenth century, belonged to a family in which, already, servants were given orders not to speak Cornish with the children. Nevertheless, deep ties continued to bind the Cornish population to its traditions.

Although it had its downsides (see chapter 2), the Celtic renaissance, one of the phenomena marking the romantic and post-romantic ages, benefited Cornish, and the German scholar G. Sauerwein even composed poems in it in 1861! The idea of remaking Cornish into a living language was suggested at the end of the nineteenth century, and a society for Cornish studies was created in 1901, which was short-lived but survived long enough to introduce the concept of a revitalization project. Studies, as much folkloric as learned, proliferated. After World War I, two determined men, A. S. D. Smith and R. M. Nance (who died in 1950 and 1959, respectively), using revised middle Cornish as a base, re-created a grammar and a vocabulary adapted to the contemporary period and rich in borrowings from Celtic languages that were still alive, even if threatened: Breton and Welsh. They also established an orthography, but not without debate or difficulties (see George 1989).

Already in 1680, a nostalgic scholar had wondered how one could retain any hope of bringing back to life a language that had vanished so long ago. Today, thanks to the efforts of the two promoters and to the persistence of a group of enthusiasts, at least 1,000 to 1,500 people speak Cornish fluently. Of course, that is a very small percentage for a county of 417,000 inhabitants. Nevertheless, it is a remarkable achievement if we consider the long period during which not a word of Cornish crossed the lips of the Cornwall people, and if we take into account the pressure from English in the world today. No one in Cornwall is unaware of the existence of "Revived Cornish." Many volunteers offer courses to spread the use of Cornish as a spoken language. Many handbooks have been developed. There are families that endeavor to use only Cornish, at least until the children reach school age, just like Ben-Yehuda did with Hebrew, all alone in Jerusalem, at the end of the nineteenth century.

SCOTTISH GAELIC AND THE PROMOTERS' STRUGGLE

Of all the Celtic languages, Scottish Gaelic is considered to be in the most advanced state of decline. One work that has helped to call the scholarly world's attention to the problem of the death of languages (see Dorian 1981) is dedicated specifically to one of its speakers. We saw earlier (see chapter 6) that, in Nova Scotia, the oldest speakers still use addresses of complicity, which only give the illusion of the language's vitality. We have also seen (see chapter 7) the terms in which those who recommend Scottish Gaelic's eradication speak of it. In Scotland, the most recent census, going back thirty years, lists only 477 monolingual speakers, all the rest (82,500) being bilingual. This language relegated to the Highlands could thus be considered seriously threatened. Nevertheless, since the 1980s, a kind of renaissance has begun to take shape. A great number of schools have been established at all levels, including kindergartens, high-quality educational works have been published, sophisticated audiovisual methods have been adopted for language teaching, the number of television shows in Gaelic has grown, and composers of popular music increasingly use Gaelic. The future will tell us if all that reflects a desire that is strong and well-organized enough to save the language from extinction.

I have already mentioned that, at the end of World War II, Yiddish was dying out, and for a good reason. So what is this language that does not wish to truly die? Around the beginning of the thirteenth century, the Jews who were fleeing northern Italy and France following the Crusades and thus abandoning their Judeo-Roman dialects had developed Yiddish on the basis of a high German dialect, but adding to it important strata from rabbinical Hebrew, that is, Hebrew and Judeo-Aramaic. Yiddish soon divided into a western branch and an eastern branch, the latter itself subdividing into three groups of dialects (see Szulmajster, forthcoming): first, those of Ukraine, white Russia and Romania; second, those of the Baltic countries; and third, those of the center, comprising Poland, western Galicia, eastern Slovakia, and Ruthenia. Slavic contributions thus further enriched Yiddish, already rendered composite by the crossbreeding of the Germanic and the Semitic.

The masses no longer spoke Hebrew, but they lived in constant contact with it. That is how an impressive symbiosis came about, visible not only in the vocabulary borrowings even for very ordinary notions, but also in the grammar, turns of phrase, idiomatic expressions, connotations, and the whole realm of thinking and references.

Yiddish is an astonishing blend that manages to deeply express the Jewish identity, but does so with a gentile language! Yiddish, which is said to be in grave danger, seems to want to take its time in arranging for its death! According to J. Fishman (1994, 434), in the album of headlines that could be imagined for the year 2050, the *Jerusalem Post* includes the following announcement: "Yiddish still dying!" Today there exists a Yiddish theater in Tel-Aviv, with concerts and poetry readings in Yiddish, although members of the audience are rarely under sixty-five years old. The same is true of the some two hundred Israeli writers and journalists who belong to the various literary associations that exist in that country. There are many Yiddish cultural activities in Israel, and a whole host of specialists at the Hebrew University in Jerusalem are devoted to Yiddish and speak it among themselves, as do a good number of students. It is a subject taught in the five Israeli universities and in fifty schools (especially religious ones).

It can no longer be said that Yiddish hardly survives anywhere anymore except in the ultra-orthodox Jewish circles of Israel and the United States. In the United States, the number of school-age children in New York who speak Yiddish only is probably much smaller than it was in the 1920s. A New York telephone company supposedly paid for an ad in Yiddish recommending that users not tie up the lines by taking their phones off the hook during the Sabbath; additionally, the Beth Israel Hospital in Manhattan is reported to provide incoming patients with an information sheet written in Yiddish (see Fishman 1994, 435). Important Yiddish cultural activities exist in New York.

Of course, none of that means that Yiddish has once more become a completely ordinary oral language used in daily life or on a vast scale. The sociocultural fabric that supported the vital usage of this language before 1939 has disappeared. But the will exists to grant Yiddish a genuine life. The twenty-first century will show if this germ of a rebirth foretells a return, or if it is only a dream.

The Birth of a European Language and
of Many Creole Languages

THE BAPTISM OF NEO-NORWEGIAN

The story of those formidable Viking sailors who made northern Europe tremble until the mid-ninth century is well known. It was thus that, like their third century Scandinavian ancestors, they invaded England especially, bringing many Nordic words into Anglo-Saxon. When Norway was Christianized in about 1000, the little Viking realms had already been united for more than a century, under Harald I (see Sturluson 2000). The Kalmar Union (1397) linked Norway to a Nordic federation under the authority of Denmark. Because of this, Norwegian was deeply permeated with Danish, to which it was already genetically very close. This influence lasted no less than 418 years, until 1815, the date of the private union between the Norwegian and Swedish crowns. This date is not only the prelude to Norway's independence, which came about in 1905, it is also when politicians and patriotic writers began to push for the creation of an authentic Norwegian language, distinct from the Dano-Norwegian of the ruling classes. The philologist I. Aasen, who published his dictionary in 1850, undertook the creation of a *Landsmål* ("language of the country") in opposition to the Danicized Norwegian that was called *Riksmål* ("language of the state"). It was based on those western dialects that were best preserved and that least resembled Danish. In use in certain rural areas, they were considered by Aasen and his friends to be more national, because they were more popular.

In 1885, this Landsmål was recognized as the second official language along with Riksmål, which has been called *Bokmål* ("language of books") since 1929. Heated conflicts set the partisans of this latter against those of the former, which is called *Nynorsk*, today, that is, Neo-Norwegian. Finally they were both recognized as education languages of equal status, and at present they constitute the two norms in Norway, their written forms fixed through various reforms in the orthography. In fact, according to the specialists (see, for example, Gundersen 1983), 90 percent of Norwegians speak Bokmål, and the minority whose language is Nynorsk is concentrated in a certain area in the western and southern parts of the country. Nevertheless, every state employee is expected to at least understand, if not speak, Nynorsk, so that its natural speakers will not be victims of discrimination if they wish to use it in their dealings with the public services. E. Haugen, a great American-Norwegian linguist, has characterized Norway's division into two linguistic norms as *schizoglossia* (see Hagège 1994, 212–213).

Whatever the antagonisms between partisans of the two norms, one fact remains: Nynorsk is a new language of the modern period, whose birth we can date precisely. Of course, Aasen did not "invent" it anymore than Ben-Yehuda invented today's Hebrew. Moreover, unlike Israeli Hebrew, Nynorsk is not a resurrected language. But, like Hebrew, it is the result of a construction beginning from existing materials. And, also like Hebrew, its success, even if it is contested by a portion of Norwegians, proves that humans can, like demiurges of the sayable, bring to life, or bring back to life, a language.

THE NINETEENTH AND THE TWENTIETH CENTURIES, GOLDEN AGES FOR NEW CREOLES
The Deprivation of Language and the Birth of Creoles
European Languages as Lenders of Vocabulary

For more than thirty years, the study of creole languages has experienced such a revival of interest in scientific circles that creole studies now appear as a leading discipline in linguistics. In most cases, these are languages that, since the seventeenth century, and no doubt earlier for some, were formed from the vocabulary of European languages. Linguists designate these European languages as *relexifiers*, because they provided their lexica, with various modifications, to users who, after varying lengths of time, had "lost" their languages. The reasons, the circumstances, and the consequences of such loss, as well as the extent of the territories of the languages involved, are the subject to debate among creolists, with no small stakes.

The example of the creoles spoken in the Caribbean clearly reveals the issues here. Their users are the descendants of slaves torn away from their African villages and transported to West Indian plantations, especially during the seventeenth and eighteenth centuries. The relexifiers were the languages of the plantation owners and white slave traders, that is, mainly English and French (from which we get, among others, the Martinique, Guadeloupan, and Guyanese creoles), as well as a few other European languages.

African Substratum or *Bioprogram?*

But we can notice traits that are completely exotic and, in any case, foreign to those of western European languages in the system that organizes this European lexical material, that is, the grammar. And secondly, these traits are found in all creoles, even though Black communities were broken up among the various locations of different plantations, as a way for the colonists to discourage contact between them. Certain linguists see in these shared grammatical traits an African substratum, that is, a group of characteristics belonging to the original languages, languages similar to each other that the slaves had not completely forgotten, and that had left traces in the form of morphological and syntactical mechanisms. Opposing these linguists, called substratists, are those who consider the African substratum to be negligible, and think the common elements of creoles are explained by the existence of a universal aptitude regarding the construction of certain grammatical categories. According to them, it would be part of the genetic code of each individual human being. Those who defend this idea call that innate aptitude *bioprogram*. Bickerton (1981) is one of them. I have tried to show (see Hagège

1993c, chapter 4) that, despite the arguments of this author and his followers, the role of the substratum cannot be ignored.

Creoles as the Human Reaction to the Death of Languages

Whichever of these two opposing theses we accept, it remains true that the creators of creoles were reacting to a situation that no human society, since the origin of Homo sapiens, has ever tolerated: being deprived of language. Creoles are not revived languages, since the ancestral languages of the peoples involved were not dead. But we must include creoles as a constituent of the human struggle against the death of languages, because they constitute the solution that communities found for preserving, within themselves, and despite violent and hostile circumstances, that activity vital to any society: verbal exchange.

The Invention of New Creoles in the Contemporary Period

It happens that in the nineteenth and twentieth centuries, new creoles are developing, under circumstances very far removed from those of the classic creoles I have just mentioned. I am referring here to languages born so recently that they can be attributed immediately to their perfectly identifiable sources. Some are a mix of local and European languages, like Michif, which I mentioned earlier (see chapter 9). Others are interesting for the ways they are different from West Indian creoles, because these other creoles do not borrow vocabulary from the languages of foreign masters who forced workers to provide slave labor. On the contrary, these are native languages adapted by their own users and users of other languages for the purposes of communication, to serve as lingua francas in multilingual environments. We can find a great number of such idioms. I will present just a few of the most prominent here. I will choose them from three continents: central and southern Africa, Asia (northeastern India), and Oceania (Timor).

New Creole-Pidgins of African Origin in Central Africa

Creolist linguists generally distinguish between creoles and pidgins. Pidgins are lingua francas that arise in the markets and other multilingual places of contact, and that are used for communication between individuals whose mother tongues are different and are often known only by their users. Having no function other than a vehicular one, pidgins are not handed down in the families. On the other hand, creoles are former pidgins that have become mother tongues. As a matter of fact, this distinction is not always clear. Tok Pisin (based on English) and Police Motu (with native origins) in Papua New Guinea are, in principle, pidgins, but they are used widely, one on the northern coast and in the capital, the other in vast regions, and they are very much more than languages responding to a need for immediate communication. The same is true for Bichelamar, a pidgin that has become the lingua franca throughout Vanuatu. A comparable case is the one of three African lingua francas, which we will turn to now.

In the Central African Republic, Sango was decreed the national language in 1963 (French, known passably well only by educated populations, has the status of official language). Sango was originally one of the dialects, called "River Sango," of a Bantu language, two others being Yakoma and Gbandi, and all three being mutually intelligible. At the end of the nineteenth century, when navigation developed on the Ubangui River to transport employees for colonial exploitations, it began to be used in a simplified form by increasing numbers of populations. Furthermore, it became a lingua franca in town marketplaces among users of many different languages. Even though it is the country's major language for communication and there is even a Sango Language Commission, it is not a creole in that traditional sense that many creolists are attached to, because, for the majority of Central Africans, it is a second language, not a mother tongue, with a vehicular function. But the situation is presently changing.

Also, in the People's Republic of the Congo, there is a pidginized form of an African language that has become the lingua franca in the capital, Kinshasa, as well as in one part of the country. This is Lingala, for which the source is Bobangi. Bobangi, originally spoken along the middle part of the Congo River, had been chosen as the language of communication by the Europeans, who had noticed its usefulness as an idiom for trade relations. In the lower Congo region, the same was true for Kikongo-Kimanyanga, on the basis of which was developed the third lingua franca considered here, that being Kituba. An example drawn from this last one can reveal the process of pidginization: at the end of the 1970s, the oldest speakers said *munu imene kuenda* (word-for-word, "I PRETERIT go"), "I went (there)," while among the youngest speakers, the expression, with the same meaning, was condensed to *mu-me-kuenda* (see Hagège 1993c, 129).

Other languages besides the three I have just cited also illustrate the development of pidginized vehicular variations in Africa in the same period, the late nineteenth and early twentieth century, especially in urban settings. That is the case with Bemba in the cities, with Swahili in Shaba (see Mufwene 2002), or with Fanagalo. Fanagalo is a pidgin based on Zulu, stocked with English and Afrikaans words, and was created in South Africa by the gold mine workers who belonged to peoples and languages with very diverse origins. The urban variations can also respond to the project of integrating only one group by excluding others. That is what is done, for example, by Isicamtho,

deliberately developed in Soweto in the South African Republic from
Afrikaans and Nguni (see Childs 1997).

Arabic Pidgins in Africa

In the early nineteenth century, Arabic also served as the basis for
various pidginized forms. In effect, the Arabic-speaking Sudanese
from northern Sudan then moved south to an area less influenced
by Arabic and Islam. They settled near military camps to do trade,
especially in slaves. After Egyptian rule was expelled, Sudanese Arabic experienced a process of restructuring among non-Arab populations, resulting in these pidginized varieties, among them the Arabic
of Juba, the language spoken by nearly half the inhabitants of the city
with that same name, and serving as lingua franca for all southern
Sudan (see Mufwene 2001, 15–16). The variations of Arabic that were
created in this way spread to the urban centers of many countries,
notably Uganda, Chad, and Kenya (see Hagège 1973, a descriptive
and interpretive monograph on the pidgin Arabic of Chad).

Nagamese, the Pidgin-Creole of the High
Indo-Burman Mountains

In 1963, the government in Delhi recognized the Indian state of
Nagaland, at the end of very violent guerrilla warfare that had long
rendered this region dangerous, with its high, dense forests, situated
at the eastern end of the country between Assam and Burma, and surrounded by recently created Indian states and territories. The twenty-
three languages of the many tribes in this little territory, even though
they all belong to the "Naga" branch of the Tibeto-Burman family —
and a portion of the Nagas speak many of them — do not always permit communication between them, and still less with the Assamese.

Barter relationships, not exempt from hostilities, existed between the Assamese and the Nagas, who went down to the Brahmaputra plain to sell their merchandise, and perhaps to capture slaves. From the early nineteenth century, these relations led to the gradual development of a kind of pidgin with a lexical base that was almost entirely Assamese, called Nagamese, undoubtedly a portmanteau (see Hagège 1987, 28) constructed from an amalgam of Naga + (Assa) mese.

A language probably born very recently, Nagamese is experiencing a period of development since the political promotion of Nagaland. Even though it is not anyone's mother tongue, and functions as a second language with a vehicular role, with varying degrees of pidginization, Nagamese is used in extensive domains. Today it seems to be a very useful language, which cannot help but bring to mind the case of Sango in the Central African Republic.

According to M. V. Sreedhar, an Indian linguist who studied the possibility of promoting Nagamese through standardization (see Bhattacharjya and Sreedhar 1994), some Naga do not know, or pretend not to know, that this language is a pidginized form of Assamese. In Nagaland, English is the official language and Hindi is the language of the Republic, taught in the schools beginning in the seventh grade. For another portion of Nagas, who are Christianized and who do not necessarily share the theories of an Indian linguist, English's prestige is very much superior to that of Nagamese. That is the position, in particular, of those who, knowing the origin of Nagamese, regard it condescendingly as a kind of rudimentary Assamese (according to F. Jacquesson). Nevertheless, the project of standardization and adaptation to the needs of a modern language, although this pidgin may have originated less than two hundred years ago, deserves to be noted, even if not all Nagas take part in it. Nagamese is not a vernacular language. It is new and its status is uncertain, but it is not without significance in Nagaland.

Tetum-Praça, the Mixed Language of Timor

Tetum, a language belonging to the large Austronesian family, is spoken by more than three hundred thousand eastern Timor inhabitants, a greater number than those who speak other languages used on this part of the island, including some Austronesian and Papuan languages, and still others whose status is more precarious. One of the three zones where Tetum is present is the region of the capital, Dili, which was the seat of Portuguese colonial power until 1974. A Lusitanized form of Tetum developed there recently, probably in the early twentieth century. It is called Tetum-Praça, that is, the Tetum of the commercial and military seat (the Portuguese word *praça* meaning "square") of Dili. The vocabulary contains a great number of Portuguese words, the sound-system is very close to that of Portuguese, from which many sounds were borrowed, and the grammar strays far from that of vernacular Tetum. As with all pidgins in the world, it tends toward analytical and invariable structures, often considered the effect of a simplification. In particular, and as in native Tetum, verbs do not have conjugated forms.

Tetum-Praça is understood by a large portion of the eastern Timor population, and consequently, among other things, it resisted Indonesian influence, to which the inhabitants of the western part of the island are submitted (see Hull 1994). The Catholic church, which remained Portuguese-speaking after the departure of the Portuguese, helped facilitate this. As we know, the Jakarta government annexed eastern Timor in about 1975, taking advantage of the Portuguese departure a year earlier. It then worked hard to undermine the significant and long-standing presence of Portuguese language and culture on that part of the island by increasingly promoting Indonesian in the western part, where pro-Indonesian militia continue to threaten the eastern Timor population that lives there.

Like Nagamese, even though it is a pidgin, Tetum-Praça is the focus of reform and standardization efforts. That is why, despite its youth, this language is considered to partially express the national identity of eastern Timor.

The Political Promotion of a Language as a Revival Factor: The Modern History of Croatian

I will not review the history of the Croatian literary language here (see Franolić 1980). Nor will I linger on the 1850 literary convention in Vienna, during which patriots from Belgrade and Zagreb, in conjunction with the Slovenians, and taking as a basis the most common dialectical form among the Serbs and Croatians, created the language that is called Serbo-Croatian (see Hagège 1994, 138–141). I will not retrace the episodes in the long antagonism that began with the foundation, following World War I, of a realm uniting the Serbs, Croatians, and Slovenians, an antagonism that increased after 1931 (the date when this realm took the name of Yugoslavia) (see Hagège, ibid.). I will not recount the well-analyzed details of the causes of the opposition between the Croatians, Roman Catholics who write their language in the Latin alphabet, and the Serbs, who are Orthodox and use the Cyrillic alphabet. I will not enumerate the measures taken by Belgrade except for the one taken in 1972 that condemned the new Croatian alphabet and forbade the public use of many Croatian words (for a list of these words and for other information, see Hagège 1993b). Nor will I analyze the well-examined points of phonetics, grammar, and vocabulary that can be considered indications of the distinction between Serbian and Croatian viewed as two different languages (see, among others, Franolić 1983, Hagège 1993a and b).

The point that seems interesting to me in the context of the present chapter is the following: by what criterion can it be claimed that two languages considered to be two variants of one and the same language are, in fact, two distinct languages? That is the problem that Croatian poses today. How can it be said that a new language was born in Croatia since the country became independent, that is, since the beginning of the 1990s? The Croatian government and intellectuals take this question seriously, and devote much time and energy to it, at least for the moment. In June 1997, finding myself in Zagreb for a linguistics colloquium to which I had been invited, I had an interview with a Croatian colleague on this problem. The interview was published in the weekly *Hrvatsko Slovo* (The Croatian Word) on June 27 with a title that could be translated as "The Difference Between Croatian and Serbian Is Not a Joke." Responding to the interviewer's questions, I indicated that a very strong desire for differentiation can justify the delineation of two distinct languages, even if intercommunication is possible.

In other words, what linguists have long called Serbo-Croatian can be considered a single language if two speakers, one of whom speaks Serbian and the other Croatian, and not using dialectal forms too distinctly marked as one or the other, succeed in understanding each other without real difficulty—without hesitations, uncertainties, or requests for repetitions. Such difficulties do appear when speakers of different Scandinavian languages (Danish, Norwegian, Swedish) converse, each in his own language, and that is why we can say that despite their strong resemblance, they constitute three distinct languages. That is not the situation today for Croatian and Serbian.

Thus, there is an internal criterion, specific to the formal systems of two languages, and deduced from the degree of ease that two speakers experience in communicating when each speaks his own language. But there is another, external, criterion that is tied to the way users regard their languages and experience them. According to this criterion, Croatian can be regarded as a different language from Serbian. Moreover, if the current efforts in Croatia to extricate a norm as distinct as possible from Serbian continue much longer, then it is possible that, one day, communication having become difficult, one will have to say that they constitute two distinct languages.

For the time being, we can consider the Croatians to be in the process of giving Europe one more language through the political promotion of Croatian, a corollary to their recently acquired independence. Language lovers will not complain, if they think back to the devastation described in the second part of this book. We will see in the conclusion, however, that phenomena of this type can look very different depending upon the perspective one adopts.

Conclusion

The pace at which languages are disappearing in the contemporary world can inspire much pessimism. In a relatively recent text, we can read (Mohan and Zador 1986, 318): "The big purge of world languages has already begun; it will continue until only a tiny crew remain, or maybe only an English payload for the new age of earth spaceships. In Hindu mythology, extinction marks the end of *kaliyuga*, the dark age in which man and his world live in hopelessness and suffering. This extinction is salutary, because it makes room for a new and better world."

I am not sure the speakers of threatened languages envision the extinction of these latter as the promise of a better world, or that they find serene wisdom in this exultant hope. As for the linguists, they are mostly very nervous about the current situation of languages. They share the feelings expressed most recently by one of them in response to a terrible report on the languages going extinct in one part of the world (Australia, Indonesia, Oceania): "Nothing can be done to reverse or arrest the continuing reduction of distinct languages spoken in the world, although the rate of reduction could be slowed. There were perhaps originally four to five thousand separate languages; by the year 2100, there will be many fewer—perhaps only a few hundred" (Dixon 1991, 234).

These figures are much more pessimistic than the ones I produced in the opening lines of the introduction to this book. I do not know what basis this author adopts for his calculations. Mine is simple: I start with the current rate of disappearance for languages, while taking into account the likely acceleration of this pace over the course of the twenty-first century.

There are circumstances that aggravate the situation. Attempts at standardization, which, as I have stressed in this book, are useful for helping to promote a language in relation to an array of dialects, also have adverse effects. Dialectal differentiation is one of the factors that specifically allow the possibility of the appearance of new languages. Under natural conditions, new languages develop out of divergent dialects. In other words, in the past, when a political power established its own dialect in a given place, it thus conferred upon that dialect, after a bit of time, the status of language, which was again reinforced, if necessary, by administrative, legal, or literary writing. But the other dialects did not cease to exist, even if they did not benefit from the same circumstances to become languages. Today, the press, radio, television, and the increasing ease by which one can travel favor the principal language to the detriment of dialect variations. When there are also attempts at deliberate promotion, the situation of dialects becomes even more precarious.

I noted, however, that new languages were born, or resuscitated, in the nineteenth and twentieth centuries. But it is clear that the number of these births does not in the least compensate for the disappearances. The only action possible, when a language is known to be on the point of extinction, is to protect what remains of it using any available means. I have emphasized the linguists' struggles in the field to revive the memory of living witnesses and record their speech. Literature also plays its role, as we have seen with Hebrew.

Even though Hebrew had fallen out of daily use, it never ceased being used in books, and the pioneers of its resurrection drew many materials from these precious deposits.

You can resuscitate a language. You can even gamble on human resurrection and, consequently, write in a moribund language. That is the cunning message of one of the winners of the Nobel Prize in literature, Isaac B. Singer, who was asked by a journalist why he wrote in Yiddish, when that language was at death's door. "I like ghost stories," replied Singer. "And I also believe in resurrection. What will all those Jews have to read when they come back to life, if I don't write in Yiddish?"

It could very well be that the use of the Internet has in store some surprises. It is possible that Anglo-American, which is believed to have invaded the network almost exclusively and worldwide, will lose its monopoly as the percentage of Internet users who speak English has dropped from 54 percent in 1999 to 43 percent in 2005. Of course, Chinese and Spanish are in strong positions among the competing languages. But they are not the only ones. The defenders of threatened languages, as well as commercial translation enterprises, have understood the advantages of establishing forums on the Web, and we can already see a great number of languages profiting by this, among them Yiddish, as well as regional French languages and many others. Thus, Internet exchanges are increased with the help of these languages. But, of course, this is not enough to reintroduce languages threatened with extinction into the living and resounding reality of daily dialogue in situations of natural communication. But this medium has provided a new voice, even in the mirage of the virtual, to idioms that we risk never hearing again. All that fosters hope, on the condition, of course, that the Internet does not become a threat for everything that makes use of writing, and that human culture does not switch entirely, as if this were progress, to writing on the screen.

The Internet struggle must certainly be taken seriously by the defenders of apparently healthy idioms, like French, German, Spanish, Italian, Portuguese — all the languages that I have called "federatives" (see Hagège 1994, chs. 1–4). If you really think about it, they are not safe from danger. Anglo-American is engaged in a process of expansion that, barring unforeseeable events, seems limitless at the moment. One could, of course, consider that this is not a bad thing for humanity, and that, on the contrary, it is good that a language exists with a calling that grows more and more manifestly international, and that would naturally be added to the mother tongue of each one of us. I have pleaded for bilingualism, or, rather, for multilingualism, but not to the benefit of Anglo-American (see Hagège 1996a).

Anglo-American cannot be a true international language, that is, a neutral instrument allowing each person to communicate everywhere. It is the vector of a culture that threatens to swallow up all others by making them objects of trade. Moreover, in an ideal universe of four billion bilingual speakers, it is not simply one member of a future partnership where it would figure harmoniously alongside a national language. It has the means, if not the vocation, to one day be the single language. This can, of course, be a long process. But one of the conclusions that ought to be drawn from this book is the following: all the factors in the death of languages, whether they are political, economic, or social, are capable of acting to the detriment of any language other than English, and to the benefit of this one language. The explicit neglect of bilingualism in the largest English-speaking countries is a striking illustration of this, among others. And, most importantly, due to modern techniques of communication, the power and speed that characterize the present diffusion of English in the entire world far surpass that which permitted other idioms in the past, like Latin two thousand years ago, to bring about the total extinction of a great number of languages.

An unexpected consequence of this situation must be noted. The promotion of languages as a reaction against a centralizing policy or former colonial domination is, whether we like it or not, a two-sided phenomenon. As an act of affirmation, of freedom, and of defense for minority languages, it can only be warmly supported. As a political act directed against the dominant language of the past, it can always be used as a weapon by the advocates for the supremacy of English. The promotion of minority languages offers two advantages: first, English has nothing to fear from local languages that express the cultural identity of a people legitimately preoccupied with a desire for recognition; and second, English has everything to gain from the wave of ideas that accuse other languages of being "instruments of oppression," especially languages like French that compete with it and have an international calling.

The threat that the supremacy of Anglo-American poses to the most commonly spoken languages in the world must, of course, be seen in the context of the present circumstances: from Mandarin Chinese (nearly 900 million speakers) to Japanese (125 million), and not forgetting Malayan, Arabic, Hindi, Bengali, Russian, these languages still have a great future before them. But the situation is evolving rapidly. I do not include here, for example, Spanish (about 266 million speakers) or Portuguese (nearly 170 million), despite these figures, which would clearly justify doing so, because the great majority of Spanish and Portuguese speakers are found in the New World, and it is enough to have lived in Mexico, Brazil, or Argentina to know how strong Americanization (by English) is, and especially how it is advancing there.

Now French, with its 100 million speakers throughout the world, of course does not even figure among the nine most commonly spoken languages. Nevertheless, it continues, now as in the past, to hold second place after English, not in terms of demographic volume, but in terms of universal diffusion, as well as presence in international institutions and in the worldwide activity of translation. Consequently, even if this second place is often more theoretical than actual, and even if, in many institutions, its equal status with English is often violated, French cannot help but appear a troublesome rival that, consciously or not, English would like to get rid of. That is why its promotion in the face of English takes on a symbolic value. Its defense and its example have long been linked to the place that French culture and speech occupy in the world.

French is an eminently political affair. Everyone knows, including those who make fun of it or try to vilify it, that the defense of cultural exception by those active in French politics is not a little operatic war. By defending the culture, that is, life, the French language defends its life. By the same token, it also defends the lives of German, Italian, and other European languages, to mention only a few.

Thus, this book's long reflection, supported by various facts, on the tragic and ignored theme of the death of languages comes to rest in full appreciation of the omnipresent danger. We could smile at these pompous predictions. We could argue that the United States, despite its everyday violence, its growing imperialism, etc., is a great democracy where many would like to visit or to live, and that English is a beautiful language, the bearer of modernity, that seduces the young people in nearly every country, since it makes them dance and sing, and makes only the outdated censors scold. Whatever argument we give, the death threat that weighs upon languages today takes the guise of English. And I wager that the wisest Anglophones would not, in fact, wish for a world with only one language.

References

Adelaar, W. F. H. 1991. "The endangered languages problem: South America." Robins and Uhlenbeck, eds.: 45–91.

Auroux, S., ed. 2000. *Histoire des idées linguistiques.* Vol. 3. "L'hégémonie du comparatisme." Philosophie et langage series. Liège: Mardaga.

Bader, F., ed. 1994. *Langues indo-européennes.* Sciences du langage series. Paris: CNRS Editions.

Bally, C. 1965. (1st ed. 1932). *Linguistique générale et linguistique française.* Bern: Francke.

Banniard, M. 1992. "*Viva voce.* Communication écrite et communication orale du IVe au IXe siècle en Occident latin." Paris: Institut des Etudes augustiniennes.

Baumgarten, J., R. Ertel, I. Niborski, and A. Wieviorka, eds. 1994. *Mille ans de culture ashkénaze.* Paris: Liana Levi.

Berthelot-Guiet, Karine. 1997. *L'apport de la publicité à la langue quotidienne des locuteurs de Paris et de la région parisienne.* Thesis for l'Ecole Pratique des Hautes Etudes, directed by C. Hagège.

Bhattacharjya, D., and M. V. Sreedhar. 1994. "Two decades of Nagamese language reform." Fodor and Hagège, eds: Vol. VI, 101–122.

Bickerton, D. 1981. *Roots of language.* Chicago: Karoma.

Blikstein, I. 1995. *Kaspar Hauser, ou a Fabricação da Realidade.* São Paulo: Editora Cultrix.

Bopp, F. 1833–1857. *Vergleichende Grammatik des Sanskrit, Zend, Griechischen, Lateinischen und Deutshen.* Berlin.

Bradley, D. 1989. "The disappearance of the Ugong in Thailand." Dorian, ed.: 33–40.

Brenzinger, M., ed. 1992. *Language death, factual and theoretical explorations with special reference to East-Africa*. Berlin and New York: Mouton de Gruyter.

Briant, P. 1996. Histoire de l'Empire perse de Cyrus à Alexandre. Paris: Fayard.

Briquel, D. 1994. "Étrusque et indo-européen." Bader, ed.: 319–330.

Brixhe, C. 1994. "Le phrygien." Bader, ed.: 165–178.

Brixhe, C., and A. Panayotou. 1994a. "Le thrace." Bader, ed.: 179–203.

———. 1994b. "Le macédonien." Bader, ed.: 205–220.

Brunot, F. 1966 (1st ed. 1906). *Histoire de la langue française des origines à nos jours*. 13 vols. Paris: A. Colin.

Buyssens, E. 1970. *La communication et l'articulation linguistique*. Brussels: Presses Universitaires de Bruxelles/Paris: P.U. F.

Calvet, L. J. 1987. *La guerre des langues et les politiques linguistiques*. Paris: Payot.

Campbell, L. 1988. Review of Greenberg 1987. *Language* 64, 3: 591–615.

Campbell L., and M. Mithun, eds. 1979. *The languages of native America: Historical and comparative assessment*. Austin: University of Texas Press.

Campbell, L., and M. C. Muntzel. 1989. "The structural consequences of language death." Dorian, ed.: 181–196.

Cerrón-Palomino, R. 1987. *Lingüística Quechua*. Cuzco: GTZ and Centro de estudios rurales andinos "Bartolomé de las Casas."

Chafe, W. L. 1962. "Estimates regarding the present speakers of North American Indian languages." *International Journal of American Linguistics* 28: 162–171.

Chamoreau, C. 1999. "Description du purepecha, une langue mexicaine menacée de disparition." *Travaux du SELF* VII: 131–146. Paris: Université René-Descartes-Paris-V, U.F.R. de Linguistique générale et appliquée.

Chavée, H. J. 1862. *Les langues et les races*. Paris.

Childs, T. 1997. "The status of Isicamtho, a Nguni-based urban variety of Soweto." In *The structure and status of pidgins and creoles*. Ed. by A. K. Spears and D. Winford. 341–367. Amsterdam and Philadelphia: John Benjamins.

Chomsky, N. 1986. *Knowledge of language: Its nature, origin and use*. New York: Praeger.

Clairis, C. 1991. "Le processus de disparition des langues." *La Linguistique* 27–2: 3–13.

Cojtí-Cuxil, D. 1990. "Lingüística e idiomas Mayas en Guatemala. Lecturas sobre la lingüística Maya." Ed. by N. C. England and S. R. Elliot. 1–25. Guatemala: Centro de Investigaciones regionales de Mesoamérica.

Craig, C. 1992. "A constitutional response to language endangerment: The case of Nicaragua." *Language* 68, 1: 17–24.

Darwin, C. 1859. *The Origin of the Species.* London.

Decimo, M. 1998. "La celtomanie au XIXe siècle." *Bulletin de la Société de Linguistique de Paris* XCIII, 1: 1–40.

Desmet, P. 1993. "La Revue de linguistique et de philogie comparée (1867–1916), organe de la linguistique naturaliste en France." Preprint nr. 147. Katholieke Universiteit Leuven.

Desmet, P., and P. Swiggers. 1993. "La nature et la fonction du langage dans l'oeuvre linguistique d'Abel Hovelaque." "Geschichte der Sprachtheorie: Studien zum Sprachbegriff der Neuzeit," ed. by U. Hoinkes, *Münstersches Logbuch zur Linguistik* 4: 129–148. Münster: Universität Münster.

Dixon, R. M. W. 1980. *The languages of Australia.* Cambridge: Cambridge University Press.

———. 1991. "The endangered languages of Australia, Indonesia and Oceania." Robins and Uhlenbeck, eds.: 229–255.

———. 1998. *The rise and fall of languages.* Cambridge: Cambridge University Press.

Dorian, N. C. 1977. "The problem of semi-speakers in language death." *International Journal of the Sociology of Language* 12: 23–32.

———. 1981. *Language death: The life cycle of a Scottish Gaelic dialect.* Philadelphia: University of Pennsylvania Press.

Dorian, N. C., ed. 1989. *Investigating obsolescence. Studies in language contraction and death.* "Studies in the social and cultural foundations of language series." Cambridge: Cambridge University Press.

Dressler, W. 1981. "Language shift and language death, a Protean challenge for the linguist." *Folia Linguistica* XV, 1–2: 5–28.

Dubois, J. 1962. *Etude sur la dérivation suffixale en français moderne et contemporain.* Paris: Librairie Larousse.

Dubuisson, M. 1980. "Toi aussi, mon fils!" *Latomus* XXXIX, 4: 881–890.

—————. 1981. "Utraque lingua." *L'antiquité classique* L, 1–2: 274–286.

Duhamel, H. 1995. *Pillotage*. Reading notes 1985–1995. Orléans: Editions Paradigme.

Durand, J. -M. 1997. *Les documents épistolaires du palais de Mari*. Paris: Editions du Cerf.

Fishman, J. A. 1968. "Some contrasts between linguistically homogenous and linguistically heterogeneous polities." In *Language problems in developing nations*. Ed. by J. A. Fishman. New York: John Wiley and Sons: 53–68.

—————. 1994. "Sociologie du yiddish." Baumgarten et al., eds.: 427–436.

Fodor, I., and C. Hagège, eds. 1983–1994. *La réforme des langues: Histoire et avenir/Language reform: History and future*. 6 vols. Hamburg: Buske.

Franolić, B. 1980. *A short history of literary Croatian*. Paris: Nouvelles éditions latines.

—————. 1983. "The development of literary Croatian and Serbian." Fodor and Hagège, eds. Vol. II: 85–112.

Gal, S. 1989. "Lexical innovation and loss: The use and value of restricted Hungarian." Dorian, ed.: 313–331.

George, K. J. 1989. "The reforms of Cornish. Revival of a Celtic language." Fodor and Hagège, eds. Vol. IV: 355–376.

Greenberg, J. H. 1987. *Language in the Americas*. Stanford: Stanford University Press.

Grenoble, L. A., and L. J. Whaley, eds. 1998a. *Endangered Languages*. Cambridge: Cambridge University Press.

—————. 1998b. "Toward a typology of language endangerment." Grenoble and Whaley, eds.: 22–54.

Guillaume, G. 1969. *Langage et science du langage*. Paris, Nizet/Quebec: Presses de l'Université Laval.

Gundersen, D. 1983. "On the development of modern Norwegian." Fodor and Hagège, eds. Vol. II: 157–173.

Haacke, W. H. G. 1989. "Nama: Revival through standardization?" Fodor and Hagège, eds. Vol. IV: 397–429.

Hadas-Lebel, M. 1976. *Manuel d'histoire de la langue hébraïque*. Paris: Publications Orientalistes de France.

—————. 1980a. "Eliezer Ben Yehuda et la renaissance de la langue hébraïque." *Yod (INALCO)* 12: 21–31.

―――. 1980b. "La sécularisation des termes religieux dans le vocabulaire politique de l'hébreu israélien." *Yod (INALCO)* 12: 63–68.

Hagège, C. 1973. *Profil d'un parler arabe du Tchad.* Groupe Linguistique d'Études chamito-sémitiques. Supplément 2. Atlas linguistique du monde arabe. Paris: Geuthner.

―――. 1975. *Le problème linguistique des prépositions et la solution chinoise (avec un essai de typologie à travers plusieurs groupes de langues).* Collection linguistique publiée par la Société de linguistique de Paris. Paris and Louvain: éditions Peeters.

―――. 1981. *Le comox lhaamen de Colombie britannique. Présentation d'une langue amérindienne. Amerindia,* special issue 2. Paris: Association d'Études Amérindiennes.

―――. 1983. "Voies et destins de l'action humaine sur les langues." Fodor and Hagège, eds. Vol. I: 11–68.

―――. 1987. *Le français et les siècles.* Paris: Odile Jacob.

―――. 1990. *The dialogic species: A linguistic contribution to the social sciences.* European Perspectives. New York: Columbia University Press.

―――. 1993a. Review of O. M. Tomić, ed. *Markedness in synchrony and diachrony.* Berlin and New York: Mouton de Gruyter. 1989. *Bulletin de la Société de Linguistique de Paris* LXXXVIII, 2: 34–44.

―――. 1993b. Review of J. Čemerikić, G. Imart, O. Tikhonova-Imart, *Paronymes russo-/serbo-croates ("amis" et "faux-amis").* Aix-en-Provence: Université de Provence. 1988. *Bulletin de la Société de Linguistique de Paris* LXXXVIII, 2: 284–290.

―――. 1993c. *The language builder, An essay on the human signature in linguistic morphogenesis.* Amsterdam studies in the theory and history of linguistic science, series IV—Current issues in linguistic theory. Amsterdam and Philadelphia: John Benjamins.

―――. 1994 (1st ed. 1992). *Le souffle de la langue.* Paris: Odile Jacob.

―――. 1995. "Le rôle des médiaphoriques dans la langue et dans le discours." *Bulletin de la Société de Linguistique de Paris* XC, 1: 1–19.

―――. 1996a. *L'enfant aux deux langues.* Paris: Odile Jacob.

―――. 1996b. *Le français, histoire d'un combat.* Paris: Editions Michel Hagège.

―――. 1998. "Grammaire et cognition. Pour une participation de la linguistique des langues aux recherches cognitives." *Bulletin de la Société de Linguistique de Paris* XCIII, 1: 41–58.

———. 2003. "Le multilinguisme dans la sphère judéo-tunisienne." J. Lentin and A. Lonnet, eds., *Mélanges David Cohen*. Paris: Maisonneuve and Larose, 305–314.

Hagège C., and A. G. Haudricourt. 1978. *La phonologie panchronique.* "Le Linguiste" series. Paris: P. U. F.

Hale, K. 1992. "Language endangerment and the human value of linguistic diversity." *Language* 68, 1: 35–42.

Hall, E. T. 1966. *The hidden dimension.* New York: Doubleday.

Hansegård, N. -E. 1968. *Tvåspråkighet eller halvspråkighet?* (= "Bilingualism or semi-lingualism?"). Stockholm: Aldus/Bonniers.

Haugen, E. 1989. "The rise and fall of an immigrant language: Norwegian in America." Dorian, ed.: 61–73.

Heath, S. B. 1972. Telling tongues: Language policy in Mexico, colony to nation. New York: Teachers College Press.

Hill, J., and K. Hill. 1977. "Language death and relexification in Tlaxcalan Nahuatl." *International Journal of American Linguistics* 12: 55–69.

Hill, J. H. 1987. "Women's speech in Mexicano." Philips et al., eds.: 121–160.

Hovelacque, A. 1878. "La vie du langage." In *Etudes de linguistique et d'ethnographie.* Ed. by A. Hovelacque and J. Vinson. Paris.

Huffines, M. L. 1989. "Case usage among the Pennsylvania German sectarians and nonsectarians." Dorian, ed.: 211–226.

Hull, G. 1994. "A national language for East Timor." Fodor and Hagège, eds. Vol. VI: 347–366.

Humboldt, W. von. 1836. Über die Kawisprache auf der Insel Jawa. Berlin.

Isebaert, L. 1994. "Le tokharien." Bader, ed.: 85–100.

Jacquesson, F. 1998. "L'évolution et la stratification du lexique. Contribution à une théorie de l'évolution linguistique." *Bulletin de la Société de Linguistique de Paris* XCIII, 1: 77–136.

Jazayery, M. A. 1983. "The modernization of the Persian vocabulary and language reform in Iran." Fodor and Hagège, eds. Vol. II: 241–267.

Jocks, C. 1998. "Living words and cartoon translations: Longhouse 'texts' and the limitations of English." Grenoble and Whaley, eds.: 216–233.

Karlgren, B. 1920. "Le proto-chinois, langue flexionelle." *Journal Asiatique.*

Kibrik, A. E. 1991. "The problem of endangered languages in the USSR." Robins and Uhlenbeck, eds.: 257–273.

King, R. 1989. "On the social meaning of linguistic variability in language death situations: Variations in Newfoundland French." Dorian, ed.: 139–148.

Klausner, I. 1935. "Halutsei ha-dibbur ha-'ivri be'artsot ha-Gola" (= "Pioneers in the expression of Hebrew in the countries of the Diaspora"). *Leshonenu la'am* XV: 1–2.

Kosztolányi, D. 1996 (1st ed. 1935). *L'étranger et la mort.* Paris: Editions IN FINE. French translation by Georges Kassai.

Krauss, M. 1992. "The world's languages in crisis." *Language* 68, 1: 4–10.

Ladefoged, P. 1992. "Another view of endangered languages." *Language* 68, 4: 809–811.

Lambert, W. E. 1967. "A social psychology of bilingualism." *Journal of Social Issues* 23: 91–109.

Landaburu, J. 1979. *La langue des Andoke (Amazonie colombienne).* Paris: Société d'Etudes Linguistique et Anthropologiques de France.

———. 1995. "Las lenguas indígenas de Colombia: lenguas en peligro." Universidad de los Andes typed report.

Launey, M. Forthcoming. "Les langues de Guyane, des langues régionales pas comme les autres?" Conference proceedings (1999).

Laycock, D. C. 1973. "Sepik languages: Checklist and preliminary classification." *Pacific Linguistics* B: no. 25.

Leroy, M. 1985. "Honoré Chavée et l'édification de la grammaire comparée." *Quaderni della cattedra di linguistica dell'università di Pisa.* Serie monografica VI: 209–225.

Mahapatra, B. P. 1991. "An appraisal of Indian languages." Robins and Uhlenbeck, eds.: 177–188.

Masson, M. 1976. *Les mots nouveaux en hébreu moderne.* Paris: Publications Orientalistes de France. "Etudes" series.

———. 1983. "La renaissance de l'hébreu." Fodor and Hagège, eds. Vol. II: 449–478.

———. 1986. *Langue et idéologie. Les mots étrangers en hébreu moderne.* Paris: Editions du CNRS.

Matisoff, J. A. 1991. "Endangered languages of mainland South-East Asia." Robins and Uhlenbeck, eds.: 189–228.

Meillet, A. 1958. *Linguistique historique and linguistique générale*. Collection linguistique publiée par la Société de linguistique de Paris. Paris: Champion.

Mertz, E. 1989. "Sociolinguistic creativity: Cape Breton Gaelic's linguistic 'tip'." Dorian, ed.: 103–116.

Mithun, M. 1989. "The incipient obsolescence of polysynthesis: Cayuga in Ontario and Oklahoma." Dorian, ed.: 243–257.

———. 1998. "The significance of diversity in language endangerment and preservation." Grenoble and Whaley, eds.: 163–191.

Mohan, P., and P. Zador. 1986. "Discontinuity in a life cycle: The death of Trinidad Bhojpuri." *Language* 62, 2: 291–319.

Mosès, S. 1985. "Une lettre inédite de Gershom Scholem à Franz Rosenzweig. A propos de notre langue. Une confession." *Archives des sciences sociales et religieuses* 60, 1: 83–84.

Mougeon, R., and E. Beniak. 1989. "Language contraction and linguistic change: The case of Welland French." Dorian, ed.: 287–312.

Mounin, G. 1992. "Discussion. Sur la mort des langues." *La Linguistique* 28, 2: 149–158.

Mufwene, S. S. 2001. *The ecology of language evolution*. Cambridge: Cambridge University Press.

———. 2002. "Language endangerment: What have pride and prestige got to do with it?" In *When Languages Collide*. Ed. by Brian Joseph, Johanna DeStefano, Neil G. Jacobs, and Ilse Lehiste. Columbus: Ohio State University Press.

Myers-Scotton, C. 1992. "Codeswitching as a mechanism of deep borrowing, language shift and language death." Brenzinger, ed.: 31–58.

Philips, S. U., S. Steele, and C. Tanz, eds. 1987. *Language, gender and sex in comparative perspective*. "Studies in the social and cultural foundations of language series." Cambridge: Cambridge University Press.

Pi Hugarte, R. 1998. *Los Indios del Uruguay*. Montevideo: Ediciones de la Banda Oriental.

Pott, A.-F. 1849. 1849 Jahrbuch. *Jahrbücher der freien Akademie zu Frankfurt*.

Poulsen, J. H. W. 1981. "The Faroese language situation." In *Minority languages today*. Ed. by E. Haugen, J. D. McLure, and D. S. Thompson. Edinburgh: Edinburgh University Press.

Pury-Toumi, S. de. 1994. "Si le nahuatl avait été langue générale . . .
Politique linguistique et idéologie nationaliste au Mexique." Fodor and
Hagège, eds. Vol. VI: 487–511.

Rey, A., ed. 1992. *Dictionnaire historique de la langue française.* 2 vols. Paris:
Dictionnaires Le Robert.

Robins, R. H., and E. M. Uhlenbeck, eds. 1991. *Endangered Languages.*
Oxford and New York: Berg.

Rosen, H. B. 1970. "La politique linguistique, l'enseignement de la langue
et la linguistique en Israël." *Ariel* 21: 93–115.

Rosetti, A. 1985. *Linguistique balkanique.* Bucarest: Editura Univers.

Rouchdy, A. 1989. "'Persistence' or 'tip' in Eygptian Nubian." Dorian, ed.:
91–102.

Sampson, G. 1980. *Making sense.* Oxford: Oxford University Press.

Sasse, H. J. 1990. "Theory of language death." *Arbeitspapier* 12. Cologne:
Universität zu Köln: Institut für Sprachwissenschaft.

Saussure, F. de. 1878. Mémoire sur le système primitif des voyelles en indo-
européen. Leipzig.

———. 1962 (1st ed. 1916). *Cours de linguistique générale.* Ed. by C. Bally,
A. Sechehaye, and A. Riedlinger. Paris: Payot.

Schilling-Estes, N., and W. Wolfram. 1999. "Alternative models of dialect
death: Dissipation vs. concentration." *Language* 75, 3: 486–521.

Schlegel, A. W. 1818. *Observations sur la langue et la littérature provençales.*
Paris.

Schlegel, F. 1808. *Über die Sprache un Weisheit der Indier.* Heidelberg.

Schleicher, A. 1860. *Die deutsche Sprache.* Leipzig.

———. 1861. *Compendium der vergleichenden Grammatik der
indogermanischen Sprachen.* Weimar.

———. 1865. *Uber die Bedeutung der Sprache für die Naturgeschichte des
Menschen.* Leipzig.

Scholem, G. 1962. *Von der mystischen Gestalt der Gottheit.* Zurich: Rhein
Verlag.

Segal, M. H. 1927. *A grammar of Mishnaic Hebrew.* Oxford: Oxford
University Press.

Séphiha, H. V. 1977. *L'agonie des Judéo-espagnols.* Paris: Editions Entente.

Singer, A. 2000. "Le net délie les langues rares." *Libération,* 12 July: 22.

Smith Stark, T. C. 1995. "El estado actual de los estudios de las lenguas mixtecas y zapotecas." In *Panorama de los estudios de las lenguas de México*. Ed. by D. Bartholomew, Y. Lastra, and L. Manrique. Vol II: 8–9. Quito: Abya-Yala.

Sturluson, S. 2000 (1st compilation 1230). *Histoire des rois de Norvège*. Translated from old Icelandic, introduction, and notes by F. -X. Dillmann. "L'aube des peuples" series. Paris: Gallimard.

Szulmajster-Celnikier, A. 1991. *Le yidich à travers la chanson populaire: Les éléments non germaniques du yidich*. Bibliothèque des Cahiers de l'Institut de linguistique de Louvain. Louvain-la neuve: Peeters.

———. Forthcoming. "Le yidiche." Perrot, ed. *Les langues de monde*. Paris: CNRS.

Tort, P. 1980. *Evolutionnisme et linguistique. L'histoire naturelle des langues*. Paris: Vrin.

Tosco, M. 1992. "Dahalo: An endangered language." Brenzinger, ed.: 137–155.

Tsitsipis, L. D. 1989. "Skewed performance and full performance in language obsolescence: The case of an Albanian variety." Dorian, ed.: 117–137.

Turniansky, C. 1994. "Les langues juives dans le monde ashkénaze traditionnel." Baumgarten et al., eds.: 418–426.

Vakhtin, N. 1998. "Copper Island Aleut: A case of language 'resurrection.'" Grenoble and Whaley, eds.: 317–327.

Vaugelas, C. F. de. 1647. *Remarques sur la langue française*. Paris: Chez la veuve Camusat.

Vendryes, J. 1934. "La mort des langues." *Conférences de l'Institut de Linguistique de l'Université de Paris:* 5–15. Paris: Boivin.

Villagra-Batoux. 1996. *Le guarani paraguayen. De l'oralité à la langue littéraire*. Villeneuve d'Ascq: Presses Universitaires du Septentrion.

Watson, S. 1989. "Scottish and Irish Gaelic: The giant's bedfellows." Dorian, ed.: 41–59.

Whitney, W. D. 1867. *Language and the study of language*. London: Trubner.

Wurm, S. A. 1991. "Language death and disappearance: Causes and circumstances." Robins and Uhlenbeck, eds.: 1–18.

Zananiri, G. 1978. "Ben Yehuda et la renaissance de la langue hébraïque." *Sens* 1: 3–17.

Zepeda, O., and J. H. Hill. 1991. "The condition of native American languages in the United States." Robins and Uhlenbeck, eds.: 135–155.

Zuckermann, G. 2003. *Language contact and language enrichment in Israeli-Hebrew*. London and New York: Palgrave Macmillan.

———. 2008. *Israelit safa yafa (Israeli, a beautiful language)*. Tel Aviv: Am Oved.

Index

347

Sakhalin Island, 166, 183

Salish languages, 37

Samaria, 249, 253, 254

Samburu, 115

San, 178

Sango, 142, 320–21, 323

San Luís Potosí, 180

Sanskrit, 12, 35, 40, 59–61, 293, 307

Santeul, J.-B., 266

Sardinian, 74

Sargon, 247

Sasanians, 152

Sauerwein, G., 312

Saussure, F. de, 20, 21, 23–28, 241

Saxons, 68, 150, 311–12

Schlegel brothers, 15

Schleicher, A., 11–18

Schleyer, Marton, 8

Scholem, G., 288–89, 290–91, 304, 308

schools, 78, 123–24, 125, 167, 216

Schulbaum, M., 280, 281

Scotland, 68, 120, 313

Scottish Gaelic, 35, 99, 120, 132, 204, 311, 313

Scutari, 72

Sejong, king of Korea, 155

Sékou Touré, Ahmed, 128

Selkup, 219

semi-lingualism, 80

semi-locutors, 80, 83

Seneca, 159

Senegal, 126, 127

Sennacherib, 249

Sephardim, 273, 299, 301

Sepik River, 185

Serbia, 70

Serbian, 131, 325–27

Serbo-Croatian, 325–26

Serbs, 72, 325

Shambala, 179

Shining Path, 107

Siberia, 120, 183, 212–14, 216, 219

Siberian languages, 147, 166

Sicily, 129

Sidetic, 72

Sikiana, 181

Simon Bar Kokhba, 258

Sind, 130

Singer, Isaac Bashevis, 330

singular, 92

Sino-Japanese, 155

Sino-Korean, 155

Sioux, 226

Slavic languages, 35, 40, 69, 70, 96

Slovakia, 314

Slovenes, 72, 325

Slovincian, 69

Smith, A. S. D., 312

Smith Island, Maryland, 189–90

Smolenski, Peretz, 273–74

sociolinguistics, 95

Sokolow, N., 268

Solomon, King, 244, 271

Somali, 91

South Africa, 138, 178, 194, 231, 321–22

Southeast Asia, 60, 184–86

South Korea, 154, 156

Soviet Union, 120, 146–47, 148, 206, 211–12

Spain, 20, 51, 54, 55, 57, 67, 119, 129,

Spain (continued)
141; Islamic, 130, 131, 265; Jews in, 262
Spanish, 25, 74, 171, 263, 330, 331; in the Americas, 81–83, 86, 88–89, 99, 104, 125, 133, 139–40, 143–46, 163–64, 180, 221–24, 332; French borrowings from, 45, 46; in the Philippines, 119
Sprachgebilde, 25
Sprechakt, 25
Sreedhar, M. V., 323
standardization, 164–65, 167, 231–32, 329
strata, 94
subordination, 91, 104
substitution, 75–76
Sudan, 115, 176, 322
Suetonius, 157
suffixation, 32–33, 91, 92
Sukuma, 179
Sumerian, 64, 244
Svans, 135
Swahili, 90, 91, 94, 115, 126–27, 179, 212, 215, 321
Sweden, 57, 91, 316
Swedish, 25, 326
Switzerland, 208, 219
Sylla, 160
syntax, 65, 82, 91
Syria, 62, 64, 130, 255, 260, 261

taboos, 34–37
Tagalog, 185
Taiwan, 185–86
Talmud, 251, 255, 259–60, 281, 293

Tambora, 106
Tamil, 18
Tang dynasty, 130
Tangut (Xixia), 107
Tanzania, 126, 127, 176, 178–79, 212, 214–15
Tarascan (Purépecha), 144, 174–75
Taruma, 175
Tasmania, 107
Taymyr Peninsula, 166
Tchernikhovsky, S., 267
Tehuelches, 142
Tell el'Amarna, 242–43
Telugu, 209
templates, 294–95
Tenochtitlán, 138, 182
tense, 27, 56, 91, 92
Tetum-Praça, 142, 324–25
Texcoco, 138
Thai, 61, 88, 184–85, 216
Thailand, 88, 119, 167–68
Theodosius II, 259
Thracian, 70–71
Tiberius, 159–60, 161
Tibetan, 73, 74
Tibeto-Burman languages, 88, 107, 184–86, 209, 322
Ticanoan languages, 182
Tigrinya, 61
Timor, 142, 324–25
Tin, 88
Tinian, 119
Titus Livius, 43, 70, 161
Tiwa tribe, 36–37
Tlapocan, 138
Tlingit, 123, 136, 199